Lease or Purchase

Dimensions of International Business

Previously published books in the series:

William A. Evans, *Management Ethics*

Frank Long, *Restrictive Business Practices, Transnational Corporations, and Development*

H. Stephen Gardner, *Soviet Foreign Trade: The Decision Process*

Lease or Purchase
Theory and Practice

Arthur C. C. Herst

Kluwer-Nijhoff Publishing
a member of the Kluwer Academic Publishers Group
Boston/The Hague/Dordrecht/Lancaster

Distributors for North America:
Kluwer Academic Publishers
190 Old Derby Street
Hingham, Massachusetts 02043, U.S.A.

Distributors outside North America:
Kluwer Academic Publishers Group
Distribution Centre
P.O. Box 322
3300AH Dordrecht, The Netherlands

Library of Congress Cataloging in Publication Data

Herst, Arthur C.C.
  Lease or purchase.

  (Dimensions of international business)
  Bibliography: p.
  Includes index.
  1. Lease or buy decisions. 2. Industrial procurement.
I. Title. II. Series.
HD39.5.H47   1984   658.1′5242   84-938
ISBN 0-89838-126-6

Printed in the United States of America

Contents

Preface   vii

1
Introduction   1

2
Concepts and Requirements   3

3
Financial Leasing: Analysis of Some Lease   15
Evaluation Models Recommended in Literature

4
Financial Leasing: Towards a Model Meeting   121
the Requirements

5
Operating Leases   147

6
Empirical Evidence   199

7
Leasing in Some West European Countries   217

8
Summary of Main Conclusions   229

Appendix 1
Financial Leasing   233

Appendix 2
Operating Leases   259

Bibliography   271

Indexes   283

Preface

Leasing of capital assets has become an important financing method, not only in the United States but in most West European countries as well. As a result, more and more often, practitioners and theorists are confronted with the lease-or-purchase issue. It may be rather difficult, however, to resolve this issue since there is a multitude of lease-or-purchase models that vary widely in assumed initial conditions, form, and content. In this book, I review and evaluate a number of these models, paying attention to financial leases as well as to operating leases. The models will be analyzed verbally, by means of a numerical example and utilizing uniform mathematical notation. After having discussed the theoretical achievements in this area, I investigate the reasons why preference is given to leasing in real-world situations and then look into any differences in legal provisions, income tax systems, and accounting regulations in various countries as they may affect the leasing of capital assets. Consequently, I feel that this book is a helpful instrument for both theorists and practitioners confronted with the lease-or-purchase decision.

Many people made valuable contributions toward developing this book, among others my colleagues of the Department of Business Finance of Erasmus University, Rotterdam. Besides, I am especially indebted to Professor Dr. A. I. Diepenhorst for his advice and suggestions, to an anonymous reviewer for helpful comments, and to Mrs. M. Leutscher-Van den Berg for her patient help in preparing the various versions of the manuscript.

Rotterdam, September 1983   A. C. C. Herst

Lease or Purchase

1 INTRODUCTION

Leasing involves many different aspects including legal, tax, accounting, and financial issues. This book examines the financial aspects of leasing and deals with the problem of how to make the lease-or-purchase decision. In answering this question I will assume that the goal of the firm is to maximize its market value on behalf of its owners: the stockholders. In other words I assume that the firm's goal is to maximize the market value of its equity. This is not to say that the interests of the firm's other participants can be neglected. Many authors demonstrate that in pursuing its goal the firm had better not act at the cost of, among others, its bondholders (see Weston and Brigham 1981, pp. 6-7).

Chapter 2 starts off by defining the word leasing and making the important distinction between financial leases and operating leases. This chapter also discusses the five requirements a model designed for making the lease-or-purchase decision should meet. Financial leases are the subject of Chapters 3 and 4, whereas Chapter 5 is devoted to operating leases. I chose this sequence of presenting the material because the insights gained in Chapters 3 and 4 are relevant for resolving the issues addressed in Chapter 5. Chapter 3 reviews and evaluates a number of models developed by various authors for solving the financial lease-versus-purchase decision. This analysis applies the five requirements discussed in Chapter 2. Taking the analysis of Chapter 3 as a basis, I develop my own model for making the financial lease-or-purchase decision in Chapter 4. Chapter 5 first applies the same five requirements to analyze a few operating lease valuation methods as suggested in the literature and then develops an alternative valuation model for resolving the operating lease-or-purchase issue. After Chapters 3, 4, and 5, with their largely theoretical background, Chapter 6 gathers empirical evidence concerning the lease-versus-purchase problem, investigating the reasons why decision makers preferred leasing to purchasing in real-world situations and examining the lease evaluation models they applied in these situations. Next, Chapter 7 pays attention to leasing in some Western European countries, exploring their legal provisions, corporate income tax systems, and accounting regulations with respect to leasing. Chapter 8 summarizes the main conclusions that can be drawn from the study. Finally, by use of a uniform mathematical notation, I illustrate the various lease-or-purchase decision models of Chapters 3, 4, and 5 (see Appendices 1 and 2).

2 CONCEPTS AND REQUIREMENTS

2.1 Introduction

This chapter goes into the meaning of the word "leasing" and into
the distinction between financial and operating leases (Section
2.2). It also discusses five requirements that lease evaluation
models have to meet (Section 2.3).

2.2 Concepts

The word "leasing" has been defined in various ways. It is interesting to see, however, that much as these definitions differ,
one can distinguish between definitions in which only one form of
leasing is illustrated and definitions in which a distinction is
made between several types of leasing. I shall characterize both
of these groups of definitions with the help of one quotation. As
for other authors who describe leasing in a similar way, I shall
refer to the bibliography on pp. 271-282. This approach seems to
be more sensible than summing up, for example in a historical
sequence, as many definitions of this concept as possible.

   A good illustration of a definition where only one form of
leasing is discussed is the one put forward by Lüssi. In his
Swiss thesis Lüssi states that he will call a contract a lease if
a specialized third party (e.g., a leasing company or a bank)
participates in it and if during a longer period of time than is
usual for a traditional rental agreement, the cash purchase price
of the lease object is to be paid off by a single lessee (Lüssi
1966, p. 9). From this definition we find that Lüssi speaks of
leasing only if a specialized third party is involved. Therefore,

a lease contract concluded with a manufacturer of an object does not fall within his definition. However, as early as 1963 Vancil makes mention of "a growing awareness by equipment manufacturers of the advantages offered by financial leases as a selling tool" (Vancil 1963, p. 183). According to this author ever more manufacturers are looking upon leasing as a device to stimulate the sale of their products. The results of the research work of McGugan and Caves appear to be in agreement with this statement. Referring to these results they observe that "guesses indicate that the manufacturers' captive lessors control more than half of the market" (McGugan and Caves 1974, p. 383).

The second restriction Lüssi introduces is that the purchase price of the lease object has to be paid off by one single user. This would be possible only if the lease cannot be cancelled or can only be cancelled if the lessor is reimbursed for any losses. Accordingly, further on in his thesis Lüssi states that a lease contract is noncancelable (p. 13). Hence it appears that contracts entered into for an indefinite period of time that can be cancelled by the lessor as well as by the lessee do not belong to the concept of leasing as employed by Lüssi. There are various other authors who define leasing in a similar way (e.g., Bibot 1966, p. 4; Kaminsky 1968, p. 64; Bierman and Smidt 1980, p. 389).

In the second category of definitions a distinction is made between several kinds of leases. For instance Vancil writes:

"All equipment-leasing plans may be categorized as either operating leases or financial leases. A financial lease is defined as a contract under which a lessee agrees to make a series of payments to a lessor which, in total, exceeds the purchase price of the equipment required. Typically, payments under a financial lease are spread over a period of time equal to the major portion of the useful life of the equipment. During this initial term of the lease, the contract is noncancelable by either party; i.e., the lessee is irrevocably committed to continue leasing the equipment. Operating leases on the other hand, may be defined as all other leasing contracts and, typically, are cancelable by the lessee upon giving due notice of cancellation to the lessor. Operating leases, therefore, do not involve any fixed future commitment by the lessee and, in this respect, are similar to most types of business expenditures" (Vancil 1963, p. 8).

In this definition Vancil distinguishes between financial and operating leases by defining the first form of leasing and calling any other lease contract an operating lease. This approach has also been utilized by Goudsmit and Keijser and by Van Horne (see Goudsmit and Keijser 1972, p. 25; Van Horne 1977, p. 493). Authors such as Voorthuysen, Schall and Haley, and Weston and Brigham make a distinction between several types of leases too (Voorthuysen 1970, p. 19 and p.26: operating and financial lease; Schall and Haley 1980, pp. 598-601: operating, financial, maintenance, and leverage lease as well as sale and leaseback; Weston and Brigham 1981, p. 851: sale and leaseback, operating and financial lease).

The first group of definitions addresses financial leasing only, whereas (especially) operating leases are left out of consideration. I disapprove of such an approach because these definitions ignore the important position operating leases have taken, at least in the Netherlands. According to Goudsmit, one of the managers of Lease Plan Holding N.V. (a large Dutch leasing company), the Dutch economy is becoming more and more interested in operating and service leases (Goudsmit 1977, p. 10). So far I agree with the writers who pay attention not only to financial leasing but to other types of lease contracts, such as operating leases, as well. On the other hand I am not an advocate of stressing the differences between various forms of leasing, as all these forms have some important characteristics in common. In the first place any lease can be looked upon as a loan in kind providing complete financing for an object (except for a first payment, if any, made at the beginning of the lease term). This object may be a consumer good or a capital asset. As observed in the introduction, this book concentrates on leasing of capital assets. Secondly, the lessee wants to obtain the right to use the asset but not to own it, as may be the case with an installment purchase. Usually the lessor owns this asset: a third charac-

teristic of leasing. I used the word "usually" because it may be
that in order to finance the asset's purchase price the lessor
has raised a loan secured by this asset. Then the lender may be
considered to be the owner of the asset. A final characteristic
feature of leasing is that the lease term corresponds with the
useful life of the leased capital asset. In a traditional rental
agreement, such a relationship does not exist: a user is going to
rent an asset for a period of time during which that asset is
needed. The user is not interested in the total service life of
that asset. A typical Dutch example is renting a machine for
digging up bulbs during harvest-time.

In the literature, a distinction is made between the technical
service life of a capital asset and its economic life. Regarding
this distinction, Van der Schroeff, a well-known Dutch author,
has observed that the technical service life is the period of
time during which the asset can be used for productive purposes,
whereas the economic life is the period during which this use is
justified from an economic point of view (Van der Schroeff 1974,
p. 128). Van der Schroeff has also argued that of the technical
service life and the economic life, the shorter should be
utilized for calculations such as computing the annual depreciation charges. Evidently Van der Schroeff has based his
argument on the standpoint that the technical service life
relates to a specific capital asset, whereas the concept of
economic life is connected with a particular kind of assets.
Otherwise, it would be hard to imagine a situation in which the
technical service life of a specific asset had already expired
whereas, from an economic perspective, making use of this asset
would still be justified. On the other hand it is possible that,
although the technical service life of an asset has expired,
operating the type of assets to which this particular asset
belongs would still be justified as seen from an economic viewpoint. The concept of economic life should be stated more precisely than Van der Schroeff has done: the economic life of a
capital asset should be defined as that period of time during
which the net present value of the cash flows generated by the
asset is highest. In an uncertain world the useful life of a

capital asset has to be estimated. Estimates are made by people and may differ from one another. For the lease-or-purchase decision, the estimates of the decision maker as to the future useful life are relevant. Considering the above exposition the following definition seems to be appropriate:

A lease is a loan in kind whereby a lessee promises to make a series of payments to a lessor in order to acquire the right to use an asset, usually owned by the lessor, during a period of time that corresponds with the useful life of the asset.

This definition recalls the problem this book will be dealing with: the lease-versus-purchase decision. While stating this problem, I use the word "lease" in a general way. In order to make this decision, it is wise to distinguish between (1) leases in which the lessee promises to pay through lease payments to the lessor at least the purchase price of the asset and (2) leases in which such a promise has not been made. Regarding the asset's purchase price: if the lessee knows the price the lessor has paid for the asset then this price is relevant. If, however, the lessee does not know the actual purchase price then the price at which the lessee could have bought the asset is relevant. As Krumbholz and Streitferdt (two German authors) observe, usually the lessee does not know what price the lessor has paid for the leased asset (Krumbholz and Streitferdt 1975, p. 23). After having signed a lease contract of the first category mentioned above, the lessee assumes a binding obligation to make the lease payments specified in the contract irrespective of the profit-ability of the leased asset. That is why with such a lease the risk of obsolescence is (largely) borne by the lessee. A lease belonging to the second category is cancelable by the lessee upon giving due notice of cancellation to the lessor. The lessee will cancel such a lease when it is of the opinion that the useful life of the asset has expired. On the other hand, if the leased asset's operation turns out to be profitable, the lessee may also continue operating this asset. In such a situation the lessee may even decide to purchase the asset. Hence, this lease term too is related to the useful life of the asset, but such a lease does not involve any fixed future commitment by the lessee. Therefore, the risk of early obsolescence is (mainly) borne by the lessor. In the following I shall call a lease belonging to the first category a financial lease, whereas a lease of the second category shall be called an operating lease.

2.3 Requirements

A model designed for solving the lease-or-purchase problem has to meet the following five requirements.

I   Taking into account the interactions of investment and financing decisions.

Various authors separate these decisions from one another assuming that the investment decision has already been made and that only the financing decision remains. Many times the latter decision is interpreted as a choice between leasing and borrowing. One may look upon this approach as an application of the so-called separation theorem first pointed out by Tobin (Tobin 1958, pp. 65-86). This theorem has also been applied by other authors, including Hirshleifer, Modigliani and Miller, and Sharpe (Hirshleifer 1958, p. 332; Modigliani and Miller 1958, p. 268; Sharpe 1981, p. 144). Starting from a number of assumptions, these authors prove that the investment decision can be made separately from the financing decision. However, there is no indication whatsoever that the authors, who are separating these two types of decisions from one another when choosing between leasing and purchasing (possibly financed by borrowing), base themselves on this separation theorem. Up to and including the fifth edition of their textbook, Weston and Brigham belonged to that group of authors. This may be evident from one of the statements in their chapter on leasing: "Note that the decision to acquire the machine is not at issue here - this decision was made previously as part of the capital budgeting process. Here we are concerned simply with whether to obtain the use of the machine by a lease or by purchase" (Weston and Brigham 1975, p. 478). Such a sharp separation between the capital budgeting decision and the financing decision may be incorrect, as can easily be explained. As Weston and Brigham observe, several decision models can be used in the capital budgeting process - among other things, the net present value (NPV) method. They then state: "Our preference is for using the NPV method to make capital budgeting decisions" (p. 285). In order to calculate the NPV of an investment project, the firm's cost of capital is needed. However, because of the market imperfections that result in managements trying to solve the lease-versus-purchase problem, the cost of capital may partly depend on the way the investment project is financed (see Schall 1974, pp. 1208-1209, footnote 14, who shows the firm's cost of capital and the NPV to be dependent on the characteristics of an individual asset). In fact Weston and Brigham propose to make an investment decision using a firm's cost of capital that can only be computed after having made the financing decision. Of course this is impossible; a simultaneous solution is essential to make both decisions.

The market imperfections mentioned above are discussed by, among others, Van Horne. In his textbook, <u>Financial Management and Policy</u>, he calls attention to market imperfections as transaction costs, information costs, and less than infinite divisibility of securities, and then he looks into bankruptcy costs and taxes (Van Horne 1983 p. 494). In his article "The Cost of Leasing with Capital Market Imperfections," Van Horne discusses various imperfections in a more analytical way (Van Horne 1977, pp. 1-12). Moreover, as Lewellen, Long, and McConnell point out, there may be "some differences in the circumstances of lessor and lessee enterprises which, even in a competitive market framework, could lead to differentially attractive asset acquisition opportunities." Among these differences they reckon discrepancies that may exist between lessor and lessee regarding their tax rates and borrowing policies, the purchase price of the capital asset to be leased or purchased, the realization of depreciation deductions, and the asset's salvage value (Lewellen, Long, and McConnell

1976, pp. 794-797). The dangers of separating the investment decision from the financing decision have been illustrated by Johnson and Lewellen, who argue: "If one unhinges the two, one can never allow a very attractive lease to reverse an original negative purchase decision; indeed, the lease analysis would never be undertaken if the NPV of purchase were unattractive" (Johnson and Lewellen 1973, p. 1025; see also Bierman 1982, pp. 97-98). Besides, combining both decisions may take less time than trying to make them separately from one another.

II   Stating the grounds for the discount rates used.

There appears to be substantial disagreement as to the discount rates to be used in a lease-purchase analysis. In particular a considerable variety of opinions exists concerning the rates to be utilized for discounting future tax savings. The following list of discount rates used for computing the present value of the tax savings is a good illustration of this variety of opinions:

. the investment opportunity rate (Vancil 1963, p. 102),
. the firm's cost of capital (Bower, Herringer, and Williamson 1966, p. 263),
. the riskless rate (Gordon 1974, p. 248),
. the required rate of return on equity (Krumbholz and Streit-ferdt 1975, p. 48),
. the borrowing rate (Levy and Sarnat 1982, p. 535),
. the borrowing rate after taxes (Bierman 1982, p. 16).

Since differences in the present value of tax savings may be relevant for choosing between leasing and buying, there is much value in a clear explanation of the grounds for using a particular capitalization rate. Of course such an explanation is necessary for other cash flows as well. When calculating the present value of payments to lessors and to lenders one needs to be well aware of the nature of these cash flows. For instance Schall explicitly states that in his illustrative example he is computing the present value of the promised payments (Schall 1974, p. 1208, footnote 13). On the other hand Schwab is capitalizing the expected values of the promised payments (Schwab 1978, p. 283). This difference exists only if risky debt is involved. In the case of riskless debt, promised payments and expected values are identical.

III Indicating whether the model has been developed for evaluating financial leases, operating leases, or both types of leases.

Bower, Herringer and Williamson commence their article, "Lease Evaluation," by discussing three groups of lease characteristics or advantages: operating, risk, and financial advantages. They then state: "Lease arrangements form a continuum. They all have some financial, operating, and risk characteristics" (Bower, Herringer, and Williamson 1966, p. 259). This starting point affects their lease evaluation model (see Section 3.4.4). Nevertheless, when illustrating this model they restrict themselves to a financial lease (p. 260). Unfortunately, the authors do not go into the usefulness of their model for evaluating an operating lease. Articles by Johnson and Lewellen and by Gordon may also lead someone to think that their models can be used for valuing any type of lease, whereas afterward these models are illustrated with the help of financial leases only (Johnson and Lewellen 1972, p. 819; Gordon 1974, p. 249). Again the reader does not obtain any information concerning the usefulness of the proposed approaches for evaluating operating leases. In order to prevent confusing the reader, it is necessary to state which type(s) of lease contracts can be evaluated using the model.

IV Quantifying the results of the lease evaluation model in net present values.

Since the lease-versus-purchase problem involves choosing between two mutually exclusive proposals, I prefer computing their net present values to computing alternative measures such as internal rates of return and benefit/cost ratios. This preference has been based on the same line of reasoning as the preference in capital

budgeting for recommending net present values rather than internal rates of return or other measures of investment worth, if
at least the profitability of more than a single investment project is to be calculated (see, among others, Weston and Brigham
1981, p. 413; Brealey and Myers 1981, pp. 61-78; Levy and Sarnat
1982, pp. 84-85). Consequently, I do not advocate lease-versus-
purchase models leading to results that are expressed in rates of
return (as developed by, among others, McEachron 1961, pp. 213-
219; Beechy 1970, pp. 769-773; and Mitchell 1970, pp. 308-314). I
may be deviating from the opinion of many practitioners who seem
to prefer the internal-rate-of-return methodology for making
capital budgeting decisions as well as financing decisions (see
Beechy 1969, p. 375; Brigham 1975, pp. 17-25; Carsberg and Hope
1976, p. 47; Van Dam 1978, pp. 232-234; Levy and Sarnat 1982, pp.
183-186). On the other hand, applying the internal-rate-of-return
method can be very troublesome as many authors point out (see for
instance Levy and Sarnat 1982, pp. 63-65, concerning reinvestment
rates, and pp. 80-85 regarding nonconventional cash flows; see
also Isom and Amembal 1982, p. 135, concerning multiple solu-
tions). If, nevertheless, a writer opts for using the internal-
rate-of-return approach, he has to prove that the problems that
may result from his employing this measure have been solved.
Likewise I do not object to using terminal (or future) values for
answering the lease-or-purchase question (see Mao 1976, pp. 471-
474 as well as Isom and Amembal 1982, p. 135), provided that the
author states his reasons for preferring this measure to the net-
present-value rule.

V   Paying attention to problems that may arise when applying
     the proposed model in practice.

The lease-or-purchase model must not only be theoretically valid
but it must also be applicable in reality. Problems may arise
when models are employed where the financing of the purchase
alternative is being accomplished by raising a loan with a
specific repayment schedule that is intended to match the lease
payment schedule: a so-called equivalent loan (as has been pro-

posed by, among others, Bower, Herringer and Williamson 1966, p. 262; by Henderson 1976, p. 148; and Brealey and Myers 1981, p. 531). If, in the situation faced by management, such a loan cannot be raised, then these models cannot be applied.

When discussing the application of lease-or-purchase models in practice one must also pay attention to the discount rates utilized. Many authors use the firm's cost of capital for discounting purposes (e.g., Bower, Herringer, and Williamson 1966, p. 261; Johnson and Lewellen 1972, p. 819; Weston and Brigham 1966, p. 856; Levy and Sarnat 1982, p. 535). Because of the very restrictive assumptions that have to be met in order to use the firm's cost of capital for discounting purposes, it may be impossible to apply this rate in the situation management faces. Myers has drawn up the following list of necessary and sufficient conditions for the firm's cost of capital, as defined in many textbooks on finance, to give the correct project hurdle rate:

. "dividend policy irrelevant,
. investment projects are perpetuities,
. project does not change firm's risk characteristics,
. project makes a permanent contribution to debt capacity,
. acceptance of project does not lead to shift of target debt ratio,
. firm's assets expected to generate a constant and perpetual earnings stream,
. firm is already at target debt ratio" (Myers 1974, p.14).

Diepenhorst goes into this subject too. Starting from perpetuities, a single-period model, and a multi-period model, he shows the firm's cost of capital to be affected by the pattern of project cash flows as well. He observes that utilizing the firm's cost of capital for capitalizing the cash flow series of an additional investment project would be justified only "if the additional cash flow, before taxes, would equal the future cash flow of the existing investment in all aspects, up to a scale factor" (Diepenhorst 1978, p. 10).

Another discount rate used is the firm's marginal borrowing rate. Employing this rate is justified only in those situations where the firm is actually able to borrow. Nevertheless, Vancil persists in applying his borrowing opportunity rate method in a situation where raising an additional loan is not possible any more (Vancil 1963, p. 172; also see p. 36).

3 FINANCIAL LEASING: ANALYSIS OF SOME LEASE EVALUATION MODELS RECOMMENDED IN LITERATURE

3.1 Introduction

The requirements that models developed for choosing between leasing and purchasing should meet were discussed in Section 2.3. Based on these requirements, I shall now look into some of these models as recommended by various authors. For this purpose, I distinguish between lease-or-borrow models and lease-or-buy models (see Section 3.2). Next I shall discuss the methods of analysis I am going to use, my assumptions, and the data of my numerical example (Section 3.3). Then, in 3.4 and 3.5, I shall analyze a number of lease-or-borrow and lease-or-buy models.

3.2 Classification of Models

Many authors have been paying attention to the financial lease-or-purchase problem. That is why it is impossible to analyze every single model they apply. Fortunately this is not necessary, because there are writers who merely advocate a variant of an approach designed by others (e.g., Ferrara 1968, p. 59; Beechy 1969, pp. 370-380; and Henderson 1976, pp. 147-151) or who think they have developed a new model when, in fact, this model already existed (such as Ferrara 1974, p. 24; Burrows 1977, p. 210; or Ooghe and de Groote 1978b, p. 434). Besides, it is interesting to note that the models set out in literature can be classified in one of the two groups defined below. The criterion for this classification is the way the purchase price of a capital asset will be financed. The importance of this criterion is evident:

the way the asset's purchase price is being financed directly influences the solution to the problem. For instance, because of a cheap method of financing the purchase price of a capital asset (whatever may be the cause of this cheapness), management may prefer purchasing this asset. The above criterion leads to the following classification:

1. Models in which the fact that management is considering to enter into a financial lease contract affects the way the purchase alternative is to be financed. In other words, advocates of these models try to shape the method of financing the purchase price of an asset in such a manner that it has a number of relevant characteristics in common with the financial lease.

2. Models in which this is not the case.

Models belonging to the first group shall be called lease-or-borrow models and those of the second group lease-or-buy models. This terminology has also been used by, among others, Johnson and Lewellen and by Myers, Dill, and Bautista (Johnson and Lewellen 1972, p. 816; Myers, Dill, and Bautista 1976, p. 801). Ferrara is one of the authors who develops a lease-or-borrow model. He states that investment and financing decisions should be kept separate. However, he argues, a financial lease is a combination of borrowing and investment. Therefore Ferrara believes "that the portions of the lease that represent borrowing cost should be removed in order to determine the portion that represents the investment in fixed assets via a long term non-cancelable lease" (Ferrara 1966, p. 113). Another train of thought that may result in a lease-or-borrow model is presented by Peirson and Bird. These writers observe that "the lessee's payments to the lessor are primarily for principal and interest which is similar to the obligations incurred under any debt instrument" (Peirson and Bird 1972, p. 241). Myers, Dill, and Bautista employ a different line of reasoning: lease-or-borrow, they state, "does not imply that the alternative to leasing an asset is to borrow an amount equal to the asset's purchase cost. It only recognizes that a firm which signs a lease contract reduces its ability to borrow through other channels" (Myers, Dill, and Bautista 1976, p. 801).

Section 3.4 discusses some lease-or-borrow models.

Authors whose approaches can be placed in the second category ordinarily describe the problem to be solved as lease-or-buy. For example Fawthrop feels that comparing a financial lease with a purchase arrangement financed with a loan is unnecessarily restrictive and may result in "quite intricate (and to this writer, ludicrous) analysis" (Fawthrop 1973, p. 125). Spittler points out that setting leasing against borrowing is not in accordance with situations encountered in reality. He goes on to state that in his own approach the purchase price is financed with 30% equity and 70% debt: a combination that, in his view, is rather customary in Germany (Spittler 1977, p. 33). Then there are authors who stress the interactions between investment and financing decisions. For instance Fawthrop and Terry argue: "The classic lease or borrow decision is concerned purely with the financial alternatives available to the company; it does not acknowledge the fundamental and concurrent inter-relationship with the associated investment decision" (Fawthrop and Terry 1976, p. 79). Section 3.5 analyzes models belonging to this second group.

3.3 Methods of Analysis, Assumptions and Numerical Example

There are several methods for analyzing lease valuation models set out in literature. The first one would be a description of the various models in a more verbal way, going into the motives for their development, describing the successive steps that have to be taken in order to choose between the alternatives, evaluating them starting from the requirements discussed in 2.3, and so forth. Another approach would be to give an illustration of every model by way of a numerical example. A third method consists of summarizing the models using mathematical notation. This probably is the most rigorous way of comparing the various models. Unfortunately, not everybody seems to appreciate such a notation, although only a couple of summations are involved. On the other hand, using mathematical notation may resemble travelling with a night-train: one knows where to get in and one sees where one leaves the train, but the route followed remains wrapped up in darkness. The verbal and the numerical method look like travelling by daylight, having the advantage that one is able to provide for a description of the route followed including the intermediate stations. We should not be afraid of travelling in the nighttime, but on the other hand we should pay attention to the route being followed before reaching our destination too. That is why the verbal and the numerical method of analysis will be applied in 3.4 and 3.5. The reader who is interested in the mathematical notation of the models analyzed in these sections should refer to the appendices.

Before starting the analysis, however, I shall discuss my assumptions and the data of the numerical example. I am assuming that:

. management of a corporation that is considering operating an additional capital asset is able to choose between purchasing it and entering into a financial lease contract,
. the cash purchase price of the asset can be paid for using debt (a loan), equity, or a combination of debt and equity,
. the repayment schedule of the loan is flexible,
. the term of the loan and the term of the lease are both equal to the tax depreciation life of the asset,
. the asset's salvage value at the end of this period is zero,
. the lease payments are tax deductible and only consist of principal payment plus implicit interest expenses (all other operating costs, e.g., cost of maintenance and insurance, are to be borne by the firm as is the case with purchasing the asset),
. any tax deductions are realized at the same time the tax deductible costs are incurred.

These assumptions are made to enable us to compare lease valuation models as developed by various authors. The majority of the authors whose models are analyzed here make the same assumptions, either explicitly or by implication. The main purpose of the numerical example employed is to form a better idea of the models to be evaluated. Therefore I tried to design an example that is as simple as possible. This has induced me to start from a relatively short asset tax depreciation life, i.e., two years, and to utilize easy figures. Here is a list of the data I shall be using:

. net cash inflow (cash revenues less cash expenses) before corporate income taxes expected from asset operation at the end of
the first year = $8,000,
. the same, at the end of the second year = $7,000,
. cash purchase price of the asset to be paid at the beginning of
the first year = $10,000,
. depreciation at the end of the first year as allowed for tax
purposes = $5,500,
. the same, at the end of the second year = $4,500,
. promised lease payments at the end of the first and the second
year = $5,850,
. corporate income tax rate = 40%,
. interest rate of a loan that can be used for financing the
purchase price of the asset = 10%,
. required rate of return on the firm's equity = 16%,
. after-tax weighted average cost of capital of the firm = 13%,
. appropriate project hurdle rate assuming perfect capital
markets and all-equity financing = 15%,
. interest rate of a risk-free cash flow = 5%.

I should like to stress that the lease payments are promised, or contractually set, payments. This also holds for any loan payments. Especially Schall has looked into this issue. Making use of his terminology, I am applying the "quasi-expected return model" instead of the "pure expected return model." In the first model, "the contractually set (promised) payments on the lease and debt obligations rather than their statistical expectations" are capitalized. The discount rates utilized are "the risk-adjusted rates used by investors in discounting the promised lease and interest streams, respectively, in determining their values" (Schall 1974, p. 1208, footnote 13). I apply the "quasi-expected return model" because, just like Schall observes, it is a "more popular, and perhaps more accurate, model than the pure expected return model."

In the next two sections I shall go into some of the more

notorious models, starting with those of the first group (lease-or-borrow models) followed by the ones of the second group (lease-or-buy models). Generally I shall discuss the various approaches consecutively, that is, in order of their date of publication, except for those models that can be looked upon as variants of approaches published before. In that case I shall analyze such a variant together with the model it has been based upon.

3.4 Lease-or-Borrow Models

This section analyzes the models developed by McEachron; Vancil; Weston and Brigham; Bower, Herringer, and Williamson; Bower; Gordon; Myers, Dill, and Bautista; and Beckman and Joosen.

3.4.1 McEachron

McEachron turns out to be an advocate of the "profitability index" for making investment decisions. This index, which he also calls the "discounted cash flow rate of return," is defined as "that interest rate that causes the entire cash flow for the project to discount to a zero present value" (McEachron 1961, p. 214). In the following I shall use the second term, because usually the profitability index is defined as the ratio between the present value of the cash inflows and the present value of the cash outflows of an investment project (see, among others, Weston and Brigham 1981, p. 435). Perhaps McEachron makes use of the same terminology as Reul does in his article "Profitability Index for Investments" (Reul 1957, pp. 116-132).

In the case of purchasing an asset, the discounted cash flow rate of return can be computed from the following variables:
. the net cash inflows after taxes,
. the tax savings on depreciation,
. the cash purchase price of the asset.
Starting from the numerical example, if the asset is purchased

McEachron's "entire cash flow for the project" can be calculated from Table 3.1.

Table 3.1
Cash Flows of Purchasing Asset as Calculated by McEachron

Year (1)	Net Cash Inflow before Taxes (2)	Net Cash Inflow after Taxes (3)= (1-0.4)x(2)	Depre- ciation (4)	Tax Saving on Depre- ciation (5)=0.4x(4)	Cash Flow (6)=(3)+(5)
0	-	-	-	-	-10,000
1	8,000	4,800	5,500	2,200	7,000
2	7,000	4,200	4,500	1,800	6,000

McEachron's discounted cash flow rate of return in the case of purchasing (r_p^{Mc}) can now be calculated from the following equation:

$$\frac{\$7,000}{(1+r_p^{Mc})^1} + \frac{\$6,000}{(1+r_p^{Mc})^2} - \$10,000 = 0$$

As can easily be seen $r_p^{Mc} = 20\%$.

McEachron holds that this method cannot be applied to financial leasing, primarily because there is no cash outflow in year 0 as when purchasing the asset (see Table 3.1, Column 6). Besides, in the lease payments there is an interest element that has to be eliminated, since when calculating r_p^{Mc} such an element was ignored. In order to solve both problems, McEachron has developed his "lease obligation procedure," in which four steps are involved (p. 218):

"1. Discount at the borrowed money interest rate the full schedule of lease payments as obligated to the point in time when the commitment is made. This gives the lump-sum debt equivalent to the lease obligation."

In our example the lease payment to be made at the end of each year of the two-year lease term is $5,850, and the borrowing rate is 10%. Therefore we obtain: lump-sum debt equivalent to the lease obligation $= \dfrac{\$5,850}{1.10^1} + \dfrac{\$5,850}{1.10^2} = \$10,153$.

"2. Compute applicable interest tax credits on debt equivalent." This step is accomplished in Table 3.2, Column 6.

"3. Starting with the project cash flow including all leasing cash effects, make these adjustments:

(a) Add in full lease payments at the time payments are made

(b) Add in debt equivalent as a negative item at time of lease commitment, and

(c) Deduct tax credits at time incurred."

These three adjustments are made in Table 3.3.

Table 3.2
McEachron's Computation of Applicable Interest Tax Credits (or Tax Savings on Interest) on Debt Equivalent

Year (1)	Lease Payment (2)	Debt Equivalent According to McEachron (3)	Interest on Debt Equivalent in Preceeding Year $(4)=0.1 \times (3)$	Lease Payment less Interest $(5)=(2)-(4)$	Tax Saving on Interest $(6)=0.4 \times (4)$
0	-	10,153	-	-	-
1	5,850	5,318	1,015	4,835	406
2	5,850	0	532	5,318	213

Table 3.3
McEachron's Adjustments

Year (1)	Net Cash Inflow less Lease Payment, before Taxes (2)=(2) in Table 3.1-(2) in Table 3.2	Net Cash Inflow less Lease Payment, after Taxes (3)= (1-0.4)x(2)	Adjust-ment (a) (4)=(3)+ Lease Payment	Adjust-ment (b) (5)=(4)- Debt Equi-valent	Adjust-ment (c) (6)=(5)- (6) in Table 3.2
0	-	-	-	-10,153	-10,153
1	2,150	1,290	7,140	7,140	6,734
2	1,150	690	6,540	6,540	6,327

"4. Compute PI on the adjusted cash flow schedule."
From Table 3.3 it can be concluded that this adjusted cash flow
schedule comprises:
. the net cash inflows after taxes,
. the tax savings on the lease payments,
. the lost tax savings on interest,
. the (present value of the) lease payments.
In our example McEachron's P(rofitability) I(ndex) or discounted
cash flow rate of return in the case of financial leasing (r_{fl}^{Mc})
can be computed from:

$$\frac{\$6,734}{(1+r_{fl}^{Mc})^1} + \frac{\$6,327}{(1+r_{fl}^{Mc})^2} - \$10,153 = 0$$

It follows that $r_{fl}^{Mc} \approx 18.79\%$. Since $r_p^{Mc}(20\%)$ exceeds $r_{fl}^{Mc}(18.79\%)$,
McEachron would recommend buying the asset. In his book Leasing
in Industry, Hamel discusses a model that is identical to
McEachron's approach, except for a somewhat different computation
of the interest tax credits (Hamel 1968, pp. 58-59). Next I shall
review McEachron's model applying the five requirements discussed
in 2.3.

Evaluation

I   McEachron does not separate the capital budgeting decision from the financing decision. With the help of his discounted cash flow rates of return (r_p^{Mc} and r_{fl}^{Mc}), he tries to quantify the profitability of a capital asset as well as to choose between purchasing and leasing that asset.

II   The author does not capitalize the various cash flows, but he utilizes these flows to determine r_p^{Mc} and r_{fl}^{Mc}. He prefers the alternative with the higher rate of return. Requirement IV will go into this issue.

III In his article, McEachron speaks of "long-term leasing" or "leasing" without mentioning the type(s) of leases he has in mind. Nonetheless, the author is restricting his analysis to financial leases, as can easily be concluded from his statement that the lease payments "must continue to be made even if the company at a later date finds it has no further use for the equipment involved," to which he adds that it "is characteristic of long-term leases that the sum total of the obligated payments over the period of the initial lease exceeds the original value of the equipment" (p. 213).

IV As observed when discussing requirement II, McEachron is choosing from two mutually exclusive arrangements using their rates of return. This procedure is correct only if any of the problems involved has been solved (see 2.3). However, in his article McEachron gives no proof of even being aware of these problems.

V   In Table 3.3 McEachron's third step has been taken: making three adjustments starting from the project cash flow including all leasing cash effects. The author describes this step by stating: "In effect, we compute the debt equivalent of the lease obligation and substitute it and its tax effects in the cash flow schedule in lieu of the lease payments themselves." He then argues that "this offsetting of a lease by retiring a debt is the essence of the lease obligation procedure" (p. 218). So McEachron attaches great value to the influence entering into a financial lease contract has on the firm's debt capacity, just as Myers, Dill, and Bautista do.[1] His debt equivalent may be looked upon as the loan that can be raised if the lease contract had not been concluded. McEachron calculates the lease's influence on debt capacity in a very specific way, completely different from the methods Myers, Dill, and Bautista and other writers are advocating. That is why McEachron's lease obligation procedure can only be applied in those cases where this influence would be computed according to this procedure. Consequently, applying McEachron's model is limited to these situations.

3.4.2 Vancil

Vancil is a well-known author on leasing whose model has been discussed by many other writers. In the first place, there is a category of authors who agree with his "borrowing opportunity rate (BOR) method" (e.g., Scheffer 1968, pp. 205-208; Goudsmit and Keijser 1972, pp. 231-232). Nevertheless, some of them develop variants of Vancil's BOR method, for example Mao (see Mao 1964, pp. 59-66; Mao 1969, pp. 322-330). Then there are authors such as Johnson and Lewellen who use the BOR method in order to develop a completely different model. I shall discuss this model in 3.5.2. Eventually at least one author, Ferrara, at first was a fervent advocate of Vancil's method (see Ferrara 1966, pp. 106-114 and Ferrara 1968, pp. 55-63) but later on characterizes the BOR method as being "overly complex" (Ferrara 1974, p. 21).

Before explaining his model, Vancil criticizes two other possible decision rules for evaluating financing alternatives: "interest-rate computations" and "discounting at the investment opportunity rate." For a better understanding of Vancil's model, it may be useful to pay some attention to these decision rules. When making use of "interest rate computations," the borrowing

---

[1] Section 3.4.7 discusses the model these authors have developed.

rate is compared with the rate implicit in the financial leasing alternative. In the illustrative example, the borrowing rate is known (10%), but the implicit financial lease rate has to be computed. Starting from the numerical example, the interest rate implicit in the financial lease, k_{fl}, can be calculated from the following equation:

$$\$10,000 - \frac{\$5,850}{(1+k_{fl})^1} - \frac{\$5,850}{(1+k_{fl})^2} = 0$$

As can easily be seen, $k_{fl} \approx 11.14\%$. If we were to apply this decision rule to the example, we would prefer to buy and borrow, as the lease rate (11.14%) exceeds the borrowing rate (10%). However, Vancil does not agree with this rule because (as he explains further on in his book) differences in permissible income tax deductions have been ignored (Vancil 1963, p. 101). In Vancil's opinion, another approach management may utilize to compare its alternatives is to capitalize cash flows at the "investment opportunity rate." Let us assume that this so-called investment opportunity rate equals the after-tax weighted average cost of capital of the corporation (13% in our example).[2] As will become evident in 3.4.3, this method for choosing between financial leasing and borrowing has been advocated by Weston and Brigham in the second edition of their well-known textbook Managerial Finance, published in 1966. In the case of purchasing and borrowing, the future cash flows consist of:
. the loan repayments,
. the loan interest payments after taxes,
. the tax savings on depreciation (see Vancil 1963, p. 96; Weston and Brigham 1966, pp. 376-378).
Assuming that the principal payments of the loan in our example are $5,000 at the end of each year of the two-year loan term, the present value of the cash flows of purchasing and borrowing (PV_p^{WB66}) can be calculated as follows (see Table 3.4):

----

[2] On pp. 34-35 when discussing the second requirement lease valuation models, like the one Vancil develops, have to meet I shall return to this assumption.

Table 3.4
Present Value of Purchasing as Calculated by Weston and Brigham in 1966

Year (1)	Loan Principal (2)	Loan Interest after Taxes (3) =(1-0.4) x0.1x(2)	Loan Repayment (4)	Tax Saving on Depreciation (5)=(5) in Table 3.1	Total Cash Flow, after Taxes (6) =(3) +(4)-(5)	Present Value at 13% (7)
1	10,000	600	5,000	2,200	3,400	3,009
2	5,000	300	5,000	1,800	3,500	2,741
						5,750

The cash flows of financial leasing are:
. the lease payments,
. the tax savings on the lease payments (Vancil 1963, p. 97; Weston and Brigham 1966, pp. 376-378).
In Table 3.5 the present value of these cash flows (PV_{fl}^{WB66}) is computed.

Table 3.5
Present Value of Financial Leasing as Calculated by Weston and Brigham in 1966

Year (1)	Lease Payment (2)	Tax Saving on Lease Payment (3)=0.4x(2)	Lease Payment after Taxes (4)=(2)-(3)	Present Value at 13% (5)
1	5,850	2,340	3,510	3,106
2	5,850	2,340	3,510	2,749
				5,855

Summarizing the results of our calculations, we obtain PV_p^{WB66} = $5,750 and PV_{fl}^{WB66} = $5,855. Since PV_{fl}^{WB66} exceeds PV_p^{WB66} Weston and Brigham would prefer to buy and borrow. Vancil feels that, although differences in permissible income tax deductions are relevant when calculating both present values (whereas in computing the lease and the loan rate these differences are ignored, see p. 26), this is also the case with differences in the amount of financing provided by leasing and by borrowing (Vancil 1963, p. 101). In his Swiss thesis on leasing, however, Bender shows that in fact there are three types of effects that intermingle: effects of differences in the amount of funds provided by leasing and by borrowing, effects of differences between the after-tax borrowing rate and the after-tax lease rate, and effects of differences in noninterest tax deductions (Bender 1973, pp. 188-189). I shall illustrate Bender's analysis with the help of our numerical example. Earlier we saw that PV_p^{WB66} = $5,750 and that PV_{fl}^{WB66} = $5,855. Consequently the total difference between these two present values is -$105. This total difference comprises the three types of effects mentioned above. In the first place there are differences in the amounts of funds provided. In Table 3.6 the amount of financing provided by the financial lease in each year of the lease term (in other words the principal of the lease) is calculated (remember that k_{fl} = 11.14%):

Table 3.6
Calculation of Lease Principal

Year (1)	Lease Principal (2)	Lease Interest (3)=0.1114x(2)	Lease Payment (4)	Lease Repayment (5)=(4)-(3)
1	10,000	1,114	5,850	4,736
2	5,264	586	5,850	5,264

Now we are able to compare the amount of funds provided by the lease with the amount of funds provided by the loan. Any differences between these amounts, costing (1-40%)x10% or 6% after taxes, can be reinvested at 13%, the firm's cost of capital. An additional dollar of funds provided, therefore, contributes 7 cents of additional profit to the company's earnings. The effects of these differences are computed in Table 3.7.

Table 3.7
Effects of Differences in Amounts of Funds Provided by Lease and Loan

Year (1)	Lease Principal (2)=(2) in Table 3.6	Loan Principal (3)=(2) in Table 3.4	Difference (4)=(2)-(3)	Effect of Difference (5)=0.07x(4)
1	10,000	10,000	0	0
2	5,264	5,000	264	18

The present value of the additional profits generated by the financial lease during the second year, discounted at the firm's cost of capital, is
$$\frac{\$18}{1.13^2} = \$14.$$

According to Bender a second category of effects is caused by differences between the after-tax loan rate and the after-tax lease rate. This is shown in Table 3.8.

Table 3.8
Effects of Differences between Loan Rate and Lease Rate, after
Taxes

Year (1)	Lease Principal (2)=(2) in Table 3.6	Lease Principal x Difference in Rates (3)=(0.1-0.1114)x(2)	Lease Principal x Difference in Rates, after Taxes (4)=(1-0.4)x(3)
1	10,000	-114	-68
2	5,264	- 60	-36

The present value of these effects is $\dfrac{-\$68}{1.13^1} + \dfrac{-\$36}{1.13^2} = -\$88$.

Finally there are effects of differences in noninterest tax deductions (see Table 3.9).

Table 3.9
Effects of Differences in Noninterest Tax Deductions

Year (1)	Lease Repayment (2)=(5) in Table 3.6	Depre- ciation (3)	Difference (4)=(2)-(3)	Tax Effect of Difference (5)=0.4x(4)
1	4,736	5,500	-764	-306
2	5,264	4,500	764	306

The present value of this third type of effects can be calculated
as
$$\dfrac{-\$306}{1.13^1} + \dfrac{\$306}{1.13^2} = -\$31.$$
The results of our calculations can be recapitulated as follows:

effects of differences in

1. amounts of funds provided by lease and by loan = $14
2. loan rate and lease rate, after taxes = -$88
3. noninterest tax deductions = -$31 +

$$-\$105$$

This -$105 equals the difference between PV_p^{WB66} ($5,750) and PV_{fl}^{WB66} ($5,855).

After having illustrated Bender's correction in the analysis of Vancil, I shall continue the discussion of the model this author develops. Vancil argues: "Recognizing that other sources of financing are available to the corporation means that it is desirable to eliminate the differences in the amount of financing provided when comparing specific proposals" (p.100). That is why Vancil develops his BOR method, which treats the minimum cost of debt capital (computed using the BOR) as an unavoidable cost of any financing plan (see also Baker and Hayes 1981, p. 114). Being unavoidable, this cost can be eliminated when comparing financing plans (p. 101). Applying Vancil's BOR method the cash flows of purchasing the capital asset are:
. the cash purchase price of the asset,
. the tax savings on depreciation (pp. 96 and 102).
Table 3.10 computes the present value of the depreciation deductions.

Table 3.10
Present Value of Tax Savings on Depreciation

Year (1)	Tax Savings on Depreciation (2)=(5) in Table 3.1	Present Value at 13% (3)
1	2,200	1,947
2	1,800	1,410
		3,357

Since the cash purchase price of the asset is $10,000, the present value of purchasing according to Vancil (PV_p^V) can be computed as follows:

$$PV_p^V = \$10,000 - \$3,357 = \$6,643$$

As can be seen from this equation the tax savings on interest have been left out of Vancil's calculation of PV_p^V. In his view only the depreciation deductions are relevant. How do we, however, determine the tax shield on the depreciation element in the case of financial leasing? To answer this question Vancil assumes that each lease payment consists of "imputed interest" and "equivalent depreciation." He then argues that "the interest cost (at the BOR) must be measured and eliminated from our calculations since we have assumed that it is an unavoidable financial cost which we can ignore for purposes of analysis" (p. 101). The tax savings on the remaining part of the lease payments are equivalent to the depreciation deductions of the purchase alternative. These tax savings are the so-called equivalent depreciation deductions. According to Vancil the relevant cash flows of leasing are:

. the lease payments,

. the tax savings on "equivalent depreciation," i.e., on the difference between the lease payments and "imputed interest" (pp. 101-103).

In order to perform Vancil's calculation, we first have to compute the tax savings on "equivalent depreciation" or the "equivalent depreciation deductions" (see Table 3.11).

Table 3.11

Vancil's Calculation of Equivalent Depreciation Deductions

Year (1)	Lease Principal According to Vancil (2)	Lease Interest (3)=0.1x(2)	Lease Payment (4)	Equivalent Depre- ciation (5)=(4)-(3)	Equivalent Depre- ciation Deduction (6)=0.4x(5)
1	10,000	1,000	5,850	4,850	1,940
2	5,150	515	5,850	5,335	2,134

Vancil capitalizes the lease payments at the BOR (in our example, this rate equals 10%) and the "equivalent depreciation deduct- ions" at the IOR or investment opportunity rate (13%). The pres- ent value of financial leasing as calculated by Vancil (PV_{fl}^{V}) is equal to the difference between the first present value (the "equivalent purchase price") and the second one:

$$PV_{fl}^{V} = (\frac{\$5,850}{1.10^1} + \frac{\$5,850}{1.10^2}) - (\frac{\$1,940}{1.13^1} + \frac{\$2,134}{1.13^2}) = \$6,765$$

Since this present value is higher than the present value of the purchase option (PV_{p}^{V} = \$6,643), Vancil would prefer to purchase the capital asset. Let us now turn to the evaluation of Vancil's BOR method applying our five requirements.

Evaluation

I   Vancil separates the investment decision from the financing decision. In the example he utilizes to illustrate his analy- sis, the investment decision has already been made. All that needs to be done is to choose between financial leasing and borrowing (p. 93).

    As can be deduced from Table 3.11, Vancil divides each lease payment into lease interest and equivalent depre- ciation. The second element of the lease payments is compa- rable with the real depreciation of the purchase arrangement.

However, under the BOR method the sum of the equivalent depreciations is not always equal to the cash purchase price of the asset. In our example (see Table 3.11) the sum of the equivalent depreciations is $10,185 ($4,850 + $5,335), whereas the asset's purchase price is only $10,000. The sum of Vancil's equivalent depreciations will equal the purchase price of the asset only if the implicit financial lease rate equals the BOR. In his 1968 article Ferrara tries to solve this problem (Ferrara 1968, pp. 55-63; see also Section 5.5).

II In the above we assumed Vancil's investment opportunity rate to be equal to the after-tax weighted average cost of capital of the firm. In his book Vancil observes that there is "still no agreed upon way of measuring the cost of capital" (p. 4). That is why he is making use of the investment opportunity rate or IOR for discounting purposes. This rate is "a prediction of the attractiveness of future investment projects" (p.72). According to Vancil there are four factors that are of relevance when determining the IOR: "cost of capital, recent investment experience, realistic aspirations, risk" (pp. 73-74). It is rather remarkable that Vancil prefers to capitalize the tax deductions at the IOR instead of at the firm's cost of capital, whereas this cost of capital, which cannot be measured in an agreed upon way, turns out to be one of the determinants of this rate. Moreover, in one of his illustrative examples the author nevertheless calculates the firm's cost of capital in the usual way: as a weighted average of the rates of the various forms of capital the firm has raised, using market values as weights and taking account of the interest tax deductibility (p. 142). Finally, applying the investment opportunity rate is not in accordance with Vancil's assumption that the corporation can draw on other sources of capital and that consequently differences in the amount of financing provided by leasing or by borrowing are irrelevant (see p. 31). The fact is that discounting at the IOR is justified only if a situation of capital rationing exists. In such a situation the cost of capital (taken as a "borrowing rate") is hardly relevant to the firm, because it is no longer able to acquire additional capital. Future cash flows should then be capitalized at the IOR (taken as a "lending rate": the rate of return an additional investment project would yield if the capital rationing constraint did not exist. See Fawthrop and Terry 1976, pp. 91-94). Since discounting the various tax savings at the IOR is not consistent with Vancil's assumption "that other sources of capital are available to the corporation," I prefer to capitalize these savings at the firm's cost of capital. There are various other writers who also utilize the cost of capital instead of the IOR when demonstrating the BOR method as developed by Vancil (see, for instance, Beechy 1969, pp. 376-377; Johnson and Lewellen 1972, p. 818; Peirson and Bird 1972, p. 242; Bender 1973, p. 48; Sartoris and Paul 1973, p. 47; Bower 1973, p. 27; Schall 1974, p. 1211; and Van Horne 1980, p. 554).

III Vancil clearly states that his BOR method has been developed to value financial leases but not to make the operating lease-or-purchase decision. In 5.2 I shall go into the approaches Vancil suggests for solving the operating lease-or-purchase problem.

IV The results of applying the BOR method are expressed in present values. The net cash inflows resulting from operating the capital asset, however, are ignored as Vancil assumes that the capital budgeting decision has already been made. Besides, the way the author states his reasons for the discount rates he employs in order to calculate the present values of the alternatives is rather disappointing (see II above).

V Vancil developes his BOR method starting from a numerical example. The company in this example, the author assumes, "had not made much use of short-term debt, and its commercial bank indicated a willingness to loan up to $20,000 at 6 per cent interest" (p. 94). For this reason Vancil considers the amount of funds provided by financing arrangements to be irrelevant and eliminates the amount of financing supplied from his computations in order to concentrate on differences in income tax savings. Hence, in situations where the assumption made by Vancil does not hold, his method cannot be applied. Nevertheless, Vancil also employs his BOR method in situations in which borrowing is no longer possible, for instance, in the Venus Air Lines case he analyzes. Concerning the BOR he then argues: "In this particular case, such a rate must be hypothesized since the airline is not in a position actually to borrow any more money" (p. 172). As we saw in the above, Vancil concentrates on differences in tax savings. With respect to this approach, Krumbholz and Streitferdt very properly observe that taking into account only the permissible income tax deductions is not sufficient, especially because in the case of leasing these deductions are based on an imaginary depreciation or amortization element. In their opinion the real financing costs and the real amounts of depreciation or amortization are relevant for choosing between leasing and purchasing (Krumbholz and Streitferdt 1975, p. 55).

3.4.3 Weston and Brigham

In this section I shall discuss some of the various leasing models Weston and Brigham advocate in the seven editions of their well-known textbook, Managerial Finance, that have been published up to now. It may strike the reader that these models differ from one another in a large measure and, moreover, that the authors do not explain the differences between their successive models. For one thing there are differences in the discount rates used. In the first edition of Managerial Finance, the relevant cash flows are capitalized at the borrowing rate and at the firm's cost of capital, in the second edition at the firm's cost of capital only, in the third and the fourth at the after-tax borrowing rate, in the fifth at the firm's cost of capital and at the (after-tax) borrowing rate, and in the sixth and the seventh editions once more at the firm's cost of capital only. In the second place the cash flows Weston and Brigham consider to be of relevance are subject to change. The same thing holds for their description of the problem to be solved. Usually the authors describe this problem as lease-or-borrow; only in the first edition (to be exact, in the appendix to the chapter on leasing) as well as in the sixth and the seventh edition is the problem described as lease-or-buy. I shall analyze these models along with other lease-or-buy approaches in 3.5.1. Now I shall look into Weston and Brigham's lease-or-borrow models. Analyzing the various lease evaluation models of the seven editions of Managerial Finance, is justified by the fact that this book may be looked upon as one of the leading textbooks and certainly as one of the best sellers in its field. Consequently, it seems that this textbook may very well have an important influence on the international exchange of views.

3.4.3.1 Weston 1962 (First Edition)

In Chapter 15 of the very first edition of Managerial Finance, which was not coauthored by Brigham, Weston assumes that the purchase price of the asset to be acquired will be financed entirely by borrowing. It is also assumed that the loan rate equals the implicit financial lease rate and that the sum of the principal payment plus interest of the loan in a given year is equal to the lease payment in that year (Weston 1962, pp. 306-307). Except for the sixth and the seventh edition, the same applies to every edition of Managerial Finance. In fact Weston starts from "a transaction in which clearly there is no benefit from a financial standpoint to leasing or owning" (p. 305) in order to investigate the influence different tax depreciation methods might have on the decision to lease or to borrow. He then pays attention to "the so-called annuity method," "straight-line depreciation," and finally "accelerated depreciation": "the sum of the digits, or the double-declining balance" (p. 307). Because of Weston's intentions, while illustrating the various Weston (and Brigham) models with a numerical example, I assume it that the equality between the loan and the lease rate and the equality between the

annual loan and lease payments are not vitally important and that
these models can also be applied in situations where one or both
of the equalities do not hold. Moreover, in the 1975 edition of
their textbook, Weston and Brigham apply their model to a situation where neither of these equalities holds (Weston and Brigham
1975, pp. 496-499).

According to Weston the relevant cash flows of buying and
borrowing are:
. the loan repayments,
. the after-tax interest payments,
. the depreciation deductions (Weston 1962, p. 306).
The author capitalizes these cash flows at the loan rate (in the
example, this rate is 10%). Assuming the loan raised to finance
the asset's purchase price is to be repaid in two equal installments, the sum of the above cash flows equals the total after-tax
cash flows of Table 3.4 Column 6 (see p. 27). Thus, the present
value of purchasing the asset as computed with the help of
Weston's 1962 model (PV_p^{W62}) is:

$$PV_p^{W62} = \frac{\$3,400}{1.10^1} + \frac{\$3,500}{1.10^2} = \$5,983$$

Since the present value of the loan principal and interest payments, capitalized at the loan rate, necessarily equals the
initial amount borrowed, and since Weston assumes that the purchase price of the asset is entirely financed by borrowing, we
can also determine PV_p^{W62} from:
. the cash purchase price of the asset,
. the tax savings on interest and depreciation.
These tax savings are calculated in Table 3.12.

Table 3.12

Tax Savings on Interest and Depreciation

Year (1)	Loan Interest (2)=(3) in Table 3.4	Depre- ciation (3)	Loan Interest plus Depreciation (4)=(2)+(3)	Tax Savings (5)=0.4x(4)
1	1,000	5,500	6,500	2,600
2	500	4,500	5,000	2,000

Now we are able to compute PV_p^{W62} in another way:

$$PV_p^{W62} = \$10,000 - (\frac{\$2,600}{1.10^1} + \frac{\$2,000}{1.10^2}) = \$5,983$$

Of course this present value is equal to the one calculated earlier. In Weston's opinion the cash flows of the financial lease arrangement are:
. the lease payments,
. the tax savings on the lease payments (p. 306).
Weston would discount these cash flows, which were computed in Table 3.5, at 10% so that their present value (PV_{fl}^{W62}) equals:

$$PV_{fl}^{W62} = (\frac{\$5,850}{1.10^1} + \frac{\$5,850}{1.10^2}) - (\frac{\$2,340}{1.10^1} + \frac{\$2,340}{1.10^2}) = \frac{\$3,510}{1.10^1} + \frac{\$3,510}{1.10^2}$$

$$= \$6,092$$

Since $PV_p^{W62} = \$5,983$ and $PV_{fl}^{W62} = \$6,092$, Weston would opt for the purchase alternative. This valuation method is also applied by Baker and Hayes. Just like Weston these writers assume that the borrowing rate equals the implicit lease rate and that the annual principal and interest payments of the loan utilized to finance the asset's purchase price equal the annual lease payments (Baker and Hayes 1981, pp. 107-109).

Evaluation

I   While discussing his lease-or-borrow model, Weston does not pay any attention to the capital budgeting decision. He only looks into the comparison of "the cost of leasing versus the cost of owning the equipment" (p. 305).

II   The author computes the present value of the financial lease and the present value of the buy-and-borrow option by making use of the borrowing rate, which in his illustrative example is equal to the implicit lease rate. He capitalizes the various cash flows at the borrowing rate without either stating the grounds for its use or indicating the rate at which to discount in situations where the borrowing rate is unequal to the lease rate. In publications on leasing it is usually assumed that the borrowing rate is less than the rate implicit in the financial lease (see, among others, Weston and Brigham 1981, p. 866; and Van Horne 1980, p. 496). In my numerical example, I made the same assumption.

III Weston does not state whether his model has been developed to value financial leases, operating leases, or both types of leases. He does not even make mention of these types of leases in his chapter on intermediate-term financing. However, the lease of his illustrative example cannot be cancelled, and the sum of the lease payments to be made during the lease term exceeds the purchase price of the leased asset. So, in my opinion, a financial lease is involved.

IV The results of Weston's approach are expressed in present values without the author taking into account the cash inflows generated by operating the asset. Moreover, as we observed in II, Weston does not state the grounds for capitalizing at the borrowing rate.

V   In his example Weston sets a financial lease against purchasing a capital asset financing its purchase price with a loan. In situations in which raising a loan is not possible, his model cannot be applied.

3.4.3.2   Weston and Brigham 1966 (Second Edition)

The lease-or-borrow model Weston and Brigham (subsequently: WB)
disclose in the second edition of Managerial Finance is a mixture
of the models described in Chapter 15 of the first edition and in
the appendix to this chapter.[3] It is a mixture because the cash
flows utilized in Chapter 15 are capitalized at the rate used in
the appendix: the firm's cost of capital (see WB 1966, pp. 376-
378). Since we already applied WB's 1966 model to our numerical
example while discussing the BOR method of Vancil, refer to
3.4.2. The results of applying the 1966 model of WB are (see pp.
26-28) PV_p^{WB66} = \$5,750 and PV_{fl}^{WB66} = \$5,855. Purchasing the asset
would be preferred.

Evaluation

I   The authors ignore interactions between the investment deci-
     sion and the financing decision just like Weston did when
     developing his model in the first edition of Managerial
     Finance.

II   As observed earlier the capitalization rate WB use is the
     same as the one Weston applies in his appendix to Chapter 15:
     the firm's cost of capital. Is is a pity WB do not account
     for their discounting at this rate. Apart from that, they
     write: "Here it has been assumed that the cost of capital is
     equal to the borrowing rate" (p. 376). They do not state the
     grounds for this assumption.

III Still WB speak of leasing in general, whereas their example
     centers upon an uncancelable lease concluded for a period of
     time (which, just like the lease of the first edition, is
     equal to the tax depreciation life of the capital asset and
     also equal to the term of the loan raised to finance the
     asset's purchase price) during which the sum of the lease
     payments to be made exceeds the purchase price of the asset.

----

3)   The model employed in this appendix is a lease-or-buy model.
     Therefore I shall discuss it in 3.5.1.1.

iv The results of WB's 1966 lease-or-borrow model are again
   expressed in present values. In determining these present
   values they apparently consider the cash inflows expected
   from asset operation to be irrelevant.

V The possibilities for applying their model may be limited
   because the authors assume that the asset's purchase price is
   entirely financed by contracting a loan. Besides, discounting
   at the firm's cost of capital would be justified only if the
   necessary and sufficient conditions discussed by Myers (and
   others) hold (see p. 13-14).

3.4.3.3 Weston and Brigham 1969 (Third Edition)

As for WB's lease analysis, there are three changes in the third
edition of Managerial Finance: the authors discount at a different rate, they do pay attention to the capital budgeting decision, and they distinguish between various types of leases (WB
1969, pp. 531-536). Regarding the first change, I would like to
point out that, although the cash flows WB start from are the
same as the ones they used in the second edition, the authors now
discount these cash flows at "the firm's after-tax cost of debt"
(p. 536) and no longer at the firm's cost of capital.[4] As we saw
in Table 3.4, Column 6, each of the purchase cash flows is made
up of the following elements:
. the loan repayments,
. the after-tax interest payments,
. the depreciation deductions.
According to WB the present value of these cash flows (PV_p^{WB69}) is
to be computed with the help of the firm's after-tax cost of
debt, in our example: $(1-40\%) \times 10\% = 6\%$. Therefore,

$$PV_p^{WB69} = \frac{\$3,400}{1.06^1} + \frac{\$3,500}{1.06^2} = \$6,323$$

----

[4] The other two changes will be discussed in evaluating WB's
    1969 model.

Since the present value of the loan repayments plus the after-tax interest payments, discounted at the after-tax interest rate, is equal to the amount initially borrowed, and since WB assume that the purchase price of the asset is entirely financed by borrowing, PV_p^{WB69} can also be calculated from:
. the cash purchase price of the asset,
. the depreciation deductions.
This enables us to calculate PV_p^{WB69} in another way:

$$PV_p^{WB69} = \$10,000 - (\frac{\$2,200}{1.06^1} + \frac{\$1,800}{1.06^2}) = \$6,323$$

This present value is of course equal to the one we computed above. In Table 3.5 it was explained that the cash flows of financial leasing consist of:
. the lease payments,
. the tax savings on the lease payments.
Discounting the differences between these cash flows (in other words, the after-tax lease payments) at the firm's after-tax cost of debt results in the present value of financial leasing as calculated by WB in 1969 (PV_{fl}^{WB69}):

$$PV_{fl}^{WB69} = \frac{\$3,510}{1.06^1} + \frac{\$3,510}{1.06^2} = \$6,435$$

WB would recommend purchasing the asset, because PV_p^{WB69} is less than PV_{fl}^{WB69}. This lease-or-borrow model is the same as the one applied by, among others, Bender, Clark, Hindelang, and Pritchard, Bierman and Smidt, Elgers and Clark, and Bierman (Bender 1973, pp. 168-183; Clark, Hindelang, and Pritchard 1979, p. 350; Bierman and Smidt 1980, pp. 391-393; Elgers and Clark 1980, pp. 89-99; Bierman 1982, p. 16).

Evaluation

I   Contrary to the two previous editions of <u>Managerial Finance,</u> WB now do make mention of the capital budgeting decision. However, in the third edition they separate this decision from the financing decision. This will be evident from their statement: "Note that the decision to acquire the machine is not at issue here - this decision was made previously as part of the capital budgeting process. Here we are concerned simply with whether to obtain the use of the machine by a lease or by purchase" (p. 534). The authors mention one exception to this procedure: "If the effective cost of the lease is substantially lower than the cost of debt ... then the cost of capital used in capital budgeting would have to be recalculated and, perhaps, projects formally deemed unacceptable might be acceptable" (p. 534). One wonders what WB would consider "substantially lower," and why "lower" in itself would not be sufficient. Apart from that, it may be taking up a lot of time first to check whether an investment project is profitable and then, if leasing turns out to be considerably less expensive than borrowing, to put the project to this test once more.

II In contrast with the second edition of 1966, WB now feel "that the discount factor that should be applied is not the weighted cost of capital. Rather, it is the cost of debt" (p. 356, footnote 3). According to the authors there is a parallel between the lease-or-borrow problem and the refunding decision, because this decision would also involve a choice being made between "two financial alternatives."[5] Therefore, WB observe, "There is essentially no risk to the firm in obtaining the savings attributable to one alternative over the other." That is why they conclude that "a discount rate that reflects the low risk is preferable to one that reflects the firm's average risk," and for that reason the authors discount at the after-tax borrowing rate instead of at the cost of capital (p. 536, footnote 3). I doubt whether WB's approach is correct. If the relevant cash flows are risk-free then they should be capitalized at the risk-free rate of

---

5) According to their statement, "The lease decision is a type of refunding decision," Dopuch and Birnberg would agree with WB (Dopuch and Birnberg 1969, p. 199).

course. If on the other hand the cash flows are not risk-free (as we saw earlier, WB use the words "essentially no risk"), then an appropriate risk premium may be added to the riskless rate. The authors do not prove, however, that adding such a premium to the riskless rate would result in a rate that equals the cost of debt. Besides, the lease-or-borrow problem involves a factor that is irrelevant for making the refunding decision: the depreciation deductions. Nonetheless WB also capitalize these deductions at the cost of debt without explaining this method of discounting. My next comment has to do with the timing of the refunding decision. In general, management may consider refunding when the present market interest rate becomes lower than the interest rate of a loan contracted in the past. The lower of the two rates may then be utilized for making the refunding decision.[6] If we apply the same approach to the lease valuation problem, then the lower of the implicit lease rate and the interest rate on debt should be used for discounting purposes. The lower of these two rates need not necessarily be the cost of debt; WB themselves do not agree with the statement that leasing always involves higher interest rates (pp. 537-538). To conclude, the authors do not explain why they discount at the "firm's after-tax cost of debt" and not simply at the "cost of debt."

III In the third edition of Managerial Finance, WB distinguish between various types of leases: "sale and leaseback, service or operating leases and financial leases" (pp. 531-533). As apparent from their illustrative example, WB apply their model to financial leases only.

IV The results of this model are expressed in present values leaving out of consideration the cash inflows generated by the capital asset.

V WB still compare a financial lease with a loan having the

----
6) For an excellent review of the refunding issue see WB 1981, pp. 835-844.

same characteristics as the loan of the previous two editions. However, because the authors now discount at the after-tax cost of debt, these characteristic features become completely irrelevant. After all, we computed PV_p^{WB69} in two different ways: the first calculation included principal and interest payments on the loan whereas the second one did not, but both calculations resulted in $PV_p^{WB69} = \$6,323$. Therefore, one wonders why WB insist on setting the lease against this loan.

3.4.3.4 Weston and Brigham 1972 (Fourth Edition)

Regarding the lease-or-borrow issue, there are very few changes in the fourth edition compared with the third one. Each lease payment now includes an element called "maintenance cost": a reimbursement for maintenance services rendered by the lessor (WB 1972, p. 462). WB assume that purchasing the asset involves precisely the same maintenance cost as leasing it. Furthermore, in the case of purchasing there is a salvage value to be realized at the end of the tax depreciation life of the asset. In my example I do not pay attention to maintenance cost and the asset's salvage value in order to be able to analyze the many other lease valuation models in which these variables are also ignored. I do, however, pay attention to those variables that the majority of the authors whose models analyzed consider to be of relevance. In view of the many similarities between the lease-or-borrow model of the third and the fourth edition, I refer to the evaluation of the third edition (see 3.4.3.3). I shall, however, look into WB's explanation with respect to the discount rate to be employed (requirement II). Although the authors still use the after-tax cost of debt for discounting purposes, their reasons for utilizing this rate have changed.

Evaluation (starting from requirement II)

II To justify their discounting at the after-tax cost of debt WB

no longer base themselves on the alleged parallel between
leasing and refunding. They now observe: "The cash flow
differentials between leasing and borrowing are known with
relative certainty.... Since the two cost figures are known
with relative certainty, the difference between them is also
a relatively certain sum, and it should be discounted at a
low interest rate to reflect its low-risk nature." For this
reason the authors capitalize the various cash flows at the
after-tax cost of debt. Although WB's argument differs from
the one they used in the third edition of their textbook, the
same questions can be asked: Why would a rate based on the
cost of debt be appropriate for discounting the cash flows
(including the depreciation deductions)? Why would the implicit lease rate not be the appropriate rate to discount at?
Finally, what is the reason for adjusting the cost of debt
for taxes?

3.4.3.5 Weston and Brigham 1975 (Fifth Edition)

If we would apply the model WB use to solve the lease-or-borrow
issue in their chapter on leasing of the fifth edition of Managerial Finance to our numerical example, then we would obtain the
same results as in 3.4.3.2, where we reviewed their 1966 model.
Nevertheless, there are some differences between both models. The
following evaluation goes into these differences.

Evaluation

I   The authors try to separate the capital budgeting decision
    from the financing decision (just like they did in the third
    and the fourth editions of their textbook). In the chapter on
    leasing in the second edition, however, they ignored the
    capital budgeting decision.
II As they did in the second edition, WB discount the relevant
    cash flows at the firm's cost of capital (p. 480). Again
    they do not state the grounds for utilizing this rate. On the
    other hand, the authors discuss their preference for applying

"risk-adjusted discount rates." In their opinion, "The appropriate discount rate to apply to an expected future cash flow
depends on the riskiness of the cash flow" (p. 480, footnote
5). In order of increasing risk, and therefore ever higher
discount rates, WB distinguish between "loan payment and
lease payment schedules, maintenance expense, tax savings"
and finally "salvage value."[7] It is a pity the authors do not
explain why in their numerical example they nonetheless discount every cash flow at the firm's cost of capital. Apart
from that, in this example the equality between the cost of
capital and the cost of debt, introduced in the second edition, no longer holds.

III In contrast to the second edition, when they discussed leasing in general, WB discriminate between "sale and leaseback,
service or operating leases and financial leases" (pp. 476-
477). From their illustrative example it becomes clear that
the lease they evaluate is a financial lease.

IV Again, WB employ present values to choose between leasing and
buying ignoring any cash benefits from operating capital
assets.

V In each of the five editions that had been published up to
1975, WB set financial leasing against purchasing financed by
contracting a loan. The interest rate of this loan is equal
to the rate implicit in the financial lease, and the sum of
the annual principal and interest payments of the loan equals
the annual lease payments (only in the appendix to the chapter on leasing in the first and the fifth editions do the
authors deviate from this approach). Since the authors now
capitalize future cash flows at the firm's cost of capital
instead of at the after-tax cost of debt, which rate they
utilized in the third and the fourth editions, the loan
repayment schedule remains of relevance. However, discounting
future project cash flows at the firm's cost of capital is

---

[7] In an appendix to their chapter on leasing WB return to this
issue. In 3.4.3.6 I shall go into this appendix.

justified only in cases in which Myers's assumptions hold (Myers 1974, pp. 1-25).

3.4.3.6 Weston and Brigham 1975 Appendix (Fifth Edition)

In "Analysis for Leasing Decisions," an appendix to their chapter on leasing, WB describe a "somewhat more refined procedure" for solving the lease-or-borrow problem (WB 1975, pp. 489-499). This procedure, they state, "draws heavily upon R.S. Bower, Issues in Lease Financing" (p. 489, footnote 1). Yet their approach differs from Bower's lease-or-borrow model, which is reviewed in 3.4.5. These differences will be discussed in the evaluation of WB's appendix model.

The criterion WB employ to choose between financial leasing and purchasing is the "Net Advantage to Lease" (NAL). They are of the opinion that "if NAL is positive, the lease should be accepted, but the loan should be used if NAL is negative" (p. 492). From this quotation it can be seen that WB's refined procedure is a "lease-versus-borrow-and-purchase-model" as they call it (p. 490). In essence NAL represents the difference between the present value of purchasing and the present value of leasing. It consists of the following cash flows:

. the cash purchase price of the asset,
. the lease payments,
. the differences between the tax savings of the lease arrangement and those of purchasing.

WB capitalize the lease payments at the before-tax borrowing rate and the differences in tax deductions at the after-tax borrowing rate. According to the authors the differences between the two sets of tax deductions should be computed as illustrated in Table 3.13.

Table 3.13
Differences in Tax Savings of Leasing and of Purchasing as
Calculated by WB in 1975

Year (1)	Tax Saving on Lease Payment (2)=(3) in Table 3.5	Tax Saving on Loan Interest plus Depreciation (3)=(5) in Table 3.12	Difference (4)=(2)-(3)
1	2,340	2,600	-260
2	2,340	2,000	340

Starting from the cash flow series mentioned above, WB would calculate NAL as:

$$\text{NAL} = \$10,000 - (\frac{\$5,850}{1.10^1} + \frac{\$5,850}{1.10^2}) - (\frac{-\$260}{1.06^1} + \frac{\$340}{1.06^2}) = -\$95$$

Since NAL turns out to be negative, WB would recommend purchasing the asset by raising a loan.

Evaluation

I   WB separate the investment decision from the financing decision stating that: "In a lease-versus-purchase decision, the
firm has already undertaken a capital budgeting decision and
concluded that the asset should be acquired. Thus, the lease
analysis is strictly a financing question...." (p.490).

II In order to determine which discount rates to utilize the
authors are of the opinion that: "Two principles must be
observed when establishing discount rates: (1) the rate must
reflect the riskiness of the stream in question, and (2) the
rate must reflect the tax status of the numerator; i.e., if
the cash flow stream is on a before-tax basis, the discount
rate should also be a before-tax rate, and conversely" (p.
493). Concerning principle (1): the technique WB prefer to
apply is only one out of many possible approaches. In their

textbook they themselves discuss, in addition to the "risk-adjusted discount rate method" mentioned above, the "certainty equivalent method." The authors explain the distinction between these approaches by observing: "Project risk can be handled by making adjustments to the numerator of the present value equation (the certainty equivalent method) or to the denominator of the equation (the risk-adjusted discount rate method)" (p. 329). That is why in my opinion it goes too far to state that "the rate must reflect the riskiness" as in WB's principle (1). In principle (2) the word "must" has been used too, but now tax deductions are involved. Applying this principle may result in tax advantages being included in the numerator as well as in the denominator, resulting in double counting of these advantages. As to capitalizing tax savings at the after-tax borrowing rate, as WB do, Bower (whose lease-or-borrow model will be discussed below) feels that "the after-tax interest rate ... is too low a rate to apply to tax shelter terms" (Bower 1973, p. 31). As we saw earlier, WB discount the lease payments at the borrowing rate, even in a situation in which this rate exceeds the interest rate implicit in the lease arrangement (p. 499). In my view this is not correct: the lower of these two rates should be used for discounting purposes (see Chapter 4).

III As appears from the numerical examples WB employ to illustrate their ideas on lease valuation, they apply their model to value financial leases only.

IV The results of the model are again expressed in present values, without the authors paying attention to any cash inflows generated by the capital asset.

V WB hold that the model explained in their chapter on leasing should be used in a situation where "each inflow and outflow was equally risky" (p. 491). In any other situation the "somewhat more refined procedure" from their appendix should be applied. Both approaches, however, can only be utilized to solve the lease-or-borrow problem. Concerning this limitation WB observe: "For purposes of our analysis, it is important to recognize that a lease is basically equivalent to a term loan

of the same length as the lease" (p. 490). The loan with
which they compare the financial lease in their examples does
not have the same repayment schedule as the one Bower compares the lease with. The fact is that this author, on whose
ideas WB claim to ground their model, starts from the loan
and the repayment schedule McEachron introduced (see 3.4.5).

3.4.4 Bower, Herringer, and Williamson

As apparent in their article "Lease Evaluation", Bower,
Herringer, and Williamson (BHW) do not want to distinguish
between financial and operating leases. This is because lease
contracts all have some characteristic features: "financial,
operating and risk characteristics." The authors argue that none
of these characteristics should be ignored when making a lease-
or-borrow decision (BHW 1966, p. 259). They define the three
characteristic features in the following way:
financial advantages: "Advantages pertaining to prior claims on
the basic cash flows,"
operating advantages: "Advantages pertaining to basic cash
flows,"
risk advantages: "Advantages pertaining to the uncertainties of basic cash flows" (p. 258).
When illustrating their model with the help of a numerical
example, BHW assume that there is no risk advantage and that the
lease cannot be cancelled (p. 260). Besides, they assume that in
the case of purchasing a capital asset its cash purchase price is
financed with a loan of which the payments are proportional to
the lease payments (p. 260). In order to determine the annual
loan payments, starting from a numerical example, we first have
to capitalize the lease payments at the borrowing rate (10%):

$$\frac{\$5,850}{1.10^1} + \frac{\$5,850}{1.10^2} = \$10,153$$

Then we have to divide the asset's purchase price by this capitalized value:

$\dfrac{\$10,000}{\$10,153} = 0.9849305$

Multiplying this ratio by the lease payments would result in the proportional loan payments:

$0.9849305 \times \$5,850 = \$5,762$

Now each loan payment has to be divided into principal payment and interest enabling us to determine the income tax savings of buying and borrowing. This step is accomplished in Table 3.14.

Table 3.14
Division of Loan Payments and Calculation of Purchase Tax Savings according to BHW

Year (1)	Loan Pay- ment (2)	Loan Princi- pal ac- cord- ing to BHW (3)	Loan Inter- est (4) =0.1x(3)	Loan Repay- ment (5) =(2)-(4)	Tax Saving on Loan Inter- est (6) =0.4x(4)	Tax Saving on Depre- ciation (7)=(5) in Table 3.1	Total Tax Saving (8) =(6)+(7)
1	5,762	10,000	1,000	4,762	400	2,200	2,600
2	5,762	5,238	524	5,238	210	1,800	2,010

BHW subtract the tax savings of buying and borrowing from the tax savings on the lease in order to calculate the so-called oper- ating advantage of the lease. The tax savings of leasing have already been computed in Table 3.5 Column 3 (see p. 27). Accord- ing to BHW, the differences between both series of tax savings are to be capitalized at the firm's cost of capital (p. 261).

Thus, the operating advantage is:

$$\frac{\$2,340 - \$2,600}{1.13^1} + \frac{\$2,340 - \$2,010}{1.13^2} = \$28$$

The financial advantage of the lease is determined by setting the cash purchase price of the asset against the capitalized value of the lease payments computed earlier. In our example the financial advantage turns out to be negative:

$$\$10,000 - \$10,153 = -\$153$$

Adding the operating advantage to the financial (dis)advantage yields -\$125. Therefore, BHW would prefer the buy-and-borrow alternative. From the above analysis it can be concluded that the cash flows involved in the BHW model are:

. the cash purchase price of the asset,

. the lease payments,

. the differences between the tax savings of the lease arrangement and those of purchasing.

This model has been utilized by Baker and Hayes in order to calculate the break-even tax rate as well as the break-even lease payments (Baker and Hayes 1981, pp. 114-116), and also by Beechy to compute the lease's effective interest rate (Beechy 1969, pp. 375-381; Beechy 1970, pp. 769-773). Just like BHW, Dopuch, Birnberg, and Demski distinguish between the financial (dis)-advantage and the operating (dis)advantage of leasing. The way in which these authors determine these (dis)advantages, however, differs from the BHW methodology (see Dopuch, Birnberg, and Demski 1982, pp. 629-631).

Evaluation

I   BHW admit having paid no attention to the investment decision. At the end of their article they discuss some of the problems that still need to be solved. One of these problems is making the investment decision (pp. 264-265).

II As was explained earlier, BHW capitalize the various cash flows at two rates: the borrowing rate is used to capitalize the lease payments, whereas the firm's cost of capital is utilized to determine the operating advantage of the lease. One wonders why the implicit lease rate rather than the borrowing rate cannot be used for discounting the lease payments, especially in cases in which the second rate exceeds the first one. Regarding the lease's operating advantage, BHW argue that the firm's cost of capital should be employed because "basic cash flows" are involved. They define these cash flows as "after-tax inflows from operations, before deduction of financing charges" (p. 258). Nevertheless, in order to compute the operating advantage, the financing charges of the loan (viz. the loan interest) as well as the financing charges of the lease (included in the lease payments) are required (see Table 3.14 and the calculation of the operating advantage of the lease). Apart from this, in BHW's article there is no explanation for their discounting the lease payments at the borrowing rate (in order to compute the present value of these payments) and the tax savings of those payments at the firm's cost of capital (to determine the operating advantage of the lease). Maybe the so-called risk characteristics of the lease, which BHW purport to ignore, are relevant after all. When Schall analyzes the BHW model he observes: "The method is also incorrect in separating the after-tax lease stream $(1-\tau)L$ into L and $-\tau L$ and discounting the former at borrowing rate k_R and the latter at rate k; the same discount rate should be applied to both parts of $(1-\tau)L$" (Schall 1974, p. 1211, footnote 18). In Schall's statement L = lease payment, τ = corporate income tax rate, and k = firm's cost of capital.

III The lease BHW set against the buy-and-borrow option of their illustrative example is a financial lease.

IV Applying their evaluation technique results in present values. Since the authors pay no attention to the capital budgeting decision, the net cash inflows of asset operation form no part of these present values. Moreover, one is surprised to find the BHW illustrative example showing a "financial advantage" at all. The authors argue that such an

advantage may arise from, among other things, the fact that
the asset's purchase price is entirely financed by the lessor
and that leasing "adds to borrowing capacity" (p. 258). In
their example, however, a financial lease is compared with a
loan that also permits 100% financing, and there is no
indication at all that the lease would add to the firm's
borrowing capacity (pp. 260-261). Obviously, in their
illustrative example there are other factors that give rise
to a financial advantage. One wonders why BHW do not make
mention of these factors. Besides, the authors do not explain
why management would be interested in distinguishing between
financial, risk, and operating advantages. After all, the sum
total of these advantages is sufficient for it to reach a
decision.

V   To my thinking BHW limit the possibilities for applying their
model in real-world situations. On one hand they characterize
the issue to be solved as "lease-or-borrow" and interpret the
latter alternative as a loan with a very specific repayment
schedule. On the other hand they capitalize some cash flows
at the firm's cost of capital without forming an idea of the
conditions necessary for utilizing this rate for discounting
purposes.

3.4.5 Bower

In his article, "Issues in Lease Financing," Bower reviews a
number of lease evaluation models that were developed before
1973. His starting point is: "It is more profitable to summarize
points of agreement, reconcile or resolve disagreements and seek
an easily used decision format" (Bower 1973, p. 25). Since
Bower's article, (which results in "a composite approach") is
rather lengthy, I shall summarize it here. In order to choose
between purchasing and leasing, the author tries to compute the
present values of these mutually exclusive alternatives. In our
illustrative example, according to Bower the cash flows necessary
to calculate the present value of purchasing are:

. the cash purchase price of the asset,
. the depreciation deductions.

In the case of financial leasing the relevant cash flows are:

. the lease payments,
. the tax savings on the lease payments,
. the tax savings on the interest payments of a loan raised to finance the asset's purchase price; these savings will be lost if the asset is leased.

The loan just mentioned has the same principal and the same repayment schedule as the loan McEachron makes use of (see 3.4.1). However, Bower attributes the introduction of this loan to Findlay (Findlay 1973, p. 136).

Bower discounts the lease payments at the loan interest rate. Since between the authors whose models Bower reviews there exists considerable disagreement concerning the rates at which to capitalize the various tax savings, he recommends performing a sensitivity analysis. This analysis consists of computing the present value of purchasing, PV_p^B, and the present value of financial leasing, PV_{fl}^B, discounting the tax savings at various rates (0%, 2%, 4%, 6%, 8%, 10%, 12%, and 14%). When applying Bower's sensitivity analysis to our example we start from:

$$PV_p^B = \$10,000 - \frac{\$2,200}{(1+k)^1} - \frac{\$1,800}{(1+k)^2}$$

$$PV_{fl}^B = \frac{\$5,850}{1.10^1} + \frac{\$5,850}{1.10^2} - \frac{\$2,340}{(1+k)^1} - \frac{\$2,340}{(1+k)^2} + \frac{\$406}{(1+k)^1} + \frac{\$213}{(1+k)^2}$$

$$= \$10,153 - \frac{\$1,934}{(1+k)^1} - \frac{\$2,127}{(1+k)^2}$$

The tax savings on depreciation ($2,200 and $1,800) have been calculated in Table 3.1, the tax savings on the lease payments ($2,340 and $2,340) in Table 3.5, and the tax savings on McEachron's interest payments ($406 and $213) in Table 3.2. In order to compute PV_p^B and PV_{fl}^B we shall discount these tax savings at the same set of rates (k) as Bower employes. Now we are able to set up Table 3.15.

Table 3.15
Present Values as Calculated by Bower Using Various
Discount Rates for the Tax Shields

k	Present Value of Purchasing	Present Value of Financial Leasing
0%	6,000	6,092
2%	6,113	6,213
4%	6,220	6,327
6%	6,323	6,435
8%	6,420	6,539
10%	6,512	6,637
12%	6,601	6,731
14%	6,685	6,820

From this table we can draw two conclusions:
. both the present value of purchasing and the present value of
  financial leasing increase if a higher rate is used to discount
  the tax savings,
. the present value of purchasing is always lower than the present value of financial leasing, so Bower would always prefer to
  purchase the capital asset.[8]

Evaluation

I   Bower appears to be aware of the interactions of investment
    and financing decisions. This is evident from his obser-

----

[8] Peirson and Bird develop a lease-or-borrow model in which they
    employ exactly the same cash flows as Bower. They do not,
    however, capitalize the various tax deductions at a series of
    discount rates as Bower does but at a single rate: the firm's
    after-tax weighted average cost of capital (Peirson and Bird
    1972, pp. 241-244).

vation: "In leasing there is a choice involving both operating flows and financial flows. In this case anything less
than a joint analysis of assets, claims and the optimal mix
of the two must limit the decision to an approximation of the
ideal" (pp. 25-26). It is a pity the author does not pay
attention to these interactions when disclosing his model.

II   In my view Bower's sensitivity analysis, with the help of
     which the impact of discounting the tax shields at different
     rates can be measured, is a very useful instrument in situ-
     ations where management does not know precisely at which rate
     to capitalize these shields. In my illustrative example the
     capitalization rate used is rather unimportant as the present
     value of purchasing is always lower than the present value of
     leasing. In Bower's example, however, there is a discount
     rate at which these present values are equal. If a lower rate
     is employed to capitalize the tax savings, leasing would be
     preferred, whereas applying a higher rate would lead to pur-
     chasing being the preferred alternative (p. 32). In such a
     situation management has to form an idea about the rate to
     use for discounting the various tax shields.

III In the first sentence of his article Bower states that he
     will be concerned with financial leasing (p. 25). From his
     illustrative example, this is obvious (p. 28).

IV   The results of Bower's evaluation model are expressed in
     present values without the author paying attention to the
     cash inflows that result from operating the asset to be
     leased or purchased.

V   In my opinion Bower reduces the practical applicability of
     his model by characterizing the problem to be solved as
     lease-or-borrow and by setting the financial lease against a
     special type of loan: the one McEachron introduced in his
     1961 article. This loan differs from the one Bower,
     Herringer, and Williamson based their 1966 model upon (see
     3.4.4). The principal of the loan Bower now wants to utilize
     is equal to the present value of the lease payments capital-
     ized at the loan rate. If this rate is lower than the inter-
     est rate implicit in the lease (as in my numerical example,

where the loan rate = 10% and the lease rate ≈ 11.14%) then the loan principal exceeds the asset's purchase price. In my example the loan principal exceeds the cash purchase price of the asset by $153. One wonders what Bower would recommend to do with this difference.

3.4.6 Gordon

Gordon begins his article on leasing by observing that the motive for writing it is formed by the article Johnson and Lewellen published in 1972 (Gordon 1974, p. 245). One of the differences between the two articles is that according to Gordon the asset's purchase price should be financed entirely by raising a loan, whereas Johnson and Lewellen reject such a lease-or-borrow approach. Thus their model belongs to the second group of lease evaluation models and will be discussed along with other lease-or-buy procedures (see 3.5.2). Here I shall go into Gordon's model. Like McEachron Gordon pays attention to the cash inflow series a capital asset generates. In order to determine the net present value of leasing that asset, NPV_{fl}^{G}, the author makes use of the following cash flows:
. the net cash inflows after taxes,
. the lease payments after taxes (p. 247).
Gordon capitalizes the first cash flow series at the project hurdle rate, assuming perfect capital markets and all-equity financing (15%), and the second one at the borrowing rate (10%):

$$NPV_{fl}^{G} = (\frac{\$4,800}{1.15^1} + \frac{\$4,200}{1.15^2}) - (\frac{\$3,510}{1.10^1} + \frac{\$3,510}{1.10^2})$$

$$= \$7,350 - \$6,092 = \$1,258$$

In this calculation the after-tax net cash inflows ($4,800 and $4,200) were copied from Table 3.1, and the after-tax lease payments ($3,510 and $3,510) come from Table 3.5. Computing Gordon's net present value of purchasing (NPV_{p}^{G}) involves much more ciphering. Gordon wants to finance the cash purchase price of the asset by raising a loan "to neutralize the tax advantage in the lease option due to the implicit debt financing" (p. 248). If the lease contract requires constant payments to be made (as in my example) then the loan, which should have the same term as the lease, ought to be redeemed "by means of equal annual payments that cover interest and principal at the interest rate at which the corporation borrows" (p. 248). Starting from my example, these "equal annual payments" are the same as the ones calculated in 3.4.4 while applying the Bower, Herringer, and Williamson methodology to this example: $5,762 to be paid at each year of the two-year loan term. Just as in Table 3.14 these loan payments have to be divided into principal payment and interest. Now we have all the elements necessary to determine NPV_p^G, for this net present value comprises:

. the net cash inflows after taxes,
. the depreciation deductions,
. the principal payments on the loan,
. the interest payments on the loan after taxes.

Gordon discounts the after-tax net cash inflows at the all-equity financing rate (15%) and the other cash flows at the loan rate (10%). Hence it appears that:

$$NPV_p^G = (\frac{\$4,800}{1.15^1} + \frac{\$4,200}{1.15^2}) + (\frac{\$2,200}{1.10^1} + \frac{\$1,800}{1.10^2})$$

$$- (\frac{\$4,762}{1.10^1} + \frac{\$5,238}{1.10^2}) - (1-0.4) \times (\frac{\$1,000}{1.10^1} + \frac{\$524}{1.10^2})$$

$$= \$7,350 + \$3,488 - \$8,658 - \$805 = \$1,375$$

The net cash inflows after taxes ($4,800 and $4,200) were also used when determining NPV_{fl}^G. The depreciation tax savings ($2,200 and $1,800) were taken from Table 3.1, whereas the other cash flows were copied from Table 3.14. Since NPV_p^G exceeds NPV_{fl}^G according to Gordon purchasing should be preferred.

Evaluation

Evaluating Gordon's model is hampered by the fact that some parts of his article are not clear. Examples are: a (typographical?)

error in the numerator of the last term of his equation (5) on p. 246, a typographical or computational error in calculating the "net present value of the buy option" (p. 249), and a mistake when reproducing an equation that was introduced by Modigliani and Miller. The fact is that Gordon states: "The after-tax cost of capital on an investment with standard risk is $qk+(1-q)(1-\tau)k$ where q is the fraction of debt in the capital structure, and k is ρ^τ in the Modigliani-Miller notation."[9] Simplifying this formula results in Gordon's after-tax cost of capital being equal to $k(1-\tau+\tau q)$. However, making use of the Gordon notation, Modigliani and Miller's equation should be: after-tax cost of capital = $k(1-\tau q)$ (see Modigliani and Miller 1963, p. 442). Let us now review Gordon's lease-or-borrow model with the help of the five requirements.

I Gordon computes the net present value of purchasing and the net present value of financial leasing. He does not try to separate the capital budgeting decision from the financing decision. In situations where the buy alternative would not be profitable, Gordon would still compute the net present value of leasing. In my opinion this is correct.

II It is rather difficult to understand which rates Gordon utilizes for discounting purposes, because some of the rates he discounts at do without a clear definition (see pp. 245-247: the rates k' and $\hat{k}$). In the second place, misspecifying one of the Modigliani-Miller equations, as discussed earlier, may create some confusion. Another rate at which Gordon capitalizes is i, defined as the "interest rate on a risk free cash flow" (p. 247). He employs this interest rate to compute the present value of the lease payments, the amortization as well as the interest payments on the loan, and the various tax deductions. The reason Gordon discounts at this rate is that he assumes that "the firm is considered to be in a strong financial position" (p. 247). In a footnote he adds:

----

9) In the above equation, τ is the corporate income tax rate.

"For the typical firm ... the lease payments have the same status as debt payments" (p. 247, footnote 3). I doubt whether in practice there are many firms that are really able to borrow at Gordon's "interest rate on a risk free cash flow." That is why in my example borrowing at this rate is not possible, and therefore I discount the above cash flows at a loan rate that comprises a risk-free element plus a risk premium (e.g., for default risk).

III From the title of Gordon's article ("A General Solution to the Buy or Lease Decision: a Pedagogical Note") and from the article itself one may get the impression that Gordon's model can be applied to financial leases as well as to operating leases. In his illustrative example, however, the author uses his model to evaluate a financial lease only. He does not look into the evaluation of operating leases.

IV As observed earlier the results of the technique Gordon develops are expressed in net present values, taking into consideration the cash inflows the capital asset is expected to generate.

V According to Gordon the problem to be solved is "lease-or-borrow." Moreover, in his view borrowing involves concluding a specific type of loan. Hence, his model can only be applied in those situations in which such a loan can actually be raised. Apart from that the usefulness of his approach has been limited by the fact that he does not explain how to determine the repayment schedule of this (equivalent) loan if the lease arrangement requires making unequal payments. Gordon assumes "that the lease calls for equal annual payments. If not, the loan payments can be made proportional to the lease payments. The two sets of payments will differ due to the implicit interest rate in each and the other costs covered by the lease payments" (p. 248, footnote 4). Unfortunately the author does not explain how the loan payments are to be made proportional to the lease payments.

3.4.7 Myers, Dill, and Bautista

In their 1976 article, Myers, Dill, and Bautista (MDB) present a solidly built model for valuing financial lease contracts. The three authors "define the value of the lease contract as the advantage of leasing vs. normal financing." The cash flows necessary for computing this value are:
. the cash purchase price of the asset,
. the lease payments after taxes,
. the tax savings on depreciation,
. the tax savings on interest of the "equivalent loan"(MDB 1976, pp. 801-802).
They believe it to be reasonable to capitalize these cash flows at the "firm's marginal borrowing rate" (p. 802). Next they argue that "if the firm employs debt financing, then the lease displaces debt" (p. 802). However, the amount of debt displaced by the lease (which amount equals the equivalent loan) "depends on how the lease's value ... changes over time" (p. 803). Hence, in order to determine the value of the lease one has to calculate the amount of displaced debt, but this amount depends on the value of the lease. Consequently, as MDB argue, these values have to be solved for simultaneously. Basing themselves on three assumptions, the authors prove that this problem can be avoided by discounting at "a weighted cost of capital, computed according to the Modigliani-Miller (MM) formula" (pp. 803-807). According to this formula: $\rho^* = \rho(1-\lambda T)$,[10] where:

"ρ^* = the weighted average cost of capital, or hurdle rate, appropriate for discounting project cash flows ...,

ρ = the appropriate project hurdle rate assuming perfect capital markets and all-equity financing" (p. 807),

T = the marginal corporate income tax rate,

λ = the proportion financed with tax deductible sources of capital, or according to MDB: "the amount of debt dis-

---

[10] While discussing Gordon's model in 3.4.6, I also used this formula.

placed or supported by a lease contract" (p. 816).
MDB observe that here ρ is equal to the firm's borrowing rate (p.
807). When applying the above formula to my example, assuming $\lambda=1$,
the discount rate to be used, ρ^*, turns out to be 10% x (1-1x40%)
= 6%. As a result of the assumption made, this rate happens to be
equal to the after-tax cost of debt, (1-40%) x 10% = 6%. In order
to calculate the value of the lease in my example, this rate
should, according to MDB, be used to determine the present value
of the following cash flows:
. the cash purchase price of the asset,
. the lease payments after taxes,
. the tax savings on depreciation.
Setting this cash flow series against the one on p. 64, we see
that the tax savings on the interest payments of the equivalent
loan are eliminated now. Starting from my numerical example, the
value of the financial lease should be computed as:

$$\text{value of lease} = \$10,000 - \left(\frac{\$3,510}{1.06^1} + \frac{\$3,510}{1.06^2}\right) - \left(\frac{\$2,200}{1.06^1} + \frac{\$1,800}{1.06^2}\right)$$

$$= -\$112$$

The after-tax lease payments (\$3,510 at the end of the first and
the second year) were calculated in Table 3.5, whereas the depreciation deductions (\$2,200 and \$1,800) were calculated in Table
3.1. Since the value of the lease turns out to be negative, purchasing the capital asset should be preferred. However, there is
another way to arrive at the same result, namely by applying the
model Weston and Brigham recommend in the third and in fourth
editions of their textbook. Back in 3.4.3 we saw that PV_p^{WB69} =
\$6,323 and that PV_{fl}^{WB69} = \$6,435. The difference between these two
present values, or using the MDB terminology, "the advantage of
leasing vs. normal financing" is -\$112 too. This is as may be
expected because in the 1969 edition of <u>Managerial Finance</u> Weston
and Brigham discount the same cash flows as MDB employ at the
"firm's after-tax cost of debt," which in my example happens to
equal the rate at which MDB discount. Just like Vancil's "borrowing opportunity rate method," the MDB model has been examined by

many authors. Among them are Ashton (1978, pp. 231-251), Clark
(1978, pp. 198-214), Franks and Hodges (1978, pp. 657-669),
Franks and Broyles (1979, pp. 322-330), Levy and Sarnat (1979,
pp. 47-54), Haley and Schall (1979, p. 466), Brealey and Young
(1980, pp. 1245-1250), Idol (1980, pp. 24-29), Brealey and Myers
(1981, pp. 528-540), and Herbst (1982, pp. 164-169).

Evaluation

I   MDB pay attention to the interactions of the firm's financing
    and investment decisions. They observe that "the decision to
    acquire a capital asset cannot in general be separated from
    the lease terms which may be offered" (p. 819).

II MDB do not prove that discounting at the firm's marginal
    borrowing rate is correct. They only believe it to be "a
    reasonable starting point" (p. 802).[11] Calculating the
    present value of the various cash flow streams utilizing one
    discount rate would be justified only, as they correctly
    argue, "when the streams fall in the same risk class." The
    authors continue by observing that "we are assuming that the
    streams of payments and tax shields have the same risk char-
    acteristics as the stream of interest and principal payments
    on the firm's debt" (p. 802). Later on in their article they
    return to this subject, stating that the various tax shields
    lost or created by the lease contract "are somewhat uncer-
    tain" (p. 816), so that capitalizing at a higher rate may be
    justified. They do not, though, explain which rate to employ.
    Finally, in their illustrative example, where MDB analyze the
    Anaconda lease of 1973, the borrowing rate exceeds the lease
    rate. Yet they discount the relevant cash flows at the
    borrowing rate (p. 808). As we observed when discussing
    Weston and Brigham's 1975 model (see p. 51), the lower of
    these two rates ought to be used for discounting purposes
    (for an explanation of this procedure see Chapter 4, p. 129).

----

11) Haley and Schall as well as Idol address this issue (Haley
    and Schall 1979, p. 466; Idol 1980, p. 28).

III The MDB model is intended for valuing financial leases, as is apparent from the title of their article ("Valuation of Financial Lease Contracts"). In their 1983 textbook, Copeland and Weston employ the MDB model to determine the competitive lease payment of a cancelable operating lease. This is accomplished by combining this model with "the present value of the American put option" (Copeland and Weston 1983, pp. 550-552; see also Copeland and Weston 1982, pp. 60-67).

IV In order to determine whether a financial lease is worthwhile, MDB utilize a present value calculation. They state that their "conclusions mostly support those presented by Bower" (p. 799), but on the other hand they reject one of Bower's most important conclusions: raising a loan equal to the present value of the before-tax lease payments to finance the purchase price of the capital asset (see 3.4.5). MDB take the view that this is an incorrect approach to represent the amount of debt displaced by leasing. Quite remarkably they attribute this approach to Vancil (p. 810). As we saw in 3.4.2, Table 3.11, according to Vancil the principal of the financial lease should be equal to the asset's purchase price and should certainly not equal the present value of the lease payments.

V Although MDB quite rightly state that we have "to get beyond the narrow lease vs. borrow problem, which limits the choice to two basically similar long-term financial claims" (p.815), they concentrate on lease versus borrow. Besides, as we saw earlier, their borrow alternative involves contracting a very special type of loan: the so-called equivalent loan. Concentrating on the lease-or-borrow question, the authors argue that this approach "only recognizes that a firm which signs a lease contract reduces its ability to borrow through other channels. In this sense the lease displaces debt; it uses up some of the 'debt capacity' created by the firm's other assets" (p. 801). As it turns out, the value of the lease they calculate is equal to the difference between the asset's purchase price, which in the case of leasing is paid for by the lessor, and the debt capacity used up by leasing, which amount equals the equivalent loan. In their opinion the debt capacity used up by leasing should be measured by means of cash flows. From a theoretical standpoint, I think they are right. In reality though, debt capacity is often measured in several other ways. To many firms, book values are important for measuring debt capacity, as Weston and Brigham observe in the 1975 edition of their textbook (Weston and Brigham 1975, p. 613, footnote 22). These values may be used for determining various leverage ratios, such as the total debt to total assets ratio. Ashton also looks into this issue. He argues that: "In general financial markets actually impose restrictions on the use of debt capacity which are closely related to reported accounting valuations. Typically the use of debt financing by a firm is restricted by such factors as current income levels and existing asset-liability structures" (Ashton 1978, p. 238). Empirical evidence gathered by Fawthrop and Terry points in the same direction. They discovered "the ratio of debt to equity in the balance sheet" and "the prior charges cover in the Profits and Losses account" to be more relevant than "the prior charges cover afforded by a cash flow forecast of some kind" (Fawthrop and Terry 1975, p. 300). In this connection I support Clark's view when he argues: "Opinions on the extent to which firms may increase their debt capacity by leasing are necessarily subjective. The views taken by individual companies and the attitudes of different financial institutions vary considerably. It is not feasible to quantify the effects of leasing on debt capacity in any particular circumstances" (Clark 1978, pp. 181-182). Clark also gives a number of reasons as to why leasing may increase the firm's debt capacity, at least in England.[12] These reasons are: "im-

----

[12] Clark cites Merrett and Sykes, who point out that there are "substantial differences in attitude to lease commitments which appear to exist between institutional lenders in the United States and in Britain" (Clark 1978, p. 180).

perfect knowledge on the part of lenders," "possible lower risks", "the potential additional rewards through retaining or sharing in the residual value of the asset," and the fact that the "fixed nature of a leasing facility gives greater security to other providers of finance" (p. 181). To conclude, as explained earlier MDB utilize λ to reflect "the amount of debt displaced or supported by a lease contract." In the above calculations, it was assumed that $\lambda=1$, i.e., that leasing displaces debt on a dollar-for-dollar basis. In their illustrative examples, MDB assume that $\lambda=1$ and $\lambda=0.8$ both for the lessee and for the lessor (p. 813). One wonders if it would be possible for λ to exceed 1. To my thinking, $\lambda>1$ may result from the capital market regarding the conclusion of a lease contract as a signal of financial weakness, arguing that only financially weak firms conclude lease contracts. Herbst too discusses the possibility of λ being larger than one. He even observes that "for high-quality, low-risk lessees it is likely that $\lambda>1.0$" (Herbst 1982, p. 169; see also pp. 166-168).

3.4.8 Beckman and Joosen

In order to develop their lease evaluation methods, Beckman and Joosen, two Dutch authors, employ the following starting points:
. they assume that the investment decision has already been made and that all that needs to be done is to select the optimal financing arrangement (Beckman and Joosen 1980, p. 67, p. 69, and p. 78),
. the Dutch fiscal authorities consider a financial lessee to be the owner of the leased asset so that, just like any other asset owner, the lessee is allowed to deduct both depreciation and interest charges when computing its taxable income (p. 69),
. differences in the amounts of funds provided by alternative financing arrangements are irrelevant (pp. 76-77).[13]

----

13) In 3.4.2 we observed that Vancil is of the same opinion.

In their illustrative example, there are two distinct financing arrangements: a bank loan and a financial lease. Beckman and Joosen (subsequently BJ) use an internal-rate-of-return method as well as a present-value method to compare these financing alternatives (pp. 69-78). We already applied the former approach when discussing Vancil's "borrowing opportunity rate method" (see 3.4.2). In my numerical example, the loan rate, k_1, is 10% and the financial lease rate, k_{fl}, equals 11.14%. From these results BJ would conclude that raising the loan and buying the asset is preferable to leasing it. BJ contend that the same choice would be made if the tax deductibility of the interest payments is taken into account. The after-tax loan rate then equals (1-40%) x 10% = 6%, and the after-tax lease rate is (1-40%) x 11.14% = 6.684%. Since the depreciation charges are identical when buying or when leasing (which follows from the second starting point of BJ), they cancel out. Therefore Vancil's objection - that apart from the interest payments there are differences in permissible income tax deductions that would be ignored when comparing financing arrangements by means of interest rate computations (see p. 26) - does not hold.

Next I shall apply the BJ present-value method to our example. They compute the present values of both financing arrangements by discounting the relevant cash flows at the after-tax loan rate because if any other rate is employed differences in the amount of financing provided would also be reflected in the present value cost of each financing plan. The cash flows BJ use to determine the present value of buying and borrowing are:
. the loan repayments,
. the after-tax loan interest payments.
When illustrating this approach with the help of a numerical example, BJ assume that the loan is to be repaid at the end of its term. We shall make the same assumption. Hence, according to BJ the present value of purchasing, PV_p^{BJ}, equals:

$$PV_p^{BJ} = \frac{\$10,000}{1.06^2} + \frac{\$600}{1.06^1} + \frac{\$600}{1.06^2} = \$10,000$$

The after-tax interest payments to be made at the end of each year of the two-year loan term are calculated from the following equation:

after-tax interest payment = (1 - tax rate) x loan interest rate x loan principal = (1-40%) x 0.1 x $10,000 = $600

BJ compute the present value of the leasing arrangement by discounting the difference between:
. the lease payments, and
. the tax savings on the lease interest payments
at the after-tax loan rate (6%). They compute the lease interest payments in the same way we did in Table 3.6. The difference between the lease payments and the tax savings on the interest portion of these payments is then capitalized at 6%. According to BJ the present value of leasing the capital asset of our example is:

$$PV_{fl}^{BJ} = \frac{\$5,850 - 0.4 \times \$1,114}{1.06^1} + \frac{\$5,850 - 0.4 \times \$586}{1.06^2} = \$10,096$$

Again, purchasing would be preferred. Nevertheless, BJ recommend utilizing the internal-rate-of-return method (pp. 77-78) because given their starting points this method results in the same order of preference as the present-value method and is easier to implement.

Evaluation

I   The authors separate the investment decision from the financing decision by stating that the former decision has already been made and that only the latter decision remains to be dealt with. Thus, when applying the BJ model it is not possible for sufficiently attractive lease terms to reverse an original negative purchase decision.

II Above it was explained that BJ capitalize the cash flows of leasing and those of borrowing at the after-tax cost of debt because differences in the amount of funds provided by these financing arrangements should be eliminated. There is another way to eliminate these differences though: setting the financial lease against some kind of equivalent loan. As we observed in 3.4.4, Bower, Herringer, and Williamson, among others, make use of such a loan. Besides, in the present value computations of BJ, the interest tax shield is reflected both in the numerator and in the denominator. Consequently, these adjustments cancel out. That is why, when explaining his lease evaluation model, Bierman observes: "The interest tax shield is omitted from the buy analysis since the inclusion of the debt flows would result in their washing out completely ... when the after-tax borrowing rate is being used as the discount rate" (Bierman 1982, p. 16). For this same reason, when performing a net-present-value analysis to make a capital budgeting decision, the interest tax savings are usually reflected in the firm's cost of capital but not in the cash flow series discounted at this rate (see, among others, Weston and Brigham 1981, p. 415 and pp. 593-594).

III BJ clearly indicate that their models can be utilized to value financial leases only. In 5.7 I shall review their methodology for analyzing operating leases.

IV As explained earlier the two authors prefer their internal-rate-of-return method to their present-value model. However, in many textbooks on finance objections are raised to comparing alternative strategies with the help of their internal rates of return, the more so as the investment decision and the financing decision usually interact. Because of these interactions the cash inflow series should be taken into consideration too.

V BJ limit their model to the lease-or-borrow question. If the purchase price of the capital asset to be acquired is financed by way of equity or by a combination of debt and equity, their model cannot be applied.

3.5 Lease-or-Buy Models

In the following I shall review a number of models that set
financial leasing against purchasing financed with a combination
of debt and equity. In turn the approaches of Weston and Brigham;
Johnson and Lewellen; Vial; Krumbholz and Streitferdt; Spittler;
Haley and Schall; Schall and Haley; and Theunissen will come up
for discussion.

3.5.1 Weston and Brigham

In this section I shall analyze the three lease-or-buy models
Weston and Brigham have developed: the first one dates from 1962,
the second one from 1978, and the third one from 1981. For the
other (lease-or-borrow) approaches Weston and Brigham developed,
refer to 3.4.3.

3.5.1.1 Weston 1962 Appendix (First Edition)

In the appendix to his chapter on leasing in the 1962 edition,
Weston recommends utilizing a lease valuation model that is quite
different from the one he uses in the chapter itself.[14] The
author pictures his appendix model to be "a more direct method of
comparison" (Weston 1962, p. 319). He argues that "the test to
apply is whether the investment that would be tied up in the
equipment would earn the firm's cost of capital" (p. 319). In our
numerical example the investment, or the cash purchase price of
the capital asset, is $10,000. This amount has to be compared
with the present value of the after-tax annual savings if the
asset is purchased instead of leased. Starting from our example,
the saving realized at the end of each year of the two-year lease
term should, according to Weston, be calculated as: lease payment

----
[14] Section 3.4.3.1 discussed the latter model.

- tax rate x (lease payment - depreciation). At the end of the
first year this would result in: $5,850 - 0.4x($5,850 - $5,500) =
$5,710. The after-tax saving at the end of the second year is:
$5,850 - 0.4x($5,850 - $4,500) = $5,310. Capitalizing these savings at 13%, the firm's cost of capital, in our example, would
result in a present value of $9,212. So, just as in Weston's
illustrative example, "the present worth of the after-tax rentals
avoided by owning rather than leasing is less than the cost of
the investment. Therefore the firm gains by leasing rather than
owning. Clearly, it is better for the firm to lease than to own
under the circumstances described" (p. 319). The cash flows
Weston uses to arrive at this result are:
. the cash purchase price of the asset,
. the lease payments after taxes,
. the tax savings on depreciation.
In fact, this is the same cash flow series as the one Myers,
Dill, and Bautista (among others) utilize, but Weston discounts
these cash flows at the firm's cost of capital and not at the
rate these three authors make use of. In our example, that is why
financial leasing would be preferred to purchasing:

$$\$10,000 - (\frac{\$3,510}{1.13^1} + \frac{\$3,510}{1.13^2}) - (\frac{\$2,200}{1.13^1} + \frac{\$1,800}{1.13^2}) = \$788$$

In 3.4.7 it was explained that the value of the lease as calculated by Myers, Dill, and Bautista is -$112, indicating that pur-
chasing should be preferred to leasing. Another difference
between the valuation model of these three writers and Weston's
approach is that they propose to employ an equivalent loan to
finance the asset's purchase price, whereas Weston does not.
Therefore, Weston's model is not a lease-or-borrow model.

Evaluation

I   No more than in his chapter on leasing does Weston pay
    attention to the calculation of the profitability of the
    combined investment and financing decision.

II In his appendix, Weston discounts the relevant cash flows at
    the firm's cost of capital instead of at the cost of debt,

the rate he applies in his chapter on leasing. I have not found out why the author now uses a different rate for discounting these cash flows. Moreover, in a footnote he even refers to Vancil's "borrowing opportunity rate method" for "a cogent argument for using the cost of debt in the calculations" (p. 319, footnote 1).

III Although neither in the appendix nor in his chapter on leasing does Weston distinguish between financial and operating leases, from his illustrative example it appears that he is concerned with the first type of leases.

IV The results of Weston's appendix model are again expressed in terms of present values (without considering the cash inflows arising from asset operation), just like the results of the evaluation method he explains in his chapter on leasing. There are differences between the two models though. In II we already paid attention to the differences in discount rates used. Another difference concerns the tax savings on interest. In the chapter on leasing, these savings form part of the cash flow series of the purchase alternative (see 3.4.3.1), but in the appendix they are left out of account. One may suggest that Weston now assumes the asset's purchase price to be entirely financed with equity instead of by contracting a loan. However, this would not be in accordance with the author's discounting at the firm's cost of capital, which rate assumes financing with a combination of debt and equity. I take it that in his appendix Weston utilizes such a combination to finance the purchase price of the capital asset and that he copes with the tax deductibility of the interest payments by adjusting the firm's cost of capital, as he does in his chapter on capital budgeting.

V Unfortunately Weston does not state in what situations to apply the model of his chapter on leasing instead of the one explained in the appendix to this chapter. The importance of such a statement may be evident from our example: applying the first valuation method results in recommending the purchase agreement, whereas according to the second model financial leasing should be preferred. Besides, many con-

ditions have to be fulfilled before the firm's cost of
capital can be used for discounting purposes as, among
others, Myers shows. Management should make sure that, when
it capitalizes at this rate, these conditions have been met.

3.5.1.2 Weston and Brigham 1978 (Sixth Edition)

The way Weston and Brigham (WB) tackle the lease valuation problem in the sixth edition of their textbook seems to be completely
new. As appears from the title of the section where they go into
this problem, namely "Cost Comparison between Lease and Purchase"
(WB 1978, pp. 549-554), they no longer try to choose between
leasing and borrowing. On the contrary, they state "that the
comparison is between leasing and the normal mix of debt and
equity financing" (p. 567). Moreover, they argue that "assuming
competitive financial markets, the terms on which leasing versus
owning will be available to the user firm will result in no
advantage to one form of acquiring the use of the assets as
compared with another" (p. 554). Next they discuss a number of
factors that may result in preferring one alternative to the
other.

The model WB now advocate for choosing between financial leasing and buying distinguishes itself from any other evaluation
method they described in the various previous editions of Managerial Finance in that the authors now also pay attention to the
net cash inflows generated by the asset to be acquired. In order
to compute the net present value of financial leasing, WB utilize
the following cash flows:
. the net cash inflows after taxes,
. the lease payments after taxes (p. 551).
The authors calculate the net present value of these cash flows
by discounting them at the firm's cost of capital. Hence, in our
illustrative example the net present value of the leasing agreement according to WB, NPV_{fl}^{WB78}, is:

$$NPV_{fl}^{WB78} = (\frac{\$4,800}{1.13^1} + \frac{\$4,200}{1.13^2}) - (\frac{\$3,510}{1.13^1} + \frac{\$3,510}{1.13^2}) = \$1,682$$

The after-tax net cash inflows ($4,800 and $4,200) have already been calculated in Table 3.1, and the after-tax lease payments ($3,510 and $3,510) were taken from Table 3.5. The cash flows necessary to compute the net present value of purchasing, i.e., NPV_p^{WB78}, are:

. the net cash inflows after taxes,
. the tax savings on depreciation,
. the cash purchase price of the asset.

Again WB discount at the firm's cost of capital. Application of their model yields:

$$NPV_p^{WB78} = (\frac{\$4,800}{1.13^1} + \frac{\$4,200}{1.13^2}) + (\frac{\$2,200}{1.13^1} + \frac{\$1,800}{1.13^2}) - \$10,000 = \$894$$

The depreciation deductions ($2,200 and $1,800) were copied from Table 3.1. Since NPV_{fl}^{WB78} ($1,682) exceeds NPV_p^{WB78} ($894), financial leasing should be preferred. When we compute the difference between these two net present values though, we find this difference to be $1,682 - $894 = $788. This result is exactly equal to the result of applying Weston's 1962 model (see 3.5.1.1). This equality arises from the fact that when we calculate the difference between NPV_{fl}^{WB78} and NPV_p^{WB78}, the after-tax net cash inflows generated by the asset cancel out. The remaining cash flows are:

. the cash purchase price of the asset,
. the lease payments after taxes,
. the tax savings on depreciation.

These are the same cash flows Weston utilizes to determine whether "the investment that would be tied up in the equipment would earn the firm's cost of capital" (Weston 1962, p. 319). The same rate is used for discounting purposes in the 1978 edition of Managerial Finance.

Evaluation

I   In contrast with the three previous editions of their textbook, which were discussed in 3.4.3, WB no longer recommend making the investment decision prior to the financing deci-

sion. By means of the net present value procedure they now
apply, the combined effects of both decisions are expressed.
II As observed earlier, the authors capitalize the relevant cash
flows at the firm's after-tax weighted average cost of capital instead of at the cost of debt. Concerning the use of
this rate, their argument can be summarized as follows:

. "a 100 per cent debt ratio for the lessor firm would not be
  realistic, so a weighted cost to reflect some use of equity
  would be required,"

. there would be a "symmetry between the position of the lessor and lessee which is generally agreed to be necessary
  for a correct analysis,"

. consequently "the use of the cost of debt alone is in-
  appropriate for analyzing the position of the lessee." (p.
  570).

As to the first statement of WB, I agree that a 100% debt
ratio of a lessor firm is not realistic. However, this does
not necessarily imply that a lessor should use his firm's
cost of capital to make capital budgeting decisions. This
depends, among other things, on the risk of the project and
on the manner in which it is financed. Regarding the second
statement of WB, I would like to stress that Lewellen, Long,
and McConnell, on whose article WB ground their argument,
demonstrate that "symmetry between the position of the lessor
and lessee" does not always hold. For instance "differences
in borrowing policies" may be a disturbing factor (Lewellen,
Long, and McConnell 1976, p. 797). Myers, Dill, and Bautista
as well as Gaumnitz and Ford and Herbst pay attention to such
disturbing factors too (Myers, Dill, and Bautista 1976, p.
812; Gaumnitz and Ford 1978, pp. 69-74; Herbst 1982, p. 169).
To conclude I should point out that WB determine the net
present value of a financial lease by discounting a "cash
flow to equity" at the firm's cost of capital. A cash flow to
equity is involved here because the difference between the
net cash inflows generated by the leased asset and the lease
payments goes to the stockholders only. A firm's cost of
capital, though, is a combination of the rates required by

stockholders and bondholders. Unfortunately, WB do not prove their discounting procedure to be correct.

III From the data of the examples WB employ to illustrate their model it can be concluded that they value financial leases.

IV Applying their valuation model results in net present values. However, when we compare their present cash flow series with the series they capitalized in the 1966 and 1975 editions of Managerial Finance, which also used the firm's cost of capital for discounting purposes, we find that the tax savings on the interest payments are left out now. The authors do not explain this difference in their methodology.

V WB no longer restrict their model to comparing financial leasing with borrowing. Since they discount at the firm's cost of capital, management should make sure that the necessary and sufficient conditions for utilizing this rate have been fulfilled.

3.5.1.3 Weston and Brigham 1981 (Seventh Edition)

When we set WB's "Cost Comparison between Leasing and Owning for Financial Leases" as described in the seventh (and up to now latest) edition of Managerial Finance against their analysis of this issue in the sixth edition, we see that the authors still compare financial leasing with buying and that once again they discount at the firm's cost of capital (WB 1981, pp. 855-859). On the other hand the net cash inflows expected from asset operation no longer form part of their calculations: in the latest edition WB calculate present values instead of net present values. The cash flows WB capitalize to calculate the present value of owning are:

. the cash purchase price of the asset,

. the depreciation deductions (p. 858).

Starting from our example, the present value of purchasing the asset as computed according to WB's 1981 approach, PV_p^{WB81}, is:

$$PV_p^{WB81} = \$10,000 - (\frac{\$2,200}{1.13^1} + \frac{\$1,800}{1.13^2}) = \$6,643$$

Again the depreciation deductions ($2,200 and $1,800) have been taken from Table 3.1. In order to determine the present value of the leasing agreement, PV_{fl}^{WB81}, WB discount the after-tax lease payments ($3,510 to be paid at the end of each year of the two-year financial lease term, see Table 3.5) at the firm's cost of capital:

$$PV_{fl}^{WB81} = \frac{\$3,510}{1.13^1} + \frac{\$3,510}{1.13^2} = \$5,855$$

The present value of purchasing ($6,643) exceeds the present value of financial leasing ($5,855), so WB would recommend leasing the capital asset. When we subtract the second present value from the first one, we obtain $6,643 - $5,855 = $788.[15] As observed when examining the sixth edition of <u>Managerial Finance,</u> this difference is exactly equal to the amount calculated when applying Weston's 1962 model to our example (see 3.5.1.2). Again this is as may be expected, because when computing the difference between PV_p^{WB81} and PV_{fl}^{WB81} the following cash flows are of relevance:

. the cash purchase price of the asset,
. the lease payments after taxes,
. the tax savings on depreciation.

As argued in 3.5.1.2 these are the same cash flows Weston discounts in order to determine whether "the investment that would be tied up in the equipment would earn the firm's cost of capital" (Weston 1962, p. 319).

Evaluation

I   With regard to the relationships between investment and financing decisions, WB describe two alternative approaches. On the one hand they argue that "the first screening test is whether, from a capital budgeting standpoint, the project passes the investment hurdle rate. The second question is

----

[15] WB perform a similar calculation on p. 858.

then whether leasing or some other method of financing is the least expensive method of financing the project." On the other hand they observe: "Alternatively, it could be argued that we do not know what the cost of capital (and therefore the investment screening rate) is until we have determined the least expensive method of financing. Having determined this method, we can determine the applicable investment screening hurdle rate for the decision of whether to undertake the project from a capital budgeting standpoint" (p. 855). The authors apply the former approach and, as observed earlier, only look into the "second question" of this approach. Hence, WB do not take into consideration the interactions of corporate financing and investment decisions they describe in the latter approach.

II WB say they are applying the lease valuation model of Myers, Dill, and Bautista, which was discussed in 3.4.7. There are some important differences between the model as utilized by WB and by Myers, Dill, and Bautista. In the first place WB do not pay attention to the equivalent loan these three authors introduced. Besides, WB discount at a rate that differs from the one Myers, Dill, and Bautista use. WB argue that "since both the lease payments and the foregone depreciation tax shields are risk-free, they can be discounted at the cost of debt. Since the debt cost is deductible to the user firm, the after-tax cost of debt is utilized" (p. 857). Regarding the former part of this statement, I doubt whether the lease payments and the depreciation tax shields are really risk-free. This is because the lease payments may have some default risk, and the "tax shields take on some of the business risk of the firm's operations, since the shields have little value if the firm's operating income evaporates" as Myers, Dill, and Bautista observe (Myers, Dill, and Bautista 1976, p. 802, footnote 9). In my view the risk of the tax shields can only be partly reduced by regulations concerning tax carry forward and back. In 4.3 I shall return to this subject. However, if we assume the lease payments and the depreciation deductions to be risk-free, then the risk-

free rate should be applied to compute their present values.
Rather than using this rate WB maintain that they discount
these cash flows at the (after-tax) cost of debt (see the
latter part of their statement quoted earlier). In their
example the before-tax cost of debt is 8% and the tax rate is
40% (p. 856), so the after-tax cost of debt should be equal
to (1-40%) x 8% = 4.8%. Nevertheless, they discount the lease
payments and the depreciation deductions at 6% (p. 858). In
their example this 6% rate is the firm's cost of capital of
the lessor calculated according to the Modigliani and Miller
formula Myers, Dill, and Bautista also apply. According to
Modigliani and Miller: $\rho^* = \rho(1-\lambda T)$. For an explanation of
this formula, refer to 3.4.7 where I discussed the valuation
method developed by Myers, Dill, and Bautista. However,
whereas these authors observe that in order to value leases
properly ρ should be equal to the firm's borrowing rate (see
Myers, Dill, and Bautista 1976, p. 807), in the example
utilized by WB ρ exceeds the borrowing rate (p. 856). Apart
from that I doubt whether the lessee knows the firm's cost of
capital of its lessor. That is why, while illustrating WB's
model, I discounted the various cash flows at the firm's cost
of capital of the lessee.

III As WB observe on p. 855: "The form of leasing to be analyzed
initially will be a pure financial lease which is fully
amortized, noncancellable, and without provision for maintenance services." Clearly their analysis concerns financial
leasing.

IV Applying the approach WB propose in the seventh edition of
their book results in present values. The cash inflows
expected from asset operation do not form part of these
present value calculations.

V If WB really capitalize the cash flows of financial leasing
and purchasing at the lessor firm's cost of capital computed
in the Modigliani and Miller fashion (as they claim they are
doing), then ρ,"the appropriate project hurdle rate assuming
perfect capital markets and all-equity financing," should be
equal to the borrowing rate (see 3.4.7). It should be borne

in mind that Modigliani and Miller's firm's cost of capital can only be used for discounting level, perpetual cash flow streams. If, on the other hand, WB discount at the firm's cost of capital of the lessee, then management should be convinced that the conditions for utilizing this rate have been met.

3.5.2 Johnson and Lewellen: Article, Comments and Reply

Johnson and Lewellen's article gave rise to the publication of a number of comments. Exactly one year after they published their article in the _Journal of Finance_, the comments of Clark, Jantorni, and Gann; Lusztig; Bierman; and Lev and Orgler were published in the same magazine. According to the editor "some fifteen additional 'Comments' were received on this article, but due to subject overlap and space limitations it was not possible to accept more than four" (_Journal of Finance_ 1973, p. 1015). Most of the writers just mentioned advocate lease-or-borrow models. However, I prefer to discuss these comments along with the lease-or-buy approach developed by Johnson and Lewellen. In 3.4.6 we reviewed the lease valuation model of Gordon, who utilizes Johnson and Lewellen's methodology as a starting point to design a completely different model. In the following I shall first of all discuss the original article of Johnson and Lewellen (3.5.2.1), then look into the four comments mentioned above (3.5.2.2 - 3.5.2.5), and finally examine Johnson and Lewellen's reply (3.5.2.6).

3.5.2.1 Johnson and Lewellen

The article of these authors (hereafter referred to as JL) comprises two parts: a review of some extant lease valuation models and an explanation of their own model. JL try to solve the lease-and-buy problem explicitly basing themselves on the firm's goal. They argue that the firm "should choose the type of asset and the form of acquisition that provide the maximum gains for the common stockholders of the enterprise" (JL 1972, p. 815). They state that this goal should result in choosing between alternative investment projects by determining their net present values. I agree with JL; their statement is in accordance with the fourth requirement we are using to evaluate lease-or-borrow as well as lease-or-buy models (see 2.3 above). JL continue by observing that a net present value should be calculated by capitalizing the cash inflows and the cash outflows at the firm's cost of capital because it is impossible to associate a specific investment project with a specific financing method even if they occur simultaneously (pp. 815-816). The firm's cost of capital should reflect "the long run debt-equity proportion chosen by the firm," they state. Consequently, if one form of finance is used for a project, then the next project ought to be financed in such a way that the long run debt-equity proportion chosen by the firm is restored (p. 816). It is a pity that the two authors do not go into the relationship between the preferred debt-equity proportion and the firm's goal, as described in the above, or into the procedure for establishing this preferred capital structure. JL consider a financial lease to be an "acquisition-of-services arrangement" that is equivalent to a purchase arrangement. That is why they compare such a lease with purchase to be financed by means of the same combination of debt and equity as the combination used to calculate the firm's cost of capital. They criticize models in which financial leasing is compared with purchasing financed with a loan, such as the "borrowing opportunity rate method" of Vancil (discussed in 3.4.2), the model of Weston and Brigham as described in the third edition of Managerial Finance (see 3.4.3.3), and the Bower, Herringer, and Williamson model (3.4.4).

After this rather lenghty introduction, I shall compute the net present value of financial leasing and of purchasing the asset of our example utilizing the JL model. The cash flows necessary to determine the former net present value, NPV_{fl}^{JL}, are:

. the net cash inflows after taxes,

. the lease payments after taxes (p. 819).

JL discount the first cash flow stream at the firm's cost of capital and the second one at the after-tax borrowing rate (p. 819):

$$\text{NPV}^{JL}_{fl} = (\frac{\$4,800}{1.13^1} + \frac{\$4,200}{1.13^2}) - (\frac{\$3,510}{1.06^1} + \frac{\$3,510}{1.06^2}) = \$7,537 - \$6,435$$

$$= \$1,102$$

JL capitalize the same cash flows as Gordon (see 3.4.6) and as Weston and Brigham in their 1978 model (3.5.1.2) but at different discount rates. According to JL the net present value of purchasing, NPV^{JL}_p, should be calculated in the same way as prescribed in many a textbook. In order to perform this calculation they utilize:
. the net cash inflows after taxes,
. the depreciation deductions,
. the cash purchase price of the asset.
As Weston and Brigham do in their 1978 textbook, this cash flow series is capitalized at the firm's cost of capital. Therefore,

$$\text{NPV}^{JL}_p = \text{NPV}^{WB78}_p = (\frac{\$4,800}{1.13^1} + \frac{\$4,200}{1.13^2}) + (\frac{\$2,200}{1.13^1} + \frac{\$1,800}{1.13^2}) - \$10,000$$

$$= \$7,537 + \$3,357 - \$10,000 = \$894$$

As to the details of this computation, refer to 3.5.1.2, where Weston and Brigham's 1978 approach was illustrated. Since $\text{NPV}^{JL}_{fl} = \$1,102$ and $\text{NPV}^{JL}_p = \$894$, JL would recommend leasing the capital asset. For their "investment and financing evaluation module," Pritchard and Hindelang make use of the JL methodology (Pritchard and Hindelang 1980, p. 97 and p. 115). In essence Elgers and Clark also apply the JL lease-or-buy model when they introduce their "lease project approach," although at first glance this approach looks quite different (Elgers and Clark 1980, pp. 98-101).

Evaluation
I JL object to separating the investment decision from the

financing decision. Quite rightly the argue: "Sufficiently attractive lease terms can in fact reverse the investment decision" (p. 822). Regarding this issue they completely disagree with Ferrara, who gives an affirmative answer to the question asked in the title of his article "Should Investment and Financing Decisions Be Separated?" (Ferrara 1966, p. 106).

II As apparent from the above calculations, JL discount the tax savings on depreciation at a rate that differs from the one they use for capitalizing the tax savings on the lease payments: the firm's cost of capital (13%) rather than the after-tax cost of debt (6%). The reason for this difference would be the "relatively greater predictability" of the lease's tax savings (p. 820). JL do not explain, however, why tax savings on one type of tax deductible costs would be more predictable than tax savings on another type. In the opinion of Bower this difference in capitalization rate used is an important cause for JL preferring leasing to purchasing the asset of their illustrative example.[16] He states: "It is difficult to avoid the conclusion that a higher discount rate for the shelter element of lease cost does a great deal more to bias the analysis in favor of leasing than it does to recognize any real difference in risk." Next Bower illustrates this statement with a numerical example (Bower 1973, pp. 29-30). Besides, JL think that it would be correct to utilize the same firm's cost of capital for determining NPV_{fl}^{JL} as well as NPV_p^{JL}. As observed earlier the firm's cost of capital is connected with the "long run debt-equity proportion chosen by the firm." A deviation from this proportion has to be corrected afterward by offsetting actions when financing other projects. In the mean time, though, discounting at the firm's cost of capital would not be justified, I think. In 3.5.2.3 I shall address this issue once

----

[16] As we saw earlier in our own example, leasing would be preferred too.

again.

III The title of the JL article is "Analysis of the Lease-or-Buy Decision," but nonetheless the authors pay attention to financial leases only. In particular this appears from the example with which they illustrate their theory.

IV JL choose between financial leasing and buying on the basis of the respective net present values.

V The authors pose the decision problem to be solved as lease-or-buy instead of lease-or-borrow. In my opinion this is a welcome and practical extension of the problem. In this manner a financial lease is no longer compared with a loan only but with other methods to finance the buy alternative as well. As JL correctly observe the issue to be resolved may also be described as "lease-versus-retain-earnings" or "lease-versus-sell-common stock" (p. 816, footnote 3). However, applying the JL model in practice may be hampered by the fact that in order to utilize the firm's cost of capital for discounting purposes many more conditions have to be fulfilled than maintaining "the long run debt-equity proportion chosen by the firm."

3.5.2.2 Clark, Jantorni, and Gann

Clark, Jantorni, and Gann object to the valuation model of JL because "there seems to be some inconsistency in the application of two discount rates – the overall cost of capital and the cost of debt" (Clark, Jantorni, and Gann 1973, p. 1015). They hold that there are two ways to meet this objection. Either the tax depreciation deductions, which "are as certain as the lease flows," are discounted at the same rate as the lease payments (p. 1015) or "the cash flows of the lease project should be discounted at one rate and that rate should be the firm's overall cost of capital" (p. 1016). The motive for the latter approach is the fact that JL argue that a lease arrangement is equivalent to any other capital project, which is usually valued by capitalizing its cash flows at the firm's cost of capital. Because of the many conditions that have to be met before the firm's cost of capital can be used for capitalizing future cash flows, the former method may be preferred to the latter.

3.5.2.3 Lusztig

Very properly Lusztig observes that JL assume the cost of capital to be unchanged whether the firm leases or purchases a capital asset. This is because when financing subsequent projects, the firm takes offsetting actions in order to restore its capital structure (Lusztig 1973, p. 1017; see also the discussion of this problem in 3.5.2.1). Like Clark, Jantorni, and Gann, Lusztig is of the opinion that the tax savings on depreciation are as certain as the lease payments and that these savings should also be discounted at the after-tax cost of debt. Hence, according to Lusztig the net present value of purchasing, NPV_p^L, should be calculated as follows:

$$NPV_p^L = (\frac{\$4,800}{1.13^1} + \frac{\$4,200}{1.13^2}) + (\frac{\$2,200}{1.06^1} + \frac{\$1,800}{1.06^2}) - \$10,000$$

$$= \$7,537 + \$3,677 - \$10,000 = \$1,214$$

The cash flow series in this calculation is the same as the one JL make use of (see 3.5.2.1 above), but Lusztig would capitalize the depreciation deductions at 6% (the after-tax cost of debt in our example) instead of at 13% (the firm's cost of capital). In order to determine the net present value of financial leasing, NPV_{fl}^L, Lusztig proposes to exclude the "imputed interest charges" from the lease payments. Otherwise, the tax deductibility of the interest portion of the lease payments would be accounted for in the numerator as well as in the denominator, and JL would "retain some measure of the double counting which they purport to avoid" (p. 1017). We need the following cash flows to compute NPV_{fl}^L:
. the net cash inflows after taxes,
. the "lease payments net of imputed interest charges" (p. 1018) after taxes.
The first group of cash flows is discounted at the firm's cost of

capital and the second one at the after-tax cost of debt:

$$NPV_{fl}^{L} = (\frac{\$4,800}{1.13^1} + \frac{\$4,200}{1.13^2}) - (1-0.4) \times (\frac{\$4,736}{1.06^1} + \frac{\$5,264}{1.06^2})$$

$$= \$7,537 - \$5,492 = \$2,045$$

The "lease payments net of imputed interest charges" ($4,736 at the end of the first year and $5,264 at the end of the second year), which are in fact the lease repayments, are copied from Table 3.6. Since these repayments are tax deductible, they are multiplied by 1 minus the corporate income tax rate. As NPV_{fl}^{L} is greater than NPV_{p}^{L} one would expect Lusztig to opt for financial leasing. This is not the case though; Lusztig proves that there must be an error in the above valuation model because leasing would always be preferred to purchasing (p. 1018). In Appendix 1 I shall show that he is correct (see p. 242). The author then points to a factor that was ignored up until now: the repayment schedule of a loan raised to finance the asset's cash purchase price. If we take this schedule into account then "we are very quickly returned to approaches suggested in the existing literature which do in fact separate the decision to 'acquire' from the decision about how the 'acquisition' is to be financed" (p. 1018). In the above we repeatedly rejected this approach.

3.5.2.4 Bierman

In his comment Bierman discusses four lease evaluation techniques that "are equivalent to each other and superior to" the model of JL (Bierman 1973, p. 1019). When illustrating these techniques with the help of our numerical example, I shall call them Bierman 1, 2, 3, and 4.

Bierman 1
Bierman's first model is characterized by "taking the present value of the cash flows for the investment and comparing this to the present value of the cash flows of leasing" (p. 1019). When explaining this model Bierman observes that the cash flows to be

discounted are identical to the cash flows JL make use of (see
3.5.2.1 above) but that the discount rate should be the after-tax
borrowing rate rather than the firm's cost of capital (p. 1020).
As a result, the net present value of financial leasing according
to Bierman's first valuation model, NPV_{fl}^{B1}, is:

$$NPV_{fl}^{B1} = (\frac{\$4,800}{1.06^1} + \frac{\$4,200}{1.06^2}) - (\frac{\$3,510}{1.06^1} + \frac{\$3,510}{1.06^2})$$

$$= \$8,266 - \$6,435 = \$1,831$$

The net present value of purchasing, NPV_p^{B1}, is:

$$NPV_p^{B1} = (\frac{\$4,800}{1.06^1} + \frac{\$4,200}{1.06^2}) + (\frac{\$2,200}{1.06^1} + \frac{\$1,800}{1.06^2}) - \$10,000$$

$$= \$8,266 + \$3,677 - \$10,000 = \$1,943$$

Since the second net present value exceeds the first one, purchasing would be preferred.

Bierman 2
Next Bierman is "including an implicit investment with leasing
equal to the present value of the leasing outlays" (p. 1019).
From the way he computes the "implicit investment with leasing"
one infers that the author applies McEachron's "lease obligation
procedure" reviewed in 3.4.1. According to Bierman and to
McEachron, the above investment equals the present value of the
lease payments discounted at the borrowing rate: $\$5,850(1.10)^{-1} +$
$\$5,850(1.10)^{-2} = \$10,153$. In order to determine the net present
value of financial leasing utilizing Bierman's second methodology, NPV_{fl}^{B2}, we need the following cash flows:
. the net cash inflows after taxes,
. the lease payments,
. the tax savings on the lease repayments calculated according to
  McEachron's "lease obligation procedure."
The lease payments are to be discounted at the before-tax borrowing rate and the other two cash flow series should be capitalized
at the after-tax borrowing rate. This would result in:

$$NPV_{fl}^{B2} = (\frac{\$4,800}{1.06^1} + \frac{\$4,200}{1.06^2}) - (\frac{\$5,850}{1.10^1} + \frac{\$5,850}{1.10^2})$$

$$+ 0.4 \times (\frac{\$4,835}{1.06^1} + \frac{\$5,318}{1.06^2}) = \$8,266 - \$10,153 + \$3,718$$

$$= \$1,831$$

The lease repayments (\$4,835 at the end of the first year and \$5,318 at the end of the second year) were taken from Table 3.2, which illustrated McEachron's lease-or-borrow model. Regarding the net present value of purchasing (NPV_p^{B2}), Bierman calculates this net present value in the same way as NPV_p^{B1}.

Bierman 3

Comparing Bierman's third model with the first one we find that NPV_{fl}^{B3} , the net present value of financial leasing according to the author's third model, is determined after the same fashion as NPV_{fl}^{B1}. In order to compute the net present value of buying Bierman is now "including borrowing cash flows in the investment analysis (implicitly including the initial outlay and initial proceeds from borrowing: they cancel each other out)" (p. 1020). The author assumes that "the total purchase price is borrowed." The cash flows necessary to compute the net present value of purchasing the capital asset, NPV_p^{B3}, are:
. the net cash inflows after taxes,
. the depreciation deductions,
. the "borrowing cash flows" after taxes.
The borrowing cash flows after taxes (loan repayments plus loan interest after taxes), discounted at the after-tax interest rate, take the place of the asset's cash purchase price as used when calculating NPV_p^{B1}. If we assume that the \$10,000 loan is to be repaid in two equal installments (\$5,000 at the end of each year of the two-year loan term) then:

$$NPV_p^{B3} = (\frac{\$4,800}{1.06^1} + \frac{\$4,200}{1.06^2}) + (\frac{\$2,200}{1.06^1} + \frac{\$1,800}{1.06^2})$$

$$- (\frac{\$5,000 + \$600}{1.06^1} + \frac{\$5,000 + \$300}{1.06^2})$$

$$= \$8,266 + \$3,677 - \$10,000 = \$1,943$$

The annual loan repayments (\$5,000) and the loan interest payments after taxes (\$600 at the end of the first year and \$300 at the end of the second year) were copied from Table 3.4. The resulting net present value necessarily equals NPV_p^{B1}. This is because when calculating the present value of the sum of the loan repayments and the after-tax interest payments making use of the after-tax interest rate we obtain the initial proceeds from borrowing. Since Bierman assumes that the purchase price of the asset is entirely financed by borrowing, these proceeds are equal to the asset's purchase price we also utilized when calculating NPV_p^{B1}. Concerning this result Bierman observes that "we now have included the debt flows of each year without affecting the analysis" (p. 1020).

Bierman 4

In his fourth model Bierman is "considering only the financing cash flows and comparing leasing and buying assuming the investment is acceptable" (p. 1020). In other words the author now computes present values rather than net present values ignoring the net cash inflows. According to this method the only cash flows needed to determine the present value of the financial lease, PV_{fl}^{B4}, are the lease payments after taxes. These payments are capitalized at the after-tax borrowing rate:

$$PV_{fl}^{B4} = (\frac{\$3,510}{1.06^1} + \frac{\$3,510}{1.06^2}) = \$6,435$$

In order to compute the present value of the purchase option PV_p^{B4}, Bierman makes use of:
. the cash purchase price of the asset,
. the depreciation deductions.
The latter cash flows are discounted at the after-tax borrowing

rate. Therefore,

$$PV_p^{B4} = \$10,000 - (\frac{\$2,200}{1.06^1} + \frac{\$1,800}{1.06^2}) = \$10,000 - \$3,677 = \$6,323$$

PV_{fl}^{B4} is higher than PV_p^{B4}, so purchasing would be recommended by
Bierman. Of course the difference between these two present
values equals the difference between the net present values of
financial leasing and buying we computed earlier: $112. This is
obvious; in Bierman's fourth model an element is left out of
consideration that the lease and the purchase arrangement have in
common: the after-tax net cash inflows. As Bierman rightly
observes this approach can only be applied if one assumes or has
ascertained that the investment project is acceptable. However,
it may be that "sufficiently attractive lease terms can in fact
reverse the investment decision" (JL 1972, p. 822). If the net
cash inflows are ignored such a reversal cannot take place.
Hence, ignoring these inflows (a procedure Bierman applies in his
recent book on leasing too)[17] may result in incorrect decisions.

However different Bierman's four models may appear to be, he
is quite right to state that they "are equivalent to each other"
(p. 1019). In fact, the models come to the same thing as the
evaluation method Weston and Brigham advocate in their 1969 and
1972 editions of Managerial Finance (see 3.4.3.3 and 3.4.3.4). In
Appendix 1 I shall prove this statement (see pp. 243-245).
Bierman is also correct in observing that one of the conditions
allowing his models to be equivalent to each other is that all
relevant cash flows are capitalized at one discount rate (p.
1021). At the same time he observes this "rate can be the after-
tax borrowing rate or something else." As we saw earlier Bierman
capitalizes the cash flows at the former rate, but he does not
explain why he uses this rate for discounting purposes. Neither
does he explain what rate is meant by "something else." At the

---

[17] In this book the author also assumes that "it has already
been decided that the equipment should be acquired" (Bierman
1982, p. 4).

end of his article, the author states that in capital budgeting
theory there is a tendency to utilize "a rate of interest that
does not include an adjustment for risk" because then problems
that arise when employing the firm's cost of capital may be
eliminated (p. 1021). Unfortunately he does not prove this statement to be correct.

3.5.2.5 Lev and Orgler

To conclude I shall discuss the comment of Lev and Orgler. These
writers address four issues. In the first place they feel that
the tax savings on depreciation should be discounted at the same
rate as the tax savings on the lease payments because "they are
at least as predictable, in terms of sizes and timing, as the
lease payments and should accordingly by discounted at the lower
rate, r" (Lev and Orgler 1973 p. 1022). Lev and Orgler do not,
however, explain why r, the after-tax cost of debt, is the appropriate discount rate here. Secondly, they contend that "a financial lease is at the same time an investment and a financing
proposal" instead of a regular investment project as JL argue.
Consequently, Lev and Orgler maintain that models developed to
value such a project are inadequate to value financial leases (p.
1023). One wonders whether the authors think these models can
only be used when the investment decision can be separated from
the financing decision. Furthermore, if such models cannot be
utilized for valuing a financial lease, what other method would
Lev and Orgler advocate and for what reasons? The following
discussion may provide an answer to these questions. Lev and
Orgler's third issue bears on the lease-or-borrow comparison.
They prefer comparing these alternatives with each other to
posing the problem as lease-or-buy because the lease and the
borrow option involve the same financial risk (p. 1023). They do
not indicate whether this equivalence holds for any arbitrary
loan or for a specific loan only. Therefore, a firm's management
has not much to go by with such a statement. Their observation
that the capital structure of a firm "would not be changed if

either leasing or purchasing the asset by borrowed funds is chosen" (p. 1023) is not of much use either, as Lev and Orgler do not discuss which factors are relevant for determining a firm's capital structure. Finally the authors point out that the JL model may give rise to incorrect decisions if management's choice rests on the difference between the net present values of financial leasing and buying, which are both negative. If management wishes to apply the evaluation method of JL, however, there is an obvious solution to this problem: calculating both NPV_{fl}^{JL} and NPV_{p}^{JL} and not just the difference between both net present values.

3.5.2.6 The Reply of Johnson and Lewellen

Since the comments on their model relate mostly to the same issues, the reply of JL has been directed at these points. First of all they address the issue of whether the problem to be solved is lease-or-buy or lease-or-borrow. JL argue that if a lease-or-borrow model is applied then (1) the entire purchase price of the asset is financed by borrowing, (2) the borrowing cost is set against "the implicit interest cost of leasing," and finally (3) the investment and the financing decisions are separated (JL 1973, p. 1024). Regarding the first consequence JL observe that in general the relationship between an investment project and a form of finance is purely accidental. They allege that if a series of assets is financed by borrowing, later series will be financed by retaining earnings or by issuing new equity (p. 1024). Presumably the long run debt-equity proportion chosen by the firm is at the bottom of this approach. JL hold that in the case of leasing, however, it is possible to establish a relationship between a project and a form of finance, for "the lease package offered by the asset's vendor ... cannot be detached for use elsewhere" (p. 1024). To my thinking this applies to other packages as well, for instance, mortgages, hire purchase contracts, installment purchases, and project financing plans. Nonetheless, I agree with JL that financing the entire

asset purchase price by means of a loan may be impossible and
that the firm's management may not want to raise such a loan. In
such a situation the lease evaluation method must also enable
management to choose between financial leasing and purchasing.

Concerning the second consequence JL attach to lease-or-
borrow, they hold that the determination of "the implicit interest cost of leasing" can only be accomplished in an arbitrary way
(p. 1025). Nevertheless, the authors explain how to compute such
a rate. This computation turns out to be identical to the one
Mitchell proposes (Mitchell 1970, pp. 308-314).

I fail to understand why lease-or-borrow results in separating
the investment decision from the financing decision, though this
is the third consequence JL attach to lease-or-borrow models. In
Bierman's third model, for instance, the purchase price of the
asset is entirely financed with a loan (hence, it is a lease-or-
borrow model), but the author does not separate the investment
from the financing decision (see 3.5.2.4).

Let us now look into the discount rates applied by JL. According to the comments discussed earlier it is incorrect to discount
the tax savings on the lease payments at a different rate than
those on depreciation. JL do not agree with these commentators.
They argue that NPV_p^{JL} is calculated "in exactly the manner urged
by received capital budgeting doctrine: all net operating flows
discounted at the firm's cost of capital" (p. 1026). On the other
hand, JL contend, lease payments "represent commitments rather
than contingencies," and therefore these payments and their tax
savings should not be capitalized at the firm's cost of capital
but at the after-tax cost of debt. I think the difference between
commitments and contigencies is irrelevant for determining the
discount rate to be used. As soon as management is allowed to
deduct definite cash flows when determining its taxable income,
these cash flows are destined to result in tax savings whether a
promised lease payment or planned depreciation is involved. In
conflict with JL's own view seems to be their statement: "We
feel, for example, that the firm's ability actually to realize
the intended package of tax-savings-cum-salvage is as uncertain
as the prospect that the project involved will work out as

predicted" (p. 1027). Since JL think they can cope with these uncertainties by capitalizing at the firm's cost of capital, the tax savings on the lease payments should also be capitalized at this rate rather than at the after-tax borrowing rate.

Finally JL pay attention to some remaining issues as discussed in the comments of Lev and Orgler and of Bierman. As these issues do not concern the heart of the matter, I refer to the JL article (pp. 1027-1028).

To summarize, JL have not succeeded in refuting the objections raised to their solution of the lease valuation problem. They make interesting contributions to the exchange of views on this problem though: they are among the very first authors who purposefully define the issue to be resolved as lease-or-buy instead of applying the rather restricted lease-or-borrow approach. In addition, the authors stress the interactions of investment and financing decisions.

3.5.3 Vial

This French author also proposes to choose between financial leasing and purchasing with the help of net present values. In order to calculate the net present value of financial leasing, NPV_{fl}^V, he uses:
. the net cash inflows after taxes,
. the depreciation deductions,
. the lease payments after taxes (Vial 1974, p. 21).
Vial utilizes two discount rates: the firm's cost of capital and the after-tax cost of debt. Starting from our numerical example, Vial would compute NPV_{fl}^V as:

$$NPV_{fl}^V = (\frac{\$4,800}{1.13^1} + \frac{\$4,200}{1.13^2}) + (\frac{\$2,200}{1.13^1} + \frac{\$1,800}{1.13^2})$$

$$- (\frac{\$3,510}{1.06^1} + \frac{\$3,510}{1.06^2}) - (\frac{\$2,200}{1.06^1} + \frac{\$1,800}{1.06^2})$$

$$= \$7,537 + \$3,356 - \$6,435 - \$3,677 = \$781$$

I employed Table 3.1 to obtain the after-tax net cash inflows ($4,800 at the end of the first year and $4,200 at the end of the second year) and the depreciation deductions ($2,200 and $1,800, respectively), and Table 3.5 to copy the after-tax lease payments ($3,510 at the end of both years). As apparent from the above equation, Vial utilizes the depreciation deductions twice: first as a positive element in the net present value calculation (discounted at 13%, the firm's cost of capital) and secondly as a negative element (discounted at 6%, the after-tax borrowing rate). I shall return to this issue when evaluating his model. As for the net present value of the purchase arrangement: Vial determines this net present value, NPV_p^V, in the same way as Weston and Brigham propose to do in the 1978 edition of their textbook (see 3.5.1.2). Thus,

$$NPV_p^V = NPV_p^{WB78} = (\frac{\$4,800}{1.13^1} + \frac{\$4,200}{1.13^2}) + (\frac{\$2,200}{1.13^1} + \frac{\$1,800}{1.13^2}) - \$10,000$$

$$= \$7,537 + \$3,356 - \$10,000 = \$894$$

Comparing NPV_{fl}^V ($781) and NPV_p^V ($894) Vial would opt for purchasing the capital asset. In the above calculations we assumed, like Vial, that the after-tax net cash inflows in the case of financial leasing ($4,800 in the first year and $4,200 in the second year) equal the after-tax net cash inflows with purchase. In the first instance Vial distinguishes between these two cash flow series (p. 12), but afterward, when simplifying his model, the author assumes that these series are identical (p. 12, footnote 9). It is a pity he does explain what can cause a difference between the two cash flow series to exist.

Vial observes that if purchasing is preferred to leasing (because of a higher net present value) the firm should utilize the most convenient financing method (e.g., retained earnings or a loan) to purchase the asset (p. 22). So the author does not confine the problem to lease-or-borrow.

Evaluation
I   According to Vial the investment decision ought to be sepa-

rated from the financing decision. This idea is based upon,
among other things, Ferrara's 1966 article "Should Investment
and Financing Decisions Be Separated?" Vial holds that when
these decisions are separated from one another, the financing
method is not reflected in the cash flows generated by the
investment project but in the firm's cost of capital employed
for capitalizing these cash flows. This approach is usually
applied in textbooks on finance (see for example Weston and
Brigham 1981, p. 415 and pp. 610-612). However, Vial also
utilizes the firm's cost of capital to capitalize the cash
flows to equity (pp. 13-14). Such a procedure can easily lead
to incorrect results. This also goes for Vial's calculation
of the internal rate of return based on the cash flows to
equity. The author quite rightly observes that, as this
internal rate of return is based on a mix of investment and
financing flows, it has no significance at all (p. 14,
footnote 14).

II Vial's definitions of the discount rates he uses are not
always clear. One rate he discounts at is defined as the rate
of return required on the type of investment projects the
firm is considering carrying out (p. 12). Since Vial argues
that Johnson and Lewellen utilize this rate too, one con-
cludes that he refers to the firm's cost of capital (13% in
our illustrative example). As to the rate for capitalizing
the depreciation tax shields, Vial states that this stream is
usually capitalized at the same rate as applied to the cash
inflows generated by the asset (p. 21, footnote 22). Nevertheless, as we saw in the above calculation of NPV_{fl}^{V}, these
tax shields are also discounted at the after-tax borrowing
rate. Vial does not explain why he makes use of two different
capitalization rates to discount the same cash flows. At the
end of his article, the author returns to this issue. He then
wonders whether the tax savings should be capitalized at the
risk-free rate. His own answer to this question is that such
a procedure would result in many theoretical and practical
problems. Unfortunately Vial does not explain exactly which
problems he foresees.

III Vial focuses his attention on financial leases only. (In France there are special laws for these crédit-bail arrangements. See Chapter 7.)

IV The results of his model are expressed in net present values.

V As observed earlier, according to Vial there is no need to finance the asset's purchase price exclusively with debt. Further on in his article he again stresses this approach (p. 19, footnote 19). It is obvious that the author does not want to restrict his evaluation technique to lease-or-borrow. When applying this technique in a real-world situation, however, management should make sure the conditions for discounting at the firm's cost of capital have been fulfilled.

3.5.4 Krumbholz and Streitferdt

The title of the book Krumbholz and Streitferdt (hereafter KS) published in Germany is <u>Leasing oder Kreditfinanzierung?</u> (<u>Leasing or Financing with Debt?</u>). From this title one may infer that their lease valuation model is to be characterized as lease-or-borrow, and therefore belongs to the first group of models discussed in 3.4. However, KS argue that whereas leasing implies (almost) 100% debt, purchasing usually involves financing with a combination of debt and equity (KS 1975, p. 13). As a result, their approach should be placed in the second group (lease-or-buy models) discussed here.

KS maintain that the rate normally used for valuing investment projects, the firm's cost of capital (or in their terminology, "die durchschnittlichen, marginalen Kapitalkosten"), is not suited for valuing the lease and the purchase opportunity (p. 46). This is because both opportunities would change the firm's capital structure (p. 47). The authors do not pay attention to the other conditions that ought to be met before one is allowed to discount at the firm's cost of capital. In order to arrive at the appropriate discount rate, KS observe that the relevant cash flows go to the company's stockholders. Consequently, one should capitalize the cash flows of the lease and the purchase agreement

at the company's equity rate (p. 48). Very properly the authors
argue that this rate will be affected by the amount of debt
financing. Since the amount of debt implicit in the financial
lease is usually higher than the amount of debt used in the
purchase arrangement, the equity rate when leasing would exceed
the equity rate when purchasing. KS contend that this difference
can hardly be measured. That is why they capitalize the cash
flows of leasing and the cash flows of purchasing at the same
rate (p. 48).

When we apply their methodology to our numerical example, we
need the following cash flows to compute the present value of
purchasing the capital asset:
. the cash purchase price of the asset,
. the principal of the loan used to finance part of this purchase
price,
. the loan repayments,
. the loan interest payments after taxes,
. the depreciation deductions (pp. 92-93).
If we assume, as KS do (pp. 92-99), that 70% of the asset's purchase price is financed with debt and 30% with equity and that
the loan is repaid in equal annual installments, then we can set
up Table 3.16.

Table 3.16
Loan according to Krumbholz and Streitferdt

Year (1)	Loan Principal according to KS (2)	Loan Interest (3)=0.1x(2)	Loan Repayment (4)
1	7,000	700	3,500
2	3,500	350	3,500

Next we have to combine the annual loan repayments, the after-tax
interest payments, and the depreciation deductions (see Table
3.17).

Table 3.17
Total Amount of Loan Repayments, After-Tax Interest Payments, and
Depreciation Deductions according to Krumbholz and Streitferdt

Year (1)	Loan Repayment (2)=(4) in Table 3.16	After-Tax Loan Interest (3)=(1-0.4)x(3) in Table 3.16	Depreciation Deduction (4)=(5) in Table 3.1	Total Amount (5)= (2)+(3)-(4)
1	3,500	420	2,200	1,720
2	3,500	210	1,800	1,910

These annual cash flows are capitalized at the firm's equity rate, 16% in our illustrative example. Now we gather all the necessary information to calculate the present value of purchasing with the help of the KS valuation model, PV_p^{KS}:

$$PV_p^{KS} = \$10,000 - \$7,000 + \frac{\$1,720}{1.16^1} + \frac{\$1,910}{1.16^2} = \$5,902$$

In order to determine the present value of financial leasing, KS discount the after-tax lease payments at the firm's equity rate. Hence, the present value of financial leasing, PV_{fl}^{KS}, equals:

$$PV_{fl}^{KS} = \frac{\$3,510}{1.16^1} + \frac{\$3,510}{1.16^2} = \$5,634$$

The after-tax lease payments were taken from Table 3.5. Comparing PV_p^{KS} ($5,902) with PV_{fl}^{KS} ($5,634) we find that, as the former present value exceeds the latter, KS would opt for leasing the asset. The same valuation model is employed by Koch and Ploog, two other German writers, who analyze the possibilities of leasing in agriculture (Koch and Ploog 1978, pp. 96-118).

Evaluation
I KS separate the investment decision from the financing decision. They argue that after having chosen a capital asset

(the investment decision) the firm's management has to make the financing decision, thereby examining its financing alternatives (i.e., financial leasing or purchase) and the profitability of these alternatives.

II   As observed above, KS argue that the cash flows they utilize in their model go to the firm's stockholders. That is why KS hold that these cash flows should be capitalized at the firm's equity rate. In 3.5.7 we shall see that Schall and Haley apply the same argument when valuing a lease contract, but that they do not capitalize the lease's cash flows at the equity rate. Schall and Haley do not explain this apparent inconsistency. It may be that they think that in practice the required rate of return on equity is difficult to estimate (see V below).

III Although in the title of their book KS speak of leasing in general the examples with which they illustrate their model relate to financial leasing only (pp. 100-101 and p. 104).

IV   Applying the KS valuation model results in present values. Since the authors assume that the cash inflows from operating a leased asset are identical to the cash inflows from operating a purchased asset, they hold that these cash inflow series can be ignored. As a result the profitability of the alternative financing arrangements cannot be determined.

V   KS do not limit their model to lease-or-borrow because to their mind in practice the purchase alternative is usually financed wih a combination of debt and equity. It is a pity, though, that the authors do not pay attention to problems that may arise when estimating the firm's equity rate in a real-world situation. Weston and Brigham discuss three procedures for "finding the basic required rate of return on common equity" (Weston and Brigham 1981, pp. 600-601). However, they then argue: "Based on our own experience in estimating equity capital costs, we recognize that both careful analysis and very fine judgments are required in this process. It would be nice to pretend that these judgments are unnecessary and to specify an easy, precise way of determining the exact cost of equity capital. Unfortunately, this is not possible" (p. 601). I think Copeland and Weston would agree with this statement, because in their recent textbook they observe that establishing "the cost of equity capital, unfortunately, is still more an art than a science" (Copeland and Weston 1983, p. 466). In the Netherlands plans have been made to divide the surplus profits of a firm among its employees and its stockholders (the so-called Vermogens- aanwasdeling or V.A.D.). In order to determine these "excess" profits it is necessary to establish the "normal" profits the stockholders are entitled to. After numerous discussions the normal rate of return on equity has for the present arbitrarily been determined to equal the average rate of return of a selected portfolio of government bonds plus 3%. In 4.3 I shall look into the possible effects of the decision to lease or to buy on the rates of return investors require (see pp. 143-145).

3.5.5 Spittler

As we observed in 3.2 Spittler argues that in reality the pur- chase price of an asset is not financed with debt exclusively but with a combination of debt and equity. Therefore, he holds that the problem to be solved is not lease-or-borrow but lease-or-buy (Spittler 1977, p. 33). In order to choose between financial leasing and buying, Spittler calculates the net present value of each alternative, thereby capitalizing the relevant cash flows at the firm's equity rate (in German: "die Eigenkapitalrendite") arguing that this is a generally accepted procedure (p. 33). For the lease arrangement the relevant cash flows are:
. the net cash inflows after taxes,
. the lease payments after taxes.
Capitalizing these cash flows at the rate of return on the firm's equity, in our example 16% results in the net present value of financial leasing as calculated by Spittler, NPV_{fl}^{S}:

$$NPV_{f1}^S = (\frac{\$4,800}{1.16^1} + \frac{\$4,200}{1.16^2}) - (\frac{\$3,510}{1.16^1} + \frac{\$3,510}{1.16^2}) = \$7,259 - \$5,63$$

$$= \$1,625$$

Spittler discounts the same cash flow series as, among others, Weston and Brigham employ in the 1978 edition of **Managerial Finance** (see 3.5.1.2). He discounts this series at a different rate though. In 3.5.7, when examining the lease-or-buy methodology of Schall and Haley, we shall return to this issue. Now we shall apply Spittler's approach in order to calculate the net present value of purchasing. Like Krumbholz and Streitferdt, Spittler assumes that 70% of the asset's purchase price is financed with a loan and 30% with equity. He also assumes that 70% of the annual depreciation is used to repay the loan and that the remaining amount is utilized to redeem the equity portion of the investment. Hence, the repayment schedule of the loan of our numerical example would look as calculated in Table 3.18.

Table 3.18
Loan according to Spittler

Year (1)	Loan Principal according to Spittler (2)	Loan Interest (3)=0.1x(2)	Loan Repayment (4)=0.7 x Depreciation	After-Tax Loan Interest (5)=(1-0.4)x(3)
1	7,000	700	3,850	420
2	3,150	315	3,150	189

This repayment schedule differs from the one Krumbholz and Streitferdt utilize (see Table 3.16). When employing Spittler's model the cash flows necessary to compute the net present value of purchasing, NPV_p^S, are:

the net cash inflows after taxes,
. the depreciation deductions,
. the loan repayments,
. the loan interest payments after taxes,
. the required returns on the equity portion of the investment,
. the redemption of this equity portion.

Concerning the last two items of this cash flow series, Spittler argues that, if the capital asset were not purchased, the equity portion of the amount invested in the asset could be used to yield the required rate of return on equity. So, purchasing the asset would result in opportunity cost (p. 38). As will be shown in Table 3.19, 30% of the annual depreciation is employed to redeem a part of the equity funds invested in the capital asset. Consequently, these opportunity costs decrease each year.

Table 3.19
Opportunity Costs of Purchasing Capital Asset with 30% Equity Funds

Year (1)	Equity Portion of Investment Outlay (2)	Required Return on Equity Portion (3)=0.16x(2)	Redemption of Equity Portion (4)=0.3 x Depreciation
1	3,000	480	1,650
2	1,350	216	1,350

Now we gather all the necessary information to apply Spittler's model to the purchase arrangement:

$$NPV_p^S = (\frac{\$4,800}{1.16^1} + \frac{\$4,200}{1.16^2}) + (\frac{\$2,200}{1.16^1} + \frac{\$1,800}{1.16^2})$$
$$- (\frac{\$3,850}{1.16^1} + \frac{\$3,150}{1.16^2}) - (\frac{\$420}{1.16^1} + \frac{\$189}{1.16^2})$$

following cash flows:
. the net cash inflows after taxes,
. the lease payments after taxes.
The first cash flow series they discount at 12% and the second
one at 8%. Hence,

$$NPV_{fl}^{HS} = (\frac{\$4,800}{1.12^1} + \frac{\$4,200}{1.12^2}) - (\frac{\$3,510}{1.08^1} + \frac{\$3,510}{1.08^2}) = \$7,634 - \$6,259$$

$$= \$1,374$$

The net present value of purchasing as determined by HS, NPV_p^{HS},
comprises the expected values of:
. the net cash inflows after taxes,
. the tax savings on depreciation,
. the tax savings on loan interest,
. the cash purchase price of the asset.
HS capitalize the first two cash flow series at 10%, and the tax
savings on interest at 8%, the same rate as used in calculating
the present value of the after-tax lease payments. This is the
first difference between their model and the one Schall develops
in his 1974 article: Schall discounts the after-tax lease payments at 8% and the tax savings on interest at 6% (Schall 1974,
p. 1210). Applying the HS model we obtain:

$$NPV_p^{HS} = (\frac{\$4,800}{1.10^1} + \frac{\$4,200}{1.10^2}) + (\frac{\$2,200}{1.10^1} + \frac{\$1,800}{1.10^2})$$

$$+ (\frac{0.4x0.08x0.8x\$10,000}{1.08^1}) + (\frac{0.4x0.08x0.8x\$10,000}{1.08^2})$$

$$- \$10,000 = \$7,835 + \$3,488 + \$237 + \$219 - \$10,000$$

$$= \$1,779$$

The net cash inflows after taxes ($4,800 at the end of the first
year and $4,200 at the end of the second year) were taken from
Table 3.1, and the depreciation tax shields ($2,200 and $1,800
respectively) were copied from Table 3.4. The tax savings on loan
interest were calculated as follows: the cash purchase price of

the asset ($10,000) was multiplied by 0.8 because, just like HS, we assume that 80% of this price was financed with debt, then by 0.08 (the interest rate on the loan HS make use of), and finally by 0.4 (the corporate income tax rate). Since HS assume the loan principal is to be repaid at the end of the useful life of the asset, the tax savings on the loan interest payments in the first and the second year are identical. Comparing NPV_{f1}^{HS} = $1,374 and NPV_{p}^{HS} = $1,779 HS would opt for purchasing the asset. To conclude I point out a second difference between the HS model and the 1974 approach of Schall it is based upon: HS also take into account the relationship between leasing and debt capacity (pp. 464-468). They then look into the assumptions of the lease valuation method Myers, Dill, and Bautista developed (see 3.4.7).

Evaluation

I   As we observed earlier HS quite rightly are of opinion that it is ordinarily incorrect to separate the investment decision from the financing decision. There is an exception to this rule though. The authors argue that "if we know without formal analysis that the asset should be acquired and the only decision is how to finance the acquisition (lease or purchase)" then determining the difference between the present value of leasing and the present value of buying is sufficient (p. 466). Again they are right; if it is obvious that acquiring an asset is profitable only the financing decision need be made.

II In the above we also observed that HS discount the expected values of the various cash flows. The authors argue that "we could just as well use promised streams ... in which case the discount rates would have to be adjusted" (p. 464, footnote 31). I prefer to capitalize promised streams rather than their statistical expectations because this is the more usual approach (see 3.3 above as well as requirement V below).

III Although the title of the part of the book we are discussing here is "Leasing," HS pay attention to financial leasing only. This is apparent from the example with which they illustrate their valuation method.

IV   Except for a situation where the asset's desirability is obvious, HS compute the net present value of financial leasing and of buying and select the arrangement with the higher net present value. However, they do not pay attention to a problem Schwab addresses. This author looks into disaggregating expected cash flows and argues "that such a disaggregation of overall net cash flows into component flows would only be permissible where the individual component flows are independent, as otherwise portfolio effects would have to be taken into consideration" (Schwab 1978, p. 282).

V   In practice it may be rather difficult to establish the rates HS discount at. In contrast with HS, Schall goes into this issue. He states: "Although in theory specific rates are associated with each distribution, in practice, at best, only a general estimate is possible. For the practitioner, therefore, the analysis here is meant to suggest that some attempt should be made to adjust for individual asset risk even though a precise determination is impossible " (Schall 1974, p. 1209). Since HS as well as Schall capitalize expected values of lease and loan payments, an additional practical problem arises: how does a firm's management determine the probabilities of the contractually set payments and of the payments that differ from these promised lease and loan payments? This practical problem is another reason to discount promised payments instead of their statistical expectations.

3.5.7 Schall and Haley

In the second edition of their textbook, <u>Introduction to Financial Management</u>, Schall and Haley (subsequently SH) employ a lease evaluation model that is also based on Schall's 1974 article but that nevertheless differs from the model just examined. SH discount the various cash flows at two rates only, and they do not distinguish between promised payments and the expected values of these payments in the way they did in the model discussed in 3.5.6. Regarding the first difference: SH capitalize the cash flows of buying the capital asset at the firm's cost of capital and those of leasing it at a higher rate (SH 1980, pp. 603-604). In their opinion this higher rate is justified since the cash flows of the lease alternative are riskier than those of the purchase agreement. This is because the lease's cash flows are "net of the firm's lease payments" (p. 604, footnote 8), whereas the purchasing cash flows are not net of the debt payments. When illustrating the evaluation method of SH by means of our example, I shall discount the former cash flow series at 16% (the firm's equity rate) and the latter at 13% (the firm's cost of capital). The second difference between the evaluation model of 3.4.6 and the one we are discussing here relates to the nature of the cash flows to be capitalized. Most probably SH capitalize the contractual lease payments instead of the expected values of the lease payments. This we infer from their statement that "CF(lease)$_t$ is the net cash flow over and above the amount payable to the lessor; that is, CF(lease)$_t$ is an equity cash flow after meeting the fixed charge in the form of the lease payment" (p. 604). From the underlined parts of this statement, I conclude that SH focus attention on the promised lease payments.

Let us now illustrate the SH model using our numerical example. In order to determine the net present value of financial leasing according to this model, NPV_{fl}^{SH}, we need the following cash flows:

. the net cash inflows after taxes,
. the lease payments after taxes.

As stated earlier we discount these cash flows at 16%:

$$NPV_{fl}^{SH} = (\frac{\$4,800}{1.16^1} + \frac{\$4,200}{1.16^2}) - (\frac{\$3,510}{1.16^1} + \frac{\$3,510}{1.16^2}) = \$7,259 - \$5,634$$

$$= \$1,625$$

SH calculate NPV_p^{SH}, the net present value of purchasing the capital asset, in a way that has become rather customary for textbooks on finance, i.e., by capitalizing:

. the net cash inflows after taxes, as well as

. the depreciation deductions
at the firm's cost of capital, and subtracting from the resulting present value:
. the cash purchase price of the asset.
This method of computing the net present value of purchasing is also used by, among others, Weston and Brigham (see 3.5.1.2). As a result:

$$NPV_p^{SH} = NPV_p^{WB78} = (\frac{\$4,800}{1.13^1} + \frac{\$4,200}{1.13^2}) + (\frac{\$2,200}{1.13^1} + \frac{\$1,800}{1.13^2})$$

$$- \$10,000 = \$7,537 + \$3,357 - \$10,000 = \$894$$

SH would prefer to lease the asset, because NPV_{fl}^{SH} ($1,625) is greater than NPV_p^{SH} ($894).

Evaluation

I   SH do not try to separate the investment from the financing decision. All relevant cash inflows and cash outflows form part of their net present value analysis.

II As was explained earlier SH discount the various cash flows at two rates: the firm's cost of capital and a higher rate. In their numerical example, the firm's cost of capital, or the rate utilized to calculate the net present value of buying, equals 10%, whereas the rate used for computing the net present value of financial leasing is equal to 12%. The authors observe: "This rate exceeds the 10 percent discount rate with purchase because we are assuming that the lease cash flow ... is riskier than the purchase cash flow...." (p. 606). They do not explain why the difference between the two rates is 2% rather than any other percentage. In the first edition of Introduction to Financial Management, SH employed exactly the same example, but they then stated that "the rate k_L for discounting CF(lease)$_t$ may approximate the firm's equity rate k_S (the rate used to discount the firm's equity cash flow ...)" (Schall and Haley 1977, p. 597). One wonders why this statement has been left out in the second edition of the SH textbook. Such a statement would give a firm's management something to go by. At the same time note that discounting at a rate that exceeds the firm's cost of capital when analyzing the lease option constitutes the only difference between the model of SH and the evaluation method Weston and Brigham advocate in the 1978 edition of **Managerial Finance**. As explained in 3.5.1.2 these authors use the firm's cost of capital not only to capitalize the purchase cash flows but also to discount the lease cash flows. When evaluating their methodology, we observed that in the case of leasing Weston and Brigham are capitalizing a cash flow to equity (since the difference between the after-tax net cash inflows the leased asset generates and the after-tax lease payments goes to the firm's stockholders) at the firm's cost of capital. Capitalizing this cash flow at the firm's equity rate would be more consistent. That is why one wonders why in the second edition of their textbook SH omit their statement concerning the capitalization rate to be applied to the lease alternative.

III Although the title of the section in the book SH we are reviewing is "Lease or Buy Analysis," SH concentrate on financial leases only.

IV Above it was explained that SH utilize the net present value method to compare the alternatives with one another. They correctly observe: "The alternative with the higher net present value of cash flows is preferred and is adopted if its net present value is positive or zero" (pp. 611-612).

V SH do not agree with authors who describe the problem to be solved as lease-or-borrow. They argue that "in actual situations, this is frequently not the relevant problem since a purchase may involve equity as well as debt financing. The approach presented here does not assume 100 percent debt financing and permits us to assume whatever is realistic with regard to the source of funds used for a purchase" (p. 602, footnote 4). Nonetheless, when illustrating their model SH assume that "the purchase is financed in the same way (same proportions of debt and equity financing) ... as the company's other assets" (p. 603). It is a pity the authors do not pay attention to other methods of financing the asset's purchase price and to the discount rates to be employed then. On the other hand, if the purchase price is financed in the same manner and the asset is of the same risk class as the firm's other assets, then this would not automatically imply that the firm's cost of capital can be used for discounting purposes. This is because many more conditions have to be fulfilled before one can discount at this rate. Also, for the practitioner it would be very useful if SH would indicate when to apply the model we are examining here instead of the one they advocate in their book The Theory of Financial Decisions, discussed in 3.5.6. Although the authors state that both models are based on the lease valuation method Schall developed in his 1974 article, the models are quite different from each other.

3.5.8 Theunissen

This Belgian author develops an interesting method to compare purchasing a capital asset with leasing it. To be able to choose between the alternatives he uses the present value methodology. According to Theunissen the cash flows necessary to determine the present value of purchasing are:
. the cash purchase price of the asset,
. the principal of the loan utilized to finance part of this purchase price,
. the loan repayments,
. the loan interest payments after taxes,
. the depreciation deductions (Theunissen 1982, p. 9).
This is the same cash flow series Krumbholz and Streitferdt start from. Theunissen, however, assumes that 20% of the asset's purchase price is financed by way of equity and 80% by negotia-ting a loan. The principal and interest payments of this loan are to be paid in equal installments. These assumptions differ from the ones Krumbholz and Streitferdt make (see 3.5.4). Starting from our example, the repayment schedule of Theunissen's loan

looks like (see Table 3.20):

Table 3.20
Loan according to Theunissen

Year (1)	Loan Principal according to Theunissen (2)	Loan Interest plus Loan Repayment (3)	Loan Interest (4)=0.1x(2)	Loan Repayment (5)=(3)-(4)
1	8,000	4,609	800	3,809
2	4,191	4,609	418	4,191

The annual sum of loan interest and loan repayment ($4,609) was calculated by dividing the amount borrowed ($8,000) by the sum of two 10%-interest factors ($1.10^{-1} + 1.10^{-2}$). The next step we have to take is to combine the annual loan repayments, the after-tax interest payments, and the depreciation deductions. See Table 3.21.

Table 3.21
Total Amount of Loan Repayments, After-Tax Interest Payments, and Depreciation Deductions according to Theunissen

Year (1)	Loan Repayment (2)=(5) in Table 3.20	After-Tax Loan Interest (3)=(1-0.4)x(4) in Table 3.20	Depreciation Deduction (4)=(5) in Table 3.1	Total Amount (5)= (2)+(3)-(4)
1	3,809	480	2,200	2,089
2	4,191	251	1,800	2,642

Capitalizing the total cash flows of Column (5) at the borrowing rate after taxes, $(1-40\%) \times 10\% = 6\%$ and taking into account the asset's purchase price ($10,000) as well as the loan principal ($8,000), we obtain the present value of purchasing according to Theunissen's procedure, PV_p^T:

$$PV_p^T = \$10,000 - \$8,000 + (\frac{\$2,089}{1.06^1} + \frac{\$2,642}{1.06^2})$$

$$= \$10,000 - \$8,000 + \$4,323 = \$6,323$$

There exists a much easier way to determine this present value though. Since Theunissen capitalizes the various cash flows at the loan rate after taxes, the present value of the loan repayments plus the after-tax loan interest payments equals the loan principal ($8,000). Consequently, the present value of the after-tax loan payments and the loan principal cancel out, and PV_p^T can also be calculated from:

. the cash purchase price of the asset,
. the depreciation deductions.

In our example, PV_p^T can therefore be computed as follows:

$$PV_p^T = \$10,000 - (\frac{\$2,200}{1.06^1} + \frac{\$1,800}{1.06^2}) = \$10,000 - \$3,677 = \$6,323$$

Applying Theunissen's approach to the lease arrangement we need:
. the lease payments,
. the tax savings on the lease payments.

The annual differences between these two cash flow series, i.e., the after-tax lease payments, are to be capitalized at 6%. Hence, according to Theunissen the present value of the financial lease, PV_{fl}^T, is computed to be:

$$PV_{fl}^T = \frac{\$3,510}{1.06^1} + \frac{\$3,510}{1.06^2} = \$6,435$$

The after-tax lease payments ($3,510 to be paid at the end of each year of the two-year lease term) were copied from Table 3.5.

Both PV_p^T and PV_{fl}^T are equal to the present values calculated according to the model Weston and Brigham apply in the 1969 edition of their textbook (see 3.4.3.3). Their model, however, starts from the lease-or-borrow concept. Comparing PV_p^T = \$6,323 with PV_{fl}^T = \$6,435, Theunissen would prefer to purchase the capital asset.

Evaluation

I   The author assumes that the capital budgeting decision has already been made and that the only problem to be solved is how to finance the asset's purchase price: with a combination of debt and equity or by leasing the asset (p. 2).

II   Theunissen is of the opinion that it would be incorrect to utilize the firm's cost of capital for calculating PV_p^T and PV_{fl}^T. He argues that the firm's cost of capital contains a risk premium as well, whereas the lease-or-buy problem does not involve any risk. That is why the author uses the risk-free rate ("risikoloze interestvoet") for discounting purposes (p. 1) and also assumes that the firm is able to raise a loan at this rate (p. 6). To my thinking, however, there usually is an element of risk in the lease-or-buy problem because it may be that the lessee or the borrower is unable to repay the debt. Apart from such default risks, other risks may be involved, for instance, the risks of inflation and, in the case of international transactions such as cross-border leasing, political risks as well as exchange rate fluctuation risks. Because of these risks, I think that most firms are not able to borrow or to lease at the risk-free rate, and this is why I utilized the (after-tax) borrowing rate rather than the (after-tax) risk-free rate to compute PV_p^T and PV_{fl}^T. I employed the same argumentation in 3.4.6 when evaluating Gordon's model.

III   Although Theunissen speaks of leasing in general, he illustrates his model with the help of financial leases only (p. 9 and p. 12).

IV   The results of his lease valuation method are expressed in present values. The author only pays attention to those cash flows that result from the financing methods that have to be compared. Therefore, the cash inflow series generated by the capital asset, which forms part of the capital budgeting decision, would be irrelevant.

V   Having shown that in actuality most firms are unable to lease or to borrow at the risk-free rate, I used the (after-tax) borrowing rate to compute PV_p^T and PV_{fl}^T. An advantage of the Theunissen valuation model is that he does not restrict it to lease-or-borrow comparisons.

4 FINANCIAL LEASING: TOWARD A MODEL MEETING THE REQUIREMENTS I - V

4.1 Introduction

Before trying to develop a lease evaluation model that meets the requirements I-V as discussed in 2.3, I shall recapitulate the models examined in Chapter 3 with the help of these requirements. When developing this new model, I shall start from this recapitulation.

4.2 A Recapitulation

Surveying the various evaluation methods reviewed in Chapter 3 and based on the requirements I-V, the following conclusions may be drawn:

I   Formerly in some publications on leasing attention was paid to the financing decision only (e.g. Weston 1962, see p. 40 above), and frequently the investment decision was separated from the financing decision (for instance, by Ferrara, who gives a clear and affirmative answer to the question asked in the title of his 1966 article: "Should Investment and Financing Decisisons Be Separated?"). In many recent publications on leasing, however, the very interactions of corporate investment and financing decisions are stressed (e.g., Johnson and Lewellen 1972, as discussed on pp. 83-87 and p. 97 above, and Haley and Schall 1979, see pp. 108-111 above). A very good illustration of these developments may be found in the successive editions of Weston and Brigham's well-known textbook. When discussing the lease-or-borrow problem in earlier

editions of Managerial Finance, Weston and Brigham do not
mention the capital budgeting decision at all (see for
example Weston and Brigham 1966 as analyzed on p. 41) and
divorce this decision from the financing decision (e.g.,
Weston and Brigham 1969, see pp. 43-44). In a more recent
edition of their textbook, however, the authors do consider
the investment decision and the interactions of investment
and financing decisions (e.g., Weston and Brigham 1978, discussed on pp. 77-78). I agree with the latter approach to the
problem because the profitability of an investment proposal
may depend on the way it is financed. Copeland and Weston
very properly argue: "A word of caution to the practitioner
is appropriate at this point. It is never advisable to
totally ignore revenues or the riskiness of the revenue
stream (even though this is frequent practice).... The
practitioner who ignores revenues and chooses the project
with the lower discounted cost may easily accept a project
with negative NPV. Costs tell only half the story. Decision
making on the basis of cost comparisons alone is inappro-
priate unless the decision maker is absolutely sure that the
mutually exclusive projects all have positive net present
value" (Copeland and Weston 1983, p. 371). Besides, combining
the investment and the financing decision may very well be
less time consuming than trying to make these decisions
separately from one another. What is more, as argued on pp.
8-10, a lot of assumptions have to be met to enable a separation of both decisions to be made.

II With respect to the discount rates to be utilized, there are
great differences of opinion among the authors whose models
were evaluated in Chapter 3. Among other things the authors
disagree as to the rates at which to capitalize the tax
savings of leasing and of purchasing. That is why I feel that
Bower's sensitivity analysis, by way of which the impact of
capitalizing these tax savings at different rates can be
measured, is such a useful instrument. Apart from this, in
many publications on leasing I have looked in vain for a
valid motivation for the discount rates applied. When

developing a new lease evaluation procedure, I shall therefore pay special attention to this issue.

III It is rather curious that various authors do not state
whether their model can be applied to both financial and operating leases or to just one of these types of leasing. Often
only from the numerical example(s) used does it become clear
which type of leasing an author has in mind. In view of the
essential differences between financial and operating leases,
I shall develop an evaluation model for each of these types
of leasing.

IV There are some authors who employ internal rates of return
(such as McEachron 1961,and Beckman and Joosen 1980) and
others who compute the net present values of financial leasing and of purchasing (e.g., Johnson and Lewellen 1972). Most
authors, however, make use of the present value methodology
without paying attention to the net cash inflows the capital
asset generates. As was explained on pp. 11-12, I prefer to
utilize net present values to compare financial leasing with
purchasing.

V Setting Section 3.4 against Section 3.5, one may conclude
that there are a lot more lease-or-borrow models than lease-
or-buy models. Regarding the first group of models, Bower
observes: "This analytic use of an equivalent loan comes very
close to removing questions of financial structure from the
lease decision. It determines the borrowing that could take
place within the debt limit if there were no commitments to
make lease payments, and it presumes that this borrowing
would take place if the lease was not signed" (Bower 1973, p.
30). Insofar as removing questions of financial structure is
justified, it may be that the presumption mentioned by Bower
is not realistic; in other words, in actuality it may be impossible to raise such an equivalent loan. In fact, it may
even be impossible to raise a loan at all, in which case
financial leasing should be compared with purchasing financed
by means of equity. It is evident that in such a situation
discounting at the borrowing rate is out of the question.
That is why the possibilities of putting a lease-or-buy model

into practice outnumber those of applying a lease-or-borrow
model. With respect to the use of the firm's cost of capital
for capitalizing future cash flows without checking whether
the necessary and sufficient conditions for utilizing this
rate have been met (e.g., Weston and Brigham 1966 as discussed on p. 42 and Johnson and Lewellen 1972, p. 87 above),
one can only say that this is a rather careless procedure. As
appears from the numerical example, applying lease-or-borrow
models results in preferring the second arrangement: borrowing and purchasing the capital asset. Most of the lease-or-
buy procedures, however, result in recommending the lease
alternative. This may be explained by the smaller tax savings
on the interest payments of the loan, which is raised to
finance only a part of the asset's purchase price. In a
lease-or-borrow model these tax savings are higher because
the entire purchase price of the asset is financed by borrowing. This may be a reason for such a model to recommend the
buy-and-borrow alternative.

4.3   A Model for Choosing between Financial Leasing and Purchas-
      ing Meeting the Requirements I-V

It is relatively easy to meet requirements I, III, and IV. In the
lease valuation model I am going to develop, the capital budgeting decision and the financing decision are made simultaneously
(this is in accordance with requirement I). At the same time I
would stress that my approach can only be used to value financial
leases (requirement III). With regard to requirement IV, this
approach will lead to results that are expressed in net present
values. I shall have to dwell a little longer on the two remaining requirements. With respect to requirement II, determining the
discount rates to be applied also depends on the nature of the
cash flows of which the present value is being calculated. I
shall calculate the present value of the cash flows to equity,
i.e., the cash flow series chargeable to or benefiting the
present owners of the firm, the stockholders. This is clear in

the case of financial leasing: the difference between the after-tax net cash inflows and the after-tax lease payments goes to the firm's stockholders. That is why Schall and Haley state: "CF(lease)$_t$ is an equity cash flow after meeting the fixed charge in the form of the lease payment" (Schall and Haley 1980, p. 604). For the other alternative, purchasing, I shall also use cash flows to equity. These cash flows are directly related to the goal of the firm as described in Chapter 1: maximizing the market value of its equity.

From the stockholders' perspective, leasing a capital asset involves the following cash flows:
. the net cash inflows after taxes,
. the tax savings on the lease payments,
. the lease payments.
The cash flows to equity in the case of purchasing an asset and financing (a part of) its purchase price by way of a loan consist of:
. the net cash inflows after taxes,
. the tax savings on depreciation,
. the tax savings on interest,
. the cash purchase price of the asset,
. the principal of the loan used to finance (a part of) this purchase price,
. the principal and interest payments of the loan.
The firm's stockholders are entitled to the balance of these cash flows. In order to determine its value, this balance can be capitalized at the rate of return the stockholders require. However, as was explained when evaluating the model of Krumbholz and Streitferdt, it may be very difficult to estimate the firm's equity rate in a real-world situation (see pp. 103-104). Moreover, the firm's equity rate need not be equal to the required rate of return appropriate to capitalize the cash flows to equity of a specific asset (see also Haley and Schall 1979, p. 462). Since in my opinion one of the five requirements a lease evaluation model has to meet is its applicability in actuality, I prefer another approach to calculate the net present value of the above cash flow series. This approach involves capitalizing every

element of the cash flow to equity at a rate commensurate with
its risk. So, in fact I am applying the risk-adjusted discount
rate approach in which the risk of a particular cash flow is
reflected in the rate utilized to compute its present value. This
risk-adjusted discount rate consists of the riskless rate plus a
risk premium appropriate to the risk of the particular cash flow.
I am also making use of the so-called value-additivity principle,
which holds that the market value of a cash flow series equals
the sum of the market values of the individual elements constituting the series. In other words: "Neither fragmenting cash
flows nor recombining them will affect the resulting values of
the cash flows" (Weston and Brigham 1981, p. 1078). As Haley and
Schall observe, the value-additivity principle "requires
perfection only in the capital markets" (Haley and Schall 1979,
pp. 459-460). Perfect capital markets do not imply that a firm's
management should be indifferent between leasing and purchasing.
There may be imperfections in other sectors of the economy as a
result of which management opts for leasing or for purchasing.
For instance the income tax rates of the firm and the lessor may
be different, or the lessor may be able to purchase a capital
asset at a lower price than the firm (see Haley and Schall 1979,
pp. 458-459). In addition, there may be imperfections in the
capital markets that result in arbitraging between the markets
being impeded. Examples of these imperfections are transaction as
well as information costs and less than infinite divisibility of
securities. Regarding such imperfections, Van Horne observes that
"it may be possible for the firm to take 'advantage' of the
situation by issuing one type of instrument or the other. Since
the advantage is likely to be small and extremely difficult to
predict in practice, we do not concentrate on these imperfections" (Van Horne 1983, p. 495). That is why I shall ignore
these imperfections too.

The next step to take is determining the value of the various
cash flow elements constituting the cash flow to equity in the
case of financial leasing and in the case of purchasing a capital
asset. For the sake of simplicity, assume that the net cash
inflows that the asset is expected to generate will be the same

whether it is leased or purchased. There may be differences
between the net cash inflows with a lease and those with purchase, however. For example, the unit cost of a product manufac-
tured using the asset may differ according to whether the asset
is leased or owned. The fact is that in the former case the lease
payments constitute a part of the unit cost of the product,
whereas in the latter depreciation plus any interest are part of
the unit cost. The lease payment does not need to equal interest,
if any, plus depreciation. Insofar as the unit cost is relevant
in determining the selling price and insofar as the selling price
is of significance to the product's sales, the net cash inflows
in the case of financial leasing may differ from the net cash
inflows in the case of purchase. When capitalizing the after-tax
net cash inflows, I shall make use of the appropriate project
hurdle rate assuming perfect capital markets and all-equity
financing (15% in my numerical example). This is in accordance
with received doctrine (see Modigliani and Miller 1963, p. 435;
Myers 1974, p. 10 and p. 18; Gordon 1974, pp. 246-248; Brealey
and Myers 1981, pp. 401-406). Nevertheless, it may be very
difficult to determine this rate in a real-world situation. On p.
137 I shall return to this issue.

Before determining the present value of the lease payments,
one must realize that a lease is in effect a loan that is
provided in kind.[1] That is why a lease is comparable with an
ordinary loan. However, there are many different kinds of loans:
debenture loans, trade credit, bank loans, installment loans,
etc. The best way of dealing with this problem is to set against
a financial lease the kind of loan that has in common with it as
many characteristics as possible and that can actually be raised.

----

[1] I do not take into consideration here the so-called percentage
leases because there are very few leases of this nature. Hamel
characterizes these percentage leases by pointing out that:
"Rentals were based on a percentage of profits or sales"
(Hamel 1968, p. 3). As a result of this characteristic, these
leases resemble equity rather than debt.

This last qualification is necessary because of requirement V -
the applicability of the proposed model in practice. From the
point of view of business finance, a financial lease is primarily
characterized by the fact that:
1. the cash purchase price of the asset is entirely financed by
   the lessor (except in cases where the first lease payment is
   made at the beginning of the lease term),
2. the lessor (usually) remains the legal owner of the asset,
3. the term of the lease is determined in the lease contract and
   corresponds with the useful life of the asset,
4. the lessee expects to meet the lease payments from the net
   cash inflows the leased asset generates.
Characteristic 2 may be relevant in respect to the risk the
lessor bears when leasing and hence for the rate of return it
requires (as expressed in the interest rate implicit in the
financial lease). I use the word "usually" because it may be
that, in order to finance the purchase price of the asset to be
leased, the lessor raises a loan secured with the asset. Even if
the lessor is the owner of the leased asset, there may be situations where the asset is seized by a third party. For example,
in the Netherlands the fiscal authorities are allowed to levy a
distress even upon leased assets if the lessee has not paid the
fiscal claim (see Chapter 7, p. 223). The expectations of characteristic 4 may be based on one of the (alleged) advantages of
leasing: pay as you earn. This may give rise to patterns of lease
payments that are supposed to follow the patterns of net cash
inflows generated by the leased asset: the so-called high-low
leases or even low-high-low leases.

   In view of these four characteristics, a loan can be set
against a financial lease when:
1. the cash purchase price of the asset is entirely financed by
   the lender (here we must also make a reservation concerning
   any payments made at the beginning of the term of the loan),
2. the loan is secured by the asset,
3. the term of the loan is equal to the term of the lease,
4. the borrower expects to meet the principal and interest payments from the net cash inflows the asset generates.

Now compare the interest rate on this loan with the interest rate
implicit in the financial lease. The present value of the lease
payments is calculated using the lower of these two rates. This
is because from an economic point of view the difference between
this rate and the higher one can be seen as a waste of money. We
find the same idea in Accounting for Leases, issued by the
Financial Accounting Standards Board. With respect to the
valuation of "capital leases," the board states that "a lessee
shall compute the present value of the minimum lease payments
using his incremental borrowing rate, unless (i) it is practi-
cable for him to learn the implicit rate computed by the lessor
and (ii) the implicit rate computed by the lessor is less than
the lessee's incremental borrowing rate. If both of those conditions are met, the lessee shall use the implicit rate" (FASB
Statement No. 13 as amended and interpreted through May 1980, p.
11). Whether the lower of the loan rate and the financial lease
rate is to be used in calculating the present value of cash flows
from purchasing a capital asset depends on the way management is
going to finance the asset's purchase price. This problem is
closely connected with the issue of a firm's optimal capital
structure, which was addressed by many famous authors (e.g.,
Modigliani and Miller 1958 and 1963, Stiglitz 1969, Hirshleifer
1970, Scott 1976, and Kim 1978). There are several methods of
financing the purchase price of an asset. If the purchase price
is entirely financed by raising the loan characterized on p. 128,
the lower of the loan rate and the lease rate can also be employed to discount the principal and interest payments of the
loan. If, on the other hand, the purchase price is all-equity
financed, the use of this discount rate is confined to the
determination of the net present value of leasing. In the case of
all-equity financing, the net present value of purchasing can be
computed from the following cash flow series:
. the net cash inflows after taxes,
. the tax savings on depreciation,
. the cash purchase price of the asset.
The reason for such a financing method could be that the company
has a cash surplus and does not intend to borrow. A third possi-

bility would be to finance the asset with a combination of debt
and equity. It follows that the amount of debt will be less than
the cash purchase price of the asset and that the present value
of the debt payments will be less than the present value of the
debt payments promised in the case of financing the entire purchase price with debt. When illustrating the model I shall return
to this issue (see pp. 131-136).

The discount rate appropriate to the tax savings resulting
from the various tax deductible costs (depreciation plus any
interest in buying, lease payments in leasing) depends to a large
extent on the tax system being in force, particularly on regulations with regard to tax deductible losses issued by fiscal
authorities such as the Internal Revenue Service. Such regulations enable a firm to realize tax savings partially or entirely, even if the tax deductible costs have not been (completely) earned. By "earned" I mean paid for out of the cash inflow
that the firm generates in that year. There are two extreme forms
of this kind of regulation, in theory at least: immediate and
full compensation for losses or no protection for losses at all.
Under the first type of loss protection the fiscal authorities
promptly pay to a company that has suffered a loss the corporate
income tax rate x amount of loss. In this context I use the
expression "loss" when the interest payments (if any) plus
depreciation or the lease payments have not been or have only
partly been earned. Under such a system the tax savings will
always be realized in full, whether the tax deductible costs have
been earned or not. Or, in other words, the realization of the
tax deductions is certain, whether the firm as a whole has
taxable income or not. It is assumed that, if the company goes
bankrupt during the asset's useful life, the fiscal authorities
pay out the present value of the future tax savings on the lease
payments or on the depreciation amounts plus any interest payments. It follows that the present value of these savings, at any
rate under immediate and full compensation for losses, can be
computed using the risk-free rate. If on the other hand there is
no compensation for losses by the fiscal authorities at all, the
tax savings will only be attained if and insofar as the relevant

tax deductible costs have been earned. If the cash inflow a company generates is the only source of funds from which these costs can be paid, it would seem reasonable to calculate the present value of tax savings using the same rate as that applicable to the lease (and debt) payments. The reason for this approach is that now there is a parallel between generating tax savings and making these payments: the tax savings will only be realized and the lease (and debt) payments will only be made if and insofar as a company's cash inflow is adequate. In other words: the probability distributions involved in realizing tax savings and that for meeting lease or debt payments are identical up to a scale factor: the corporate income tax rate. In the foregoing I discussed the discount rate to be used in computing the present value of the lease and debt payments. In view of the parallel just mentioned, this discount rate can also be used for calculating the present value of the tax savings where there is no loss protection at all.

Let us now illustrate the above model with the help of the numerical example of Chapter 3. We shall be utilizing four different sets of assumptions. First, we assume that the asset's purchase price is entirely financed by contracting a loan having characteristics 1, 2, 3 and 4 discussed on p. 128 and that there is instantaneous and full compensation for losses by the fiscal authorities. The present value of the various tax savings can therefore be calculated using the risk-free rate: 5% in our example. Since in this example it was assumed that the implicit financial lease rate (11.14%) exceeds the loan rate (10%), we shall employ the latter rate to capitalize the lease and the loan payments. We are now able to compute the net present value of financial leasing by discounting:

. the after-tax net cash inflows at the project hurdle rate assuming perfect capital markets and all-equity financing (15%),
. the tax savings on the lease payments at the risk-free rate (5%),
. the lease payments at the loan rate (10%).

Therefore the net present value of the financial lease ($NPV_{fl,1}$)

is:

$$NPV_{fl,1} = (\frac{\$4,800}{1.15^1} + \frac{\$4,200}{1.15^2}) + 0.4 \times (\frac{\$5,850}{1.05^1} + \frac{\$5,850}{1.05^2})$$

$$- (\frac{\$5,850}{1.10^1} + \frac{\$5,850}{1.10^2}) = \$7,350 + \$4,351 - \$10,153$$

$$= \$1,548$$

Summing the present value of the after-tax net cash inflows ($7,350) and the present value of the tax savings on the lease payments ($4,351), we obtain the gross present value of the financial lease: $11,701. The net present value of the buy-and-borrow alternative can be computed from:

. the after-tax net cash inflows capitalized at 15%,
. the tax savings on depreciation capitalized at the risk-free rate (5%),
. the tax savings on interest also capitalized at the risk-free rate (5%),
. the cash purchase price of the asset,
. the principal of the loan used to finance this purchase price,
. the principal and interest payments of the loan capitalized at the loan rate (10%).

Assuming that the principal payments of the loan are $5,000 at the end of the first and the second year of the two-year loan term, so that the interest payments are 10% × $10,000 = $1,000 at the end of the first year and 10% × $5,000 = $500 at the end of the second year, the net present value of purchasing the capital asset ($NPV_{p,1}$) can now be calculated to be:

$$NPV_{p,1} = (\frac{\$4,800}{1.15^1} + \frac{\$4,200}{1.15^2}) + 0.4 \times (\frac{\$5,500}{1.05^1} + \frac{\$4,500}{1.05^2})$$

$$+ 0.4 \times (\frac{\$1,000}{1.05^1} + \frac{\$500}{1.05^2}) - \$10,000 + \$10,000$$

$$- (\frac{\$5,000 + \$1,000}{1.10^1} + \frac{\$5,000 + \$500}{1.10^2})$$

$$= \$7,350 + \$3,728 + \$562 - \$10,000 + \$10,000 - \$10,000$$

= $1,640

The gross present value of purchasing can be computed by summing the present value of the after-tax net cash inflows ($7,350) and the present value of the tax savings on depreciation ($3,728) and on interest ($562): $11,640. Comparing $NPV_{f1,1}$ ($1,548) with $NPV_{p,1}$ ($1,640), we prefer the purchase alternative.

Let us now look into the second set of assumptions. This set is equal to the first one except for the lease payments and the interest rate of the lease. We now assume that each lease payment is $5,723 (rather than $5,850) and consequently that the lease rate is 9.5% (instead of 11.14%). Since the loan rate (10%) exceeds this rate, the latter rate should be used for determining the present value of the lease and the loan payments. The other cash flows will be capitalized at the rates we used when starting from the first set of assumptions. The net present value of the financial lease ($NPV_{f1,2}$) can now be calculated as:

$$NPV_{f1,2} = (\frac{\$4,800}{1.15^1} + \frac{\$4,200}{1.15^2}) + 0.4 \times (\frac{\$5,723}{1.05^1} + \frac{\$5,723}{1.05^2})$$

$$- (\frac{\$5,723}{1.095^1} + \frac{\$5,723}{1.095^2}) = \$7,350 + \$4,257 - \$10,000$$

$$= \$1,607$$

The net present value of financial leasing has increased because of the lower lease payments. The gross present value, however, has decreased to $7,350 + $4,257 = $11,607 due to the lower present value of the tax savings on the lease payments ($4,257 rather than $4,351). The net present value of the purchase arrangement ($NPV_{p,2}$) can be computed from:

$$NPV_{p,2} = (\frac{\$4,800}{1.15^1} + \frac{\$4,200}{1.15^2}) + 0.4 \times (\frac{\$5,500}{1.05^1} + \frac{\$4,500}{1.05^2})$$

$$+ 0.4 \times (\frac{\$1,000}{1.05^1} + \frac{\$500}{1.05^2}) - \$10,000 + \$10,000$$

$$- (\frac{\$5,000 + \$1,000}{1.095^1} + \frac{\$5,000 + \$500}{1.095^2})$$

$$= \$7,350 + \$3,728 + \$562 - \$10,000 + \$10,000 - \$10,067$$

$$= \$1,573$$

The net present value of purchasing has decreased, whereas its gross present value has remained the same (\$11,640). Since $NPV_{fl,2}$ (\$1,607) exceeds $NPV_{p,2}$ (\$1,573), the leasing proposal should be recommended.

Our third set of assumptions is completely different from the second one. We now assume that the purchase price of the asset is entirely financed by way of equity, that the lease payments are \$5,850 just like they were in the first set of assumptions (hence the financial lease rate is 11.14% again), and that the fiscal authorities do not provide for any loss protection at all. As was explained on p. 131, the present value of the tax savings can now be computed utilizing the same rate as that applicable to the lease and debt payments. We assume this rate to be 10%: the interest rate of a loan having the four features described on p. 128. Based on the above assumptions, the net present value of financial leasing ($NPV_{fl,3}$) equals:

$$NPV_{fl,3} = (\frac{\$4,800}{1.15^1} + \frac{\$4,200}{1.15^2}) + 0.4 \times (\frac{\$5,850}{1.10^1} + \frac{\$5,850}{1.10^2})$$

$$- (\frac{\$5,850}{1.10^1} + \frac{\$5,850}{1.10^2}) = \$7,350 + \$4,061 - \$10,153$$

$$= \$1,258$$

The net present value of the financial lease just calculated is lower than those calculated under the two sets of assumptions employed earlier. The same holds for the gross present value of leasing (which equals \$7,350 + \$4,061 = \$11,411). Since the financing of the buy alternative is being accomplished with equity funds, the following cash flows are involved:

. the after-tax net cash inflows discounted at 15%,
. the depreciation deductions discounted at 10%,
. the cash purchase price of the asset.
Therefore we obtain:

$$NPV_{p,3} = (\frac{\$4,800}{1.15^1} + \frac{\$4,200}{1.15^2}) + 0.4 \times (\frac{\$5,500}{1.10^1} + \frac{\$4,500}{1.10^2}) - \$10,000$$

$$= \$7,350 + \$3,488 - \$10,000 = \$838$$

The net present value of purchasing as well as the gross present value ($7,350 + $3,488 = $11,838) are lower than they were before. As can be seen from the above calculations, the net present value of leasing exceeds the net present value of purchasing; hence the lease option is to be preferred.

To conclude we shall apply the fourth set of assumptions. This set is equal to the third one except for the financing method of the purchase opportunity; we now assume that the asset's purchase price is financed half with a 10% loan and half with equity. The principal of the loan is $5,000. The loan repayments are $2,500 at the end of the first and the second year, and the interest payments are 10% x $5,000 = $500 at the end of the first year and 10% x $ 2,500 = $250 at the end of the second year. This change does not affect the net present value of financial leasing, so $NPV_{fl,4} = NPV_{fl,3} = \$1,258$. The same goes for the gross present value of this alternative, which remains at $11,411. In order to determine the net present value of the purchase option, we need the following cash flows:

. the after-tax net cash inflows discounted at 15%,
. the tax savings on depreciation discounted at 10%,
. the tax savings on interest discounted at 10%,
. the cash purchase price of the asset,
. the principal of the loan used to finance half this purchase price,
. the principal and interest payments of the loan discounted at 10%.

The net present value of purchasing the asset ($NPV_{p,4}$) is:

$$NPV_{p,4} = (\frac{\$4,800}{1.15^1} + \frac{\$4,200}{1.15^2}) + 0.4 \times (\frac{\$5,500}{1.10^1} + \frac{\$4,500}{1.10^2})$$

$$+ 0.4 \times (\frac{\$500}{1.10^1} + \frac{\$250}{1.10^2}) - \$10,000 + \$5,000$$

$$- (\frac{\$2{,}500 + \$500}{1.10^1} + \frac{\$2{,}500 + \$250}{1.10^2})$$

$$= \$7{,}350 + \$3{,}488 + \$264 - \$10{,}000 + \$5{,}000 - \$5{,}000$$

$$= \$1{,}102$$

As $NPV_{f1,4}$ ($1,258) exceeds $NPV_{p,4}$ ($1,102), we opt for leasing the asset (the gross present value of the lease also exceeds the gross present value of purchasing: $11,411 > $11,102). From the above calculations we may conclude that the more debt is utilized to finance the asset's purchase price the higher will be the net present value of the purchase alternative. For management trying to maximize the market value of the firm's equity this may be a matter for consideration.

In all of these calculations we assumed the financial lease payments to be tax deductible. We made this assumption after the authors whose lease evaluation models were examined in Chapter 3. If, however, the fiscal authorities consider a financial lessee to be the owner of the leased asset (as in the Netherlands for example), the lessee has to deduct depreciation and interest charges instead of the lease payments when computing its taxable income.[2] This affects the net present value of the lease arrangement, which should now be calculated from:
. the after-tax net cash inflows,
. the tax savings on depreciation,
. the tax savings on lease interest,
. the lease payments.
Calculating the net present value of the financial lease, we start from the first set of assumptions we used on p. 131. Thus the purchase price of the asset is entirely financed by raising a loan having the features 1-4 discussed on p. 128, there is full and instantaneous compensation for losses by the fiscal authorities so that the various tax savings can be discounted at the

----

[2] The discussion of the model of Beckman and Joosen touched on this subject (see 3.4.8).

risk-free rate (5%), and the financial lease rate (11.14%) exceeds the loan rate (10%) so that the latter rate can be used for
capitalizing the lease payments. Therefore, the net present value
of financial leasing ($NPV_{fl,5}$) is:

$$NPV_{fl,5} = (\frac{\$4,800}{1.15^1} + \frac{\$4,200}{1.15^2}) + 0.4 \times (\frac{\$5,500}{1.05^1} + \frac{\$4,500}{1.05^2})$$
$$+ 0.4 \times (\frac{\$1,114}{1.05^1} + \frac{\$586}{1.05^2}) - (\frac{\$5,850}{1.10^1} + \frac{\$5,850}{1.10^2})$$
$$= \$7,350 + \$3,728 + \$637 - \$10,153 = \$1,562$$

The lease interest payments ($1,114 at the end of the first year
and $586 at the end of the second year) have been copied from
Table 3.6 on p. 28 . The above net present value exceeds the one
computed on p. 132 ($NPV_{fl,1}$ = $1,548). The difference between the
two present values can be explained from the higher present value
of the tax savings in the above net present value calculation.
The purchase arrangement, however, is still to be preferred
because of its higher net present value ($NPV_{p,1}$ = $1,640, see pp.
132-133).

In the above calculations we utilized the appropriate project
hurdle rate assuming perfect capital markets and all-equity
financing to capitalize the after-tax net cash inflows (15%). As
observed on p. 127, it may be very difficult to determine this
rate in a real-world situation because in fact it is an imaginary
rate: it is the rate of return investors would require in view of
the risk characteristics of a project if this project were financed exclusively with equity funds. One may reproach me with
preferring the use of the value-additivity principle, thereby
discounting part of the cash flow to equity series (i.e., the
after-tax net cash inflows) at an imaginary equity rate, rather
than capitalizing the series itself at the real required rate of
return on equity. To be brief, one may argue that it would be
harder to determine an imaginary rate than a real rate. No more
than Schall do I mean "to gainsay the practical difficulties in
ascertaining" the capitalization rates to be used (Schall 1974,
p. 1209). Nonetheless I feel that the above analysis can be con-

sidered to be a useful instrument for making the lease-or-purchase decision, as this analysis allows us to determine any of the required capitalization rates except for the (imaginary) all-equity financing rate. This rate, however, is to be applied to the net cash inflows after taxes, usually a common element in the net present value calculations. Hence, if a firm's management is unable to provide anything more than a rough estimate of the all-equity financing rate, the net present values of leasing and of purchasing can no longer be calculated in an exact way, but management is still able to select the alternative with the higher net present value.

Up until now we have been employing two different regulations concerning tax deductible losses: immediate and full compensation for losses or no protection for losses at all. Other regulations concerning the tax deductible losses fall between these two extreme forms of regulation. If follows that the discount rate to be applied to the tax savings will then be between the risk-free rate and the rate used for calculating the present value of the lease and the debt payments. The problem is how to determine the correct tax discount rate. This rate may very well be rather low, because as Bierman and Smidt observe: "Even if the firm does not have taxable income in any particular year, the tax-loss carry-forward and carry-back provisions of the law provide a high degree of assurance that tax savings will result, although their timing might change slightly" (Bierman and Smidt 1980, p. 393). Where the fiscal authorities provide no compensation for losses at all, the present value of the tax savings has been computed using the same discount rate as that utilized for discounting the lease and debt payments. Doing so assumes that the total cash inflow generated by the firm is the only source of funds from which these payments can be met. However, when there are other ways of dealing with these costs if the cash inflow of the firm is inadequate, e.g., cash reserves, this approach is no longer correct. There may now be situations where, although these costs have been covered, the tax savings have not been realized. Because of these situations, realizing the tax savings may be less certain than meeting the lease and debt payments. This greater uncertainty may lead to a higher discount rate being employed for computing the present value of the tax savings. There may yet be other complications with respect to tax savings: the corporate income tax rate may change in the future just as the regulations concerning the tax deductible losses and the tax deductible costs may change.[3] Of course the uncertainty caused by these complications can be reflected in the use of higher discount rates too. Again the question is how to determine those rates. According to Schall the discount rate to be utilized can be determined "by observing market rates on comparable streams." Nevertheless, the author has to admit that for the practitioner this will not be an easy method (Schall 1974, pp. 1208-1209). Besides, starting from a multivariate regression analysis Crawford, Harper, and McConnell very convincingly argue that an "appropriate risk-adjusted discount rate" to be used for lease evaluation presumably is "a function of the risk of the lessee, but it also may be a function of lease prepayment requirements, lease maturity, and the prevailing structure of interest rates" (Crawford, Harper, and McConnell 1981, p. 13). Therefore and because of requirement V (the applicability of the model in practice), I recommend performing a sensitivity analysis. In such an analysis one can trace the effects of using different discount rates in calculating the present value of the tax savings for the lease-or-purchase decision. This approach to the problem has also been applied by Bower (Bower 1973, pp. 31-32). In order to illustrate such a sensitivity analysis, we assume that the purchase price of the asset is entirely financed by raising the same 10% loan used on p. 132 and that the lease payments ($5,850 to be paid at the end of the first and the second year) are tax deductible. The loan rate, being lower than the lease rate, is employed for discounting the lease and the loan payments. The net present value of the financial lease can therefore be determined from:

----

[3] Earlier I looked into those cases where the lease payments are not tax deductible.

$$NPV_{fl} = (\frac{\$4,800}{1,15^1} + \frac{\$4,200}{1,15^2}) + 0.4 \times (\frac{\$5,850}{(1+k)^1} + \frac{\$5,850}{(1+k)^2})$$
$$- (\frac{\$5,850}{1,10^1} + \frac{\$5,850}{1,10^2})$$

We shall start from various discount rates to capitalize the tax savings on the lease payments: k = 0%, 5%, 10%, 15%, and 20%. The net present value of the purchase opportunity can be computed from:

$$NPV_p = (\frac{\$4,800}{1.15^1} + \frac{\$4,200}{1.15^2}) + 0.4 \times (\frac{\$5,500}{(1+k)^1} + \frac{\$4,500}{(1+k)^2})$$
$$+ 0.4 \times (\frac{\$1,000}{(1+k)^1} + \frac{\$500}{(1+k)^2}) - \$10,000 + \$10,000$$
$$- (\frac{\$5,000 + \$1,000}{1,10^1} + \frac{\$5,000 + \$500}{1,10^2})$$

Again starting from the tax discount rates 0%, 5%, 10%, 15% and 20%, we arrive at the following results:

Table 4.1
Net Present Values Using Various Discount Rates for the Tax Shields

k	Net Present Value of Financial Leasing	Net Present Value of Purchasing
0%	1,877	1,950
5%	1,548	1,640
10%	1,258	1,367
15%	1,001	1,123
20%	772	906

These results can also be presented graphically, as shown in Figure 4.1.

Figure 4.1

Net Present Values Using Various Discount Rates for the Tax
Shields (Original Data)

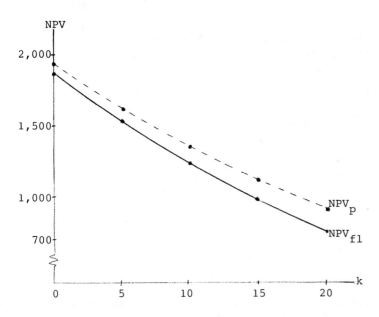

From the tabular and the graphic presentation it can be concluded
that, for any of the tax discount rates employed, management
should opt for purchasing the asset; NPV_p exceeds NPV_{fl} for each
tax discount rate. So, even if management does not exactly know
at which rate to capitalize the tax deductions it does know which
alternative to select. If, however, we were to use another method
to depreciate the asset, for example, if depreciation at the end
of the first year were $2,000 and at the end of the second year
$8,000, then the net present value of purchasing can be calcu-
lated from:

$$NPV_p = (\frac{\$4,800}{1.15^1} + \frac{\$4,200}{1.15^2}) + 0.4 \times (\frac{\$2,000}{(1+k)^1} + \frac{\$8,000}{(1+k)^2})$$

$$+ 0.4 \times (\frac{\$1,000}{(1+k)^1} + \frac{\$500}{(1+k)^2}) - \$10,000 + \$10,000$$

$$- (\frac{\$5,000 + \$1,000}{1.10^1} + \frac{\$5,000 + \$500}{1.10^2})$$

Inserting k = 0%, 5%, 10%, 15%, and 20% in this equation results
in Table 4.2.

Table 4.2
Net Present Value of Purchasing Using Various
Discount Rates for the Tax Shields

k	Net Present Value of Purchasing
0%	1,950
5%	1,577
10%	1,250
15%	964
20%	711

If we present NPV_{fl} and NPV_p graphically, we obtain Figure 4.2.

Figure 4.2
Net Present Values Usirg Various Discount Rates for the Tax
Shields (Modified Data)

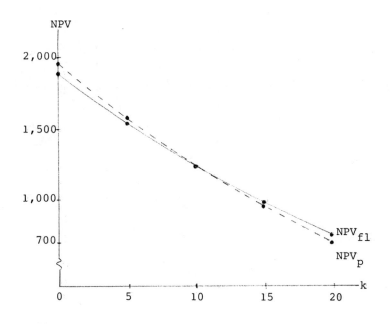

Now NPV_p exceeds NPV_{fl} at tax discount rates below about 10%, but the reverse holds at rates above 10%. If management is of the opinion that the realization of the tax savings is rather certain and therefore uses a low discount rate to capitalize these savings (for example, 6% or 7%), purchasing the asset is preferable. If, on the other hand, it thinks a higher discount would be more appropriate (e.g., 18% or 19%), it should choose to lease. Up until now the present value of any of the tax savings resulting from depreciation and interest as well as from the lease payments has been calculated using the same tax discount rate. If for a particular category of tax savings there should be specific uncertainties, I recommend performing a sensitivity analysis for each category. Summing up, the above sensitivity analysis enables management to choose between financial leasing and purchasing even it does not know exactly at which rates to capitalize the tax savings. A sensitivity analysis, however, can also be performed if there is uncertainty about other factors that may influence the net present value of the alternatives, for instance, salvage values and net cash inflows (see Pritchard and Hindelang 1980, Chapter 9).

In conclusion I would like to discuss three issues. The first one concerns the approach to the lease-or-purchase problem. In many publications on this problem, the authors commence by discussing the conditions for management to be indifferent between leasing and purchasing a capital asset. They then go into the imperfections that cause management to prefer one alternative over the other (e.g., Lewellen, Long, and McConnell 1976, pp. 787-798; Haley and Schall 1979, pp. 455-467; Weston and Brigham 1981, pp. 855-859). I did not apply this approach but immediately looked into situations where the rather unrealistic conditions for indifference between leasing and purchasing do not hold.

Secondly, entering into a financial lease or financing the purchase price of an asset in a specific way might influence the rates of return investors require. In the literature on leasing little attention is paid to this potential influence. One exception is formed by two German authors, Krumbholz and Streitferdt, who state that in the case of leasing the part of the purchase price of the asset that is financed with nonequity funds will in practice usually be larger than it would be in the case of buying. Therefore, they argue, the cash flows of the lease have to be discounted using a higher rate than the one used for calculating the present value of the cash flows of the purchase alternative (Krumbholz and Streitferdt 1975, p. 48; see 3.5.4 for an evaluation of their model). Terborgh is another author who pays attention to this problem. He states that "since lease obligations, like the more conventional forms of debt, increase the risk of equity, you may wish to add a 'loading' for this reason" (Terborgh 1967, p. 307). As Weston and Brigham show, a required rate of return consists of a risk-free element, a premium for business risk, and a premium for financial risk (Weston and Brigham 1981, p. 607). As for business risk, it is conceivable that the lessor has a different influence upon the user continuing the operation of the asset than the investors would have had in the case of purchasing. The fact is that the lessor usually remains the legal owner of the leased asset, and if the lessee fails to make the lease payments or gets into trouble in some way the lessor may be inclined to repossess the asset sooner than the other investors would think of disposing the asset by forced sale. The likelihood of the lessor's recovering the asset, however, also depends on the possibility of its selling or leasing it to another user. In addition to the impact leasing could have upon business risk, entering into a lease contract may influence financial risk. This may apply where, in the present investors' view, the way the asset's purchase price is financed has different consequences for their position as investors than leasing the asset would have had. In this connection Franks and Broyles discuss the concept of the hidden or implicit cost of debt. They explain this concept by pointing out "that introducing debt...increases the discount rate on the equity" (Franks and Broyles 1979, p. 291). On the other hand, a well-known Dutch author, Wytzes, turns his attention to the reactions of the present bondholders. He illustrates these reactions with an example in which a firm would finance the purchase price of an asset with a combination of debt and equity funds. In the case of leasing, however, the asset would be entirely financed by the lessor. This may be a motive for the bondholders to require more equity in proportion to debt, at least if the company is going to lease on a large scale rather than purchase assets financed with a combination of debt and equity (Wytzes 1981, p. 451). Wytzes also states that management is responsible for examining the capital structure of its firm, taking into consideration the liabilities resulting from entering into lease contracts (p. 454). This is correct of course; the discussion on the optimal capital structure (referred to on p. 129) is also relevant here. Bouma, another Dutch author, discusses the implicit cost of capital too. What is involved in this cost is the adverse effect of a financing transaction on the cost of existing or future financing transactions. If, for instance, a firm enters into a lease, investors may require higher rates of return because leasing would add to the burden of fixed financing charges that the firm must bear (Bouma 1980, p. 415). However, as Bierman and Smidt show, in the case of leasing a proper balance to the firm's capital structure can be restored by reducing other fixed charges, say, by repaying debt applying (part of) the equity funds available for purchase of the asset (Bierman and Smidt 1980, p. 391).

In the third place I would point out that in choosing between financial leasing and buying I have hitherto considered only quantitative factors (i.e., factors that can be measured in percentages, sums of money, and the like). In making this choice, however, nonquantifiable considerations may be of relevance too. For instance, whereas it may be that a financial lease is preferable according to the calculations, management may nevertheless favor buying the asset owing to the pride of ownership. The reverse is imaginable too: purchasing may be preferable on account of a higher net present value, but management may choose to lease in order to keep up the contacts it has previously made with the lessor. Qualitative considerations of this nature do not, however, render calculating net present values a useless pastime. On the contrary, such calculations show management how much it is going to cost to give in to such motives. In Chapter 6 it will appear that qualitative considerations are relatively unimportant in real-world situations.

As may be evident from the preceding pages, I am not an advocate of blindly applying the same model to the lease-or-purchase decision in every conceivable situation where this would mean that binding instructions are given regarding the discount rates to be used or the method of financing the purchase price of the capital asset. This decision must be made taking into account the firm's goal, the position the firm is in (among other things, its income tax status), and the financing alternatives open to it.

5 OPERATING LEASES

5.1 Introduction

After having discussed the financial lease-versus-purchase decision, I shall now address operating leases. Back in Chapter 2 it
was explained that an operating lease is cancelable by the lessee
upon giving due notice of cancellation to the lessor (see p. 7).
That is why such a lease does not involve a large fixed future
commitment by the lessee. The lessee may cancel an operating
lease contract if the continued operation of the leased capital
asset is no longer economically justified.[1] Therefore, the risk
of obsolescence is (for the greater part) borne by the lessor.
This risk, however, may differ from the risk the lessee is
avoiding by entering into an operating lease arrangement. In
contrast with the lessee, the lessor may be able to sell the
leased asset or to lease it again to another user. Of course it
is easier to find another user if the asset can be utilized for
various purposes and has been serviced in a correct way.
    In the following I shall be applying the same working method
as the one used for financial leasing. Utilizing the requirements
I-V I shall first examine a number of operating lease evaluation
models as recommended by several authors and then I shall try to
develop my own model. The first part of this task will not take

----

[1] On the other hand, however, the lessee may also continue
operating the leased asset if its operation turns out to be
profitable. The lessee may even decide to purchase the asset
in such a situation (see also 2.2). Thus, an operating lease
is a very flexible financing method.

much time because, contrary to financial leases, the literature
on operating leases is scant. Models for valuing operating leases
can be distinguished into two groups. This classification has
been based on one of the characteristic features of an operating
lease: its flexibility. Employing this feature, one is able to
distinguish between:
1. models in which the flexibility of an operating lease is not
   quantified, and
2. models in which this advantage is quantified.
When discussing the first group of models, I shall evaluate the
approach of Vancil (see section 5.2), of Peirson and Bird (5.3),
and of Goudsmit and Keijser (5.4). Next I shall go into some
models of the second group and review the model of Jenkins (5.5),
of Hax (5.6), and of Beckman and Joosen (5.7). Then, in 5.8, I
shall discuss my own model. When illustrating these models with
the help of a numerical example, I shall assume that:
. management of a corporation considering operating an additional
  capital asset is able to choose between purchase of the asset
  and an operating lease,
. the cash purchase price of the asset can be paid for using debt
  (a loan), equity, or a combination of debt and equity,
. the repayment schedule of the loan is flexible,
. the salvage value of the asset at the end of the tax depreciation life of the asset is zero,
. the tax deductible lease payments consist only of principal
  payment plus interest (all other operating costs, e.g., cost of
  maintenance and insurance, are to be borne by the user of the
  capital asset, as in the case of purchasing that asset),
. any tax deductions are realized at the same time the tax deductible costs are incurred.
Comparing this set of assumptions with the one on p. 18, we see
that now we are no longer assuming that the lease term equals the
asset's tax depreciation life. This is because an operating lease
is a flexible financing instrument, which results in there being
uncertainty concerning the lease term at the moment the firm's
management enters into such a lease. Regarding the fifth assumption, I would like to observe that since in the case of an oper-

ating lease the lessor assumes (in full or in part) the risk of obsolescence, the lessor is interested in the way the maintenance services are performed. The possibilities of the lessor finding another user for an asset that has been returned by a former lessee also depend on the way the asset has been serviced. That is why the lessor may prefer to service the leased asset, making the service costs a part of the lease payments. Hence, a so-called service lease is involved. In order to keep this exposition as simple as possible, however, I shall assume that the user performs the necessary maintenance services whether it leases or purchases the asset. Moreover, as Copeland and Weston argue "the maintenance contract is economically separable" from the lease contract, which implies that a financial as well as an operating lease "may involve a separable contract for various types of maintenance on the leased asset" (Copeland and Weston 1983, p. 541). Consequently, I assume that each lease payment consists of principal payment and interest only. If a firm's management has to evaluate a service lease agreement, then it may try to eliminate the maintenance costs the lessor has incurred. In order to determine these costs, management may gather information from the lessor or may estimate the costs of servicing the leased asset itself. These costs can then be deducted from the lease payments. The same goes for any insurance costs forming a part of these payments. Another service a lessor may perform is putting a replacement asset at its lessee's disposal if the leased asset breaks down. Again, I shall ignore the costs of performing this service in order to concentrate on the flexibility of an operating lease and on the effects of this advantage for choosing between such a lease and purchasing the asset. If management has to value a lease where the lessor provides a substitute if the leased asset breaks down, it may try to estimate the cost of this service in the same manner as discussed in the above.

Just as I did in Chapters 3 and 4 I shall illustrate the lease evaluation models I am about to discuss with the help of a simple numerical example. In this example I assume that the maximum service life of a capital asset, which can be leased or purchased, is two years. The tax depreciation life is equal to this maximum service life. However, the asset's actual service life is uncertain: it may be one year or it may be two years. If it turns out to be one year, then the lessee is allowed to cancel the lease. If the asset has been purchased, however, it is sold by the former user for the salvage value at the end of the first year. Other data to be used are:

. net cash inflow before corporate income taxes expected from asset operation at the end of the first year = $4,000,
. the same, at the end of the second year = $3,800,
. cash purchase price of the asset to be paid at the beginning of the first year = $5,000,
. depreciation at the end of the first year as allowed for tax purposes = $3,000,
. the same, at the end of the second year = $2,000,
. residual value of the asset at the end of the first year = $1,000 (the residual value at the end of the second year is zero),
. promised lease payments at the end of the first and the second year as long as the lease is not cancelled = $3,200,
. corporate income tax rate on ordinary firm income = corporate income tax rate on gains and losses from disposing of assets = 40%,
. interest rate of a loan that can be used for financing the asset's purchase price = 11%,
. after-tax weighted average cost of capital of the firm = 14%,
. appropriate project hurdle rate assuming perfect capital markets and all-equity financing = 16%.

5.2 Vancil

In his book, Leasing of Industrial Equipment, Vancil not only pays attention to financial leases but to operating leases as well. As he did when explaining his "borrowing opportunity rate method," Vancil illustrates his ideas by means of numerical examples. The author commences by observing that transferring the

risk of early obsolescence is an important function of an operating lease, to which he adds: "If the lessee wishes to avoid transferring this risk, his alternative is to purchase the equipment outright" (Vancil 1963, p. 55). That is why Vancil holds that the problem to be solved is lease-or-buy (rather than lease-or-borrow, which issue he intended to solve when developing his "borrowing opportunity rate method") and that the decision to be made "is similar to many other types of capital investment decisions." Therefore, he first looks into "evaluating capital investments" discussing two evaluation methods: "return on investment" and "profitability measured in present-value dollars" (pp. 56-75). Vancil utilizes both measures for answering the operating lease-or-buy question. I shall evaluate each of these measures, starting with the return on investment. When calculating this return, Vancil uses the following cash flows:
. the cash purchase price of the asset,
. the lease payments,
. the differences between the tax savings on the lease payments and the tax savings on depreciation,
. the residual value of the asset,
. the tax effect of any differences between the asset's book value and its residual value (p. 88).
In order to compute the return on investment (k_{ol}^{V}), Vancil initially assumes that the operating lease term equals the asset's tax depreciation life: two years in our numerical example. Starting from this two-year period, we shall first calculate the tax savings on depreciation and the tax savings on the lease payments. These calculations are performed in Table 5.1.

Table 5.1.

Tax Savings on Depreciation and on Lease Payments

Year (1)	Depreciation (2)	Depreciation Deduction (3)=0.4x(2)	Lease Payment (4)	Tax Saving on Lease Payment (5)=0.4x(4)
1	3,000	1,200	3,200	1,280
2	2,000	800	3,200	1,280

Since at the end of the second year the asset's salvage value and its book value are both zero, we can determine k_{ol}^V from the following equation:

$$\$5,000 - (\frac{\$3,200}{(1+k_{ol}^V)^1} + \frac{\$3,200}{(1+k_{ol}^V)^2}) + (\frac{\$1,280 - \$1,200}{(1+k_{ol}^V)^1}$$

$$+ \frac{\$1,280 - \$800}{(1+k_{ol}^V)^2}) = 0$$

Hence:

$$\$5,000 - \frac{\$3,120}{(1+k_{ol}^V)^1} - \frac{\$2,720}{(1+k_{ol}^V)^2} = 0$$

It follows that $k_{ol}^V \approx 11.28\%$. However, it may be that the asset becomes obsolete before the end of the two-year tax depreciation life. If management had opted for purchasing the asset, it "accepts the risks of ownership" Vancil observes (p. 88). In one of his numerical examples, $k_{ol}^V \approx 30\%$, and the author then argues that "this rate of return is high enough to justify ... accepting the risks of ownership" (p. 89). It is a pity Vancil does not mention the rate he compares with this 30%. Maybe this rate is the weighted average cost of capital the author also utilizes when calculating the so-called profitability in present-value dollars. On the other hand, Ferrara sets the return on investment as computed by Vancil against the after-tax borrowing rate of the firm. In any of Ferrara's illustrative examples, this return exceeds the after-tax borrowing rate. The difference between both rates is called the "premium." In his opinion, choosing between an operating lease and purchasing amounts to answering the question, "How large a premium should I pay to avoid various ownership risks?" (Ferrara 1974, p. 26). Next I shall evaluate Vancil's model with the help of requirements I-V.

Evaluation

I   Starting from his numerical example Vancil has tried to choose between an operating lease and a purchase arrangement, but he does not calculate the profitability of the preferred alternative. In another part of his book, however, he does make an attempt at setting up such a calculation (pp. 75-76). The author then performs a "two-step analysis," and first looks into the choice between "continuing the status quo" and leasing a capital asset to replace the present asset. If the former proposal is chosen, then this proposal is set against purchasing the new capital asset employing Vancil's return on investment or profitability measured in present-value dollars. If, on the other hand, an operating lease would be preferred to "continuing the status quo," then the lease and the purchase option are compared with one another. Unfortunately Vancil does not illustrate this second analysis. Besides, one wonders why the problem has to be solved in two steps. In my opinion a direct comparison of the three alternatives would be less time consuming.

II   The author does not capitalize future cash flows to arrive at a present value but uses the cash flow series to derive an internal rate of return or, using his own terminology, a return on investment. He does not state which rate to set against the return on investment. Therefore, the meaning of this result is still in the air. Moreover, even if the author did mention the rate to be set against his return on investment, a direct comparison of both rates in order to select the preferred alternative may very well result in severe problems. This is because of the difficulties attached to choosing from alternative strategies with the help of rates of return.

III Vancil clearly indicates that the above model can only be used for valuing operating leases. In another chapter of his book he discusses his "borrowing opportunity rate method" to be utilized for valuing financial leases (analyzed in 3.4.2).

IV Vancil's first approach to resolving the operating lease-or-purchase issue has been based on internal rates of return and not on a net present value procedure. The author does not appear to be aware of the dangers that may result from using these rates when choosing from alternative arrangements.

V Applying Vancil's model in practice is hampered by his settling the operating lease-versus-purchase problem with the statement concerning the result of his calculations quoted earlier: "This rate of return is high enough to justify ... accepting the risks of ownership" (p. 89). Even if the author did state which rate to compare with his return on investment, the ultimate decision is left to management. This is because management has to check whether the possibility of the operating lease being more expensive than purchasing the required capital asset offsets the advantage of being able to avoid the risk of early obsolescence.

After having explained his "borrowing opportunity rate method," Vancil returns to the operating-lease-or-buy problem. He now looks into "economic life and residual value" (pp. 127-160). Quite rightly the author observes that both factors are inter-related (p. 128). He now employs the second measure of investment worth as discussed in his chapter on capital budgeting: "profitability measured in present-value dollars." The capitalization rate he makes use of is the so-called investment opportunity rate (p. 119). Back in 3.4.2, it was explained that when there is no capital rationing this rate equals the firm's cost of capital (see pp. 34-35). Starting from the profitability measured in present-value dollars, Vancil performs two break-even analyses. In the first place he calculates the service life of a capital asset, which causes the present value of the cash flows of leasing to be equal to the present value of the cash flows of purchasing; in other words, the difference between both present values is zero. This service life he calls the "break-even economic life." In his second analysis Vancil computes the "break-even residual value": the asset's residual value that causes the present value of leasing to be equal to the present value of purchasing or, alternatively, the residual value that causes the difference between both present values to be zero. I shall illustrate these two analyses by way of a numerical example.

Vancil's break-even economic life can be determined from the following cash flow series:
. the cash purchase price of the asset,
. the lease payments,
. the differences between the tax savings on the lease payments and the tax savings on depreciation,
. the residual value of the asset,
. the tax effect of any differences between the asset's book value and its residual value.

We shall capitalize these cash flows at the firm's after-tax weighted average cost of capital, which in our example equals 14%. Assuming the service life of the capital asset to be two years, we obtain:

$$\$5,000 - (\frac{\$3,200}{1.14^1} + \frac{\$3,200}{1.14^2}) + (\frac{\$1,280 - \$1,200}{1.14^1} + \frac{\$1,280 - \$800}{1.14^2})$$

$$= \$170$$

Since at the end of the second year of the asset's service life the book value and the residual value are both zero, there is no tax effect. The result of our calculations is a positive $170, indicating that leasing the asset is less expensive than purchasing it. Let us now start from a service life of one year:

$$\$5,000 - \frac{\$3,200}{1.14^1} + \frac{\$1,280 - \$1,200}{1.14^1} - \frac{\$1,000}{1.14^1}$$

$$- 0.4 \times \frac{(\$5{,}000 - \$3{,}000) - \$1{,}000}{1.14^1}$$

$$= \$5{,}000 - \$2{,}807 + \$70 - \$877 - \$351 = \$1{,}035$$

At the end of the first year there is a difference between the salvage value of the asset ($1,000, as can be seen from the fourth term of the above equation) and its book value. The asset's book value is equal to the cash purchase price of the asset ($5,000) less the amount of depreciation at the end of the first year ($3,000), so the asset's book value is $2,000. Multiplying this difference ($2,000 - $1,000 = $1,000) by the tax rate (40%), we obtain the tax effect resulting from the asset's book value being unequal to its residual value (0.4 x $1,000 = $400). Finally, this tax effect has to be capitalized at 14% (resulting in a present value of $351). The result of our computations is a positive $1,035 indicating that, starting from a one-year service life, leasing is again less expensive than purchasing.

From the above calculations we can conclude that the break-even economic life as calculated by Vancil would be slightly longer than two years. If it would be possible for management to lease the asset for a period of time that is equal to this break-even economic life, the present value of the cash flows of the operating lease would be equal to the present value of the cash flows of purchasing the asset. If management expected the service life of the asset to be longer than its break-even economic life, then purchasing should be preferred. Otherwise management should opt for entering into an operating lease. However, since we assumed that the maximum service life of the capital asset is two years, leasing it should be preferred.

Next I shall discuss Vancil's calculation of the break-even residual value S_n^*. The cash flows necessary to determine S_n^* are the same as the ones utilized for computing the break-even economic life of the capital asset. Starting from a two-year service life, the break-even salvage value, S_2^*, causing the present value of the purchase opportunity to equal the present value of the operating lease alternative (in other words, the difference between both present values is zero), can be calculated from:

$$\$5,000 - (\frac{\$3,200}{1.14^1} + \frac{\$3,200}{1.14^2}) + (\frac{\$1,280 - \$1,200}{1.14^1} + \frac{\$1,280 - \$800}{1.14^2})$$

$$- \frac{S_2^*}{1.14^2} - 0.4 \times \frac{(\$5,000 - \$3,000 - \$2,000) - S_2^*}{1.14^2} = 0$$

The amounts between the parentheses in the last term of this equation indicate that the asset's book value at the end of the second year - that is, the difference between its purchase price ($5,000) and the depreciation amount at the end of the first year ($3,000) and the depreciation amount at the end of the second year ($2,000) - is zero. The above equation can be simplified as follows:

$$\$5,000 - \$5,269 + \$440 - 0.77 \, S_2^* + 0.31 \, S_2^* = 0$$

$$\$171 - 0.46 \, S_2^* = 0$$

$$S_2^* = \$372$$

For the present value of purchasing to equal the present value of leasing or, alternatively, for management to be indifferent between the purchase and the operating lease option, Vancil's break-even residual value at the end of the second year, S_2^*, has to be equal to $372. Since the salvage value at the end of this year is expected to be zero, a value much lower than S_2^*, management should prefer to lease the asset.[2]

Assuming the useful service life of the asset to be one year,

----

[2] In their textbook, The Capital Budgeting Decision, Bierman and Smidt also utilize the break-even salvage value to determine whether to lease or to buy. However, the lease contract of their numerical example is a financial lease (see Bierman and Smidt 1980, pp. 401-402).

Vancil's break-even salvage value, S_1^*, can be computed from the following equation:

$$\$5,000 - \frac{\$3,200}{1.14^1} + \frac{\$1,280 - \$1,200}{1.14^1} - \frac{S_1^*}{1.14^1}$$

$$- 0.4 \times \frac{(\$5,000 - \$3,000) - S_1^*}{1.14^1} = 0$$

$$\$5,000 - \$2,807 + \$70 - 0.88 \, S_1^* - \$702 + 0.35 \, S_1^* = 0$$

$$\$1,561 - 0.53 \, S_1^* = 0$$

$$S_1^* = \$2,945$$

Hence, the present value of purchasing the asset would be equal to the present value of leasing it if $S_1^* = \$2,945$. Since management expects the residual value at the end of the first year to be only \$1,000, it should again opt for leasing the asset.

Evaluation

I Applying Vancil's break-even analyses, it is possible to choose between an operating lease and buying, but the profitability of both arrangements remains unknown. It does not become clear whether Vancil would again recommend employing his "two-step analysis" discussed earlier (see p. 153).

II The author does not state the grounds for his capitalizing at the after-tax weighted average cost of capital of the firm. When illustrating his "borrowing opportunity rate method," Vancil also makes use of this rate (see 3.4.2). As argued on pp. 31-33, the tax deductibility of interest is an important factor when applying this method. However, when explaining his break-even analyses, Vancil completely ignores this factor. Unfortunately he does not explain this difference of approach.

III Vancil clearly states that his break-even analyses have been developed to value operating leases.

IV As was explained in the above, both the break-even economic life and the break-even residual value have been based on Vancil's profitability in present-value dollars, without paying attention to the cash inflows the capital asset generates.

V   Vancil observes that in actuality it often is rather difficult to estimate the future service life of a capital asset. In his opinion it is easier for management to find out whether the estimated service life does or does not exceed the break-even economic life. The same would hold for the residual value in proportion to the break-even residual value. To a certain extent I agree with Vancil: both break-even values give management something to go by. However, Vancil maintains that the break-even economic life is especially of interest in situations where technological factors determine the asset's service life. He then states: "If it becomes economically feasible to replace a piece of equipment because the cost savings provided by more modern equipment are sufficient to justify the acquisition of the modern equipment, then it is also likely that the residual value of the old equipment will be rather small" (p. 129). I do not agree with this statement. In the case of computers, where technological changes frequently occur, it is conceivable that the present generation of computers is still fit for use by less exacting users after a new and more advanced generation has been introduced. Generally speaking, out of date for one category of users does not imply out of date for another category. That is why "the residual value of the old equipment" may still be substantial. On the other hand Vancil is of the opinion that if commercial factors affect the service life of an asset, "the residual value of the equipment at the end of its economic life will not necessarily be so small as it might be in the case of technological obsolescence" (p. 150). This statement is correct only when the asset can be utilized for various purposes. I think Vancil would agree to this condition; in his illustrative example the firm's management assumes that it "will be able to sell the equipment to someone who might use it to manufacture another product" (p.

150).

In Vancil's book I have looked in vain for an attempt to integrate his return on investment and his break-even analyses. Then a question like, "Do we have to utilize these approaches along with one another or instead of each other?" may be answered. Such an exposition can only add to the possibilities of applying these models in real-world situations.

5.3 Peirson and Bird

Just like Vancil, Peirson and Bird (subsequently PB) pay attention to the evaluation of financial and operating leases. Moreover, they also contend that: "the analysis of an operating lease is merely a special type of investment decision" (PB 1972, p. 238). In order to compute the present value of purchasing a capital asset, PB utilize the following cash flows:
. the cash purchase price of the asset,
. the depreciation deductions,
. the residual value of the asset,
. the tax effect of a difference, if any, between the asset's book value and its residual value (pp. 239-240).
These cash flows are capitalized at the firm's cost of capital (14% in our example). In order to calculate the present value of leasing an asset, the authors use:
. the lease payments,
. the tax savings on the lease payments (pp. 239-240).
These cash flows are discounted at the firm's after-tax weighted average cost of capital too. When illustrating their model with a numerical example, PB start from two different useful service lives of the capital asset to be acquired: the first one is comparatively short and the second one is somewhat longer. When explaining the PB model, I shall give an example first assuming that the asset's useful life is one year and then assuming that this life is two years. Starting from a one-year service life the present value of the purchase arrangement as calculated by PB,

PV_{p1}^{PB}, equals:

$$PV_{p1}^{PB} = \$5,000 - \frac{\$1,200}{1.14^1} - \frac{\$1,000}{1.14^1} - 0.4 \times \frac{\$2,000 - \$1,000}{1.14^1}$$

$$= \$5,000 - \$1,053 - \$877 - \$351 = \$2,719$$

The depreciation deduction at the end of the first year (\$1,200) has been copied from Table 5.1. In the last term of the above equation, the tax effect of the difference between the asset's book value (\$2,000) and its salvage value (\$1,000) is calculated. Applying the methodology of PB and assuming a one-year lease term, the present value of the operating lease, PV_{o11}^{PB} , is:

$$PV_{o11}^{PB} = \frac{\$3,200}{1.14^1} - \frac{\$1,280}{1.14^1} = \$2,807 - \$1,123 = \$1,684$$

Since PV_{p1}^{PB} (\$2,719) exceeds PV_{o11}^{PB} (\$1,684), the authors would recommend leasing the asset.

If we assume the service life of the asset to be two years, then the present value of purchasing it, PV_{p2}^{PB} , can be determined from:

$$PV_{p2}^{PB} = \$5,000 - (\frac{\$1,200}{1.14^1} + \frac{\$800}{1.14^2}) = \$5,000 - \$1,053 - \$616 = \$3,331$$

Based on a two-year service life, we find the asset's book value, its salvage value, and consequently the tax effect to be zero. If the operating lease arrangement would be continued for two years we obtain PV_{o12}^{PB} :

$$PV_{o12}^{PB} = (\frac{\$3,200}{1.14^1} + \frac{\$3,200}{1.14^2}) - (\frac{\$1,280}{1.14^1} + \frac{\$1,280}{1.14^2})$$

$$= \$5,269 - \$2,108 = \$3,161$$

Again leasing would be preferred to purchasing the capital asset, as PV_{o12}^{PB} (\$3,161) is lower than PV_{p2}^{PB} (\$3,331).

Subtracting PV_{o11}^{PB} from PV_{p1}^{PB} we find the difference between both present values to be \$2,719 - \$1,684 = \$1,035. Performing the same calculation starting from a two-year useful service life, we obtain $PV_{p2}^{PB} - PV_{ol2}^{PB} = \$3,331 - \$3,161 = \$170$. These differences exactly equal the ones we obtained when determining Vancil's break-even economic life (see pp. 155-156). This is as may be expected, as the same cash flows and the same capitalization rate are utilized both by Vancil and by PB.

Evaluation

I   PB separate the investment decision from the financing decision. This may be evident from their statement: "Prior to any evaluation of the lease plans it is necessary for the basic investment decision to have already been made. We will proceed on the assumption, therefore, that management considers it advantageous to acquire the use of the equipment" (p. 238).

II The authors do not state the grounds for their capitalizing the various cash flows at the "lessee's cost of capital." It may be that utilizing this rate results from their considering the operating lease-versus-purchase problem to be "merely a special type of investment decision" (p. 238). When making the investment decision, PB also employ the cost of capital (pp. 79-80). On the other hand, when choosing from financial leasing and purchasing the authors utilize the cost of capital too, although they hold that this "decision boils down to a lease or borrow decision - a financial decision not an investment decision" (p. 241).

III PB explicitly state that their model has been developed to value operating leases.

IV The results of this model are expressed in present values. The authors do not pay attention to the cash inflow series the capital asset generates.

V   Just as Vancil did when demonstrating his first model (see p. 154), PB leave the question of whether to lease or to buy to management, observing: "The answer will depend on the circumstances of the particular case and the judgement of the financial manager" (p. 241). Management has to ascertain whether the disadvantage of an operating lease being more expensive than purchasing outweighs the advantage of being

able to transfer the risk of obsolescence to the lessor.
Apart from that, PB do not appear to be aware of the conditions that have to be met before the firm's cost of capital
can be utilized for discounting purposes.

5.4 Goudsmit and Keijser

Goudsmit and Keijser, two Dutch authors, also pay attention to
financial as well as operating leases. Like Vancil they say they
will capitalize the relevant cash flows at the so-called investment opportunity rate. Goudsmit and Keijser (GK) define this rate
as the return management requires an investment project as
carried out by its firm to yield based on experiences from the
past and expectations in future developments and expressed as a
percentage of that investment (GK 1972, p. 213). As argued when
discussing Vancil's model, the investment opportunity rate equals
the firm's cost of capital if there is no capital rationing (see
p. 154).

When computing the present value of purchasing an asset, GK
make use of:
. the principal payments on a loan used to finance the asset's
  purchase price,
. the after-tax interest payments on this loan,
. the depreciation deductions.
GK assume that the cash purchase price of the capital asset to be
acquired is entirely financed by raising the loan. The loan term
is equal to the asset's economic life as estimated by management,
which in their numerical examples equals the tax depreciation
life of the asset (p. 214). In our example this life is two
years. When illustrating their model, GK start from two types of
loan financing: under the first one the loan is repaid by means
of equal principal payments, whereas under the second one principal and interest are to be paid in equal installments (pp. 214-
216). In the examples GK employ, the firm's cost of capital
equals the loan rate (p. 214). In Table 5.2 we compute the cash
flows necessary to determine the present value of the purchasing

agreement according to GK assuming equal annual loan repayments.

Table 5.2
Cash Flows of Purchasing as Calculated by GK

Year (1)	Loan Prin- cipal (2)	Loan Inter- est (3)= 0.11x(2)	Loan Interest after Taxes (4)= (1-0.4)x(3)	Loan Repay- ment (5)	Depre- ciation Deduction (6)=(3) in Table 5.1	Cash Flow (7)= (4)+ (5)-(6)
1	5,000	550	330	2,500	1,200	1,630
2	2,500	275	165	2,500	800	1,865

Capitalizing the cash flows of Column 7 of Table 5.2 at the cost of capital of the firm (14%) results in the present value of purchasing the capital asset as calculated by GK, PV_p^{GK} :

$$PV_p^{GK} = \frac{\$1,630}{1.14^1} + \frac{\$1,865}{1.14^2} = \$2,865$$

In order to determine the present value of leasing, GK start from the following cash flows:
. the lease payments,
. the tax savings on the lease payments.
In their illustrative examples GK assume the operating lease term to equal the asset's tax depreciation life. Discounting the above cash flows at 14% yields the present value of the operating lease according to GK, PV_{ol}^{GK} :

$$PV_{ol}^{GK} = (\frac{\$3,200}{1.14^1} + \frac{\$3,200}{1.14^2}) - (\frac{\$1,280}{1.14^1} + \frac{\$1,280}{1.14^2})$$

$$= \$5,269 - \$2,108 = \$3,161$$

Comparing PV_{ol}^{GK} with PV_{ol2}^{PB} as calculated according to the Peirson and Bird methodology (see 5.3), we find these present values to be equal: \$3,161. This is because in the case of operating leasing GK and PB make use of the same cash flow series and apply the same capitalization rate.

Since PV_p^{GK} is less than PV_{ol}^{GK}, GK would recommend purchasing the asset. They argue that three types of factors may cause the present values to differ from one another. First, there are differences in the way the asset's purchase price is financed: by raising a loan or by leasing. In order to compute the present value of these differences GK employ:

. the repayments on the loan used to finance the purchase price of the asset,
. the interest payments on this loan,
. the lease payments.

These cash flows are discounted at the firm's cost of capital:

$$\frac{\$2,500 + \$550 - \$3,200}{1.14^1} + \frac{\$2,500 + \$275 - \$3,200}{1.14^2}$$

$$= -\$132 - \$326 = -\$458$$

In the second place there are tax differences that GK quantify by capitalizing at the firm's cost of capital:

. the tax savings on the lease payments,
. the tax savings on depreciation and on interest.

The present value of these differences is:

$$\frac{\$1,280 - \$1,200 - \$220}{1.14^1} + \frac{\$1,280 - \$800 - \$110}{1.14^2}$$

$$= -\$123 + \$285 = \$162$$

Finally, according to GK other cash flow differences may cause PV^{GK} to deviate from PV_{ol}^{GK} , for instance, differences in maintenance costs. Since we assumed that the user firm performs the maintenance services whether the capital asset is purchased or leased (see p. 149), these differences are irrelevant in our numerical example. From the above calculations we find that the disadvantage of financing the asset by way of an operating lease is -\$458. On the other hand the lease's tax deductions exceed the tax savings of purchasing by $162. Therefore the net disadvantage of the operating lease is -$458 + $162 = -$296, which amount equals the difference between PV_p^{GK} and PV_{ol}^{GK} : $2,865 - $3,161 = -$296. As can easily be seen the GK analysis differs from the analysis of Bender as discussed in 3.4.2 (see pp. 28-31).

After having explained their model with some numerical examples, GK discuss a formula that can be utilized for making the operating lease-versus-purchase decision (p. 217). There are, however, some differences between the model illustrated by means of their numerical examples and the one represented by their formula.

. In this formula the various cash flows are capitalized at an unspecified rate of interest, whereas in the examples the so-called investment opportunity rate is used for discounting purposes.

. GK perform their formula analysis starting from the lease term (p. 217), that is, the period of time during which management expects to make use of the cancelable lease (p. 240, footnote 4); they do not explain the relationship between this period and the asset's economic life as estimated by the firm's management, which in their examples would be equal to the tax depreciation life of the asset and to the loan term.

. In their formula GK introduce the asset's value at the end of the lease term as well as the remaining balance of a loan utilized to finance the purchase price of the asset. In their examples they did not make use of these factors.

It is a pity GK do not illustrate the model represented by their formula with the help of one or more numerical examples. Then these differences might have been elucidated.

Evaluation

I   In their chapter, "Operational Leasing," GK do not pay attention to the capital budgeting decision.

II In their illustrative examples, GK employ the so-called investment opportunity rate, which is equal to the borrowing rate. It does not become clear whether the investment opportunity rate corresponds with the rate of discount used in the

GK formula discussed earlier. Regarding the definition of the investment opportunity rate as reproduced in the beginning of this section, I would like to observe that this rate should represent the opportunity loss (quantified as a rate of return) caused by capital rationing, by a shortage of managers, or by other factors rather than the rate of return management requires an investment project to yield based on experiences from the past and expectations in future developments.

III GK observe that their model has been developed to value operating leases. In another part of their book the authors go into the financial lease-versus-purchase decision. They then utilize a formula that differs somewhat from the one employed for operating leases in that the asset's value at the end of the lease term and the remaining balance of the loan utilized to finance the asset's purchase price are missing (p. 230). I could not find an explanation for these differences.

IV Applying the GK model results in present values. The authors ignore the cash inflows operating the capital asset generates.

V In their illustrative examples GK assume the cash purchase price of the asset to be financed with a loan. It does not become clear whether other financing methods can be employed too. When discussing financial leases, however, they do look into several alternative ways to finance the capital asset's purchase price (pp. 232-240).

As observed in the above, when representing their approach with a formula GK start from the period of time during which management expects to make use of the cancelable lease (p. 240). They question the model of Bierman and Smidt who, basing themselves on a probability distribution of the numbers of years the asset may be utilized, set the expected present value of the lease payments against the asset's cash purchase price (Bierman and Smidt 1960, pp. 203-204; see also Bierman and Smidt 1980, pp. 395-396). GK doubt whether this method really facilitates the calculations because deter-

mining the probabilities of the possible service lives of the
leased asset will be as difficult as directly estimating the
asset's service life (p. 218). At the end of their argument
they conclude quite in the same spirit that they did not
value a very important difference between operating and
financial leases - the greater flexibility that management
has as a result of being able to cancel an operating lease -
arguing that this greater flexibility can hardly be quantified (p. 239). The authors add that management expects a
calculation concerning the lease-or-buy issue to be exact.
After having performed such a calculation, it has to weigh
qualitative considerations like flexibility: this would be an
essential part of management's task (pp. 239-240). To my
thinking, however, it is very useful for management to
realize that the expected service life of an asset is only
one out of several possible service lives. Management has to
realize that the results of its analyses to a large extent
depend on the assumptions made regarding factors such as the
future service life of an asset.

5.5 Jenkins

Jenkins applies Ferrara's 1968 financial lease-or-borrow model to
the operating lease valuation issue. He tries to quantify the
advantage of being able to cancel an operating lease by estimating the probabilities of various useful lives of a capital asset
to be purchased or leased (Jenkins 1970, pp. 30-31). Consequently
his model belongs to the second group of models discussed in 5.1.
   In order to determine the present value of the purchasing
arrangement, Jenkins starts from the following cash flows:
. the cash purchase price of the asset,
. the depreciation deductions,
. the residual value of the asset,
. the tax effect of a possible difference between the asset's
  book value and its residual value (p. 30).
Just like Ferrara, Jenkins capitalizes these cash flows at the

firm's after-tax weighted average cost of capital (14% in our numerical example). If the useful life of the capital asset is two years, the present value of purchasing, applying Jenkins' model, PV_{p2}^J , equals:

$$PV_{p2}^J = \$5,000-(\frac{\$1,200}{1.14^1} + \frac{\$800}{1.14^2}) = \$5,000 - \$1,053 - \$616 = \$3,331$$

The depreciation deductions ($1,200 at the end of the first year and $800 at the end of the second year) were calculated in Table 5.1. If the asset is operated for two years, its residual value and its book value are both zero. Hence, the tax effect is zero. If, however, the asset's useful service life turns out to be only one year, Jenkins would compute the present value of purchasing it, PV_{p1}^J , as:

$$PV_{p1}^J = \$5,000 - \frac{\$1,200}{1.14^1} - \frac{\$1,000}{1.14^1} - 0.4 \times \frac{\$2,000 - \$1,000}{1.14^1}$$

$$= \$5,000 - \$1,053 - \$877 - \$351 = \$2,719$$

Now not only the cash purchase price of the asset and the depreciation deduction at the end of the first year are relevant, but we also have to know its salvage value and the tax effect of the difference between this value and the asset's book value. Notice that up until now the calculations are equal to the ones Peirson and Bird performed: $PV_{p2}^J = PV_{p2}^{PB}$ and $PV_{p1}^J = PV_{p1}^{PB}$ (see 5.3).

Next comes the rather complicated step of computing the present value of the operating lease. According to Jenkins the cash flows necessary te determine this present value are:

. the lease payments,

. the tax savings on the difference between the lease payments and the lease interest payments as computed by Ferrara in his 1968 article (p. 29).

In this 1968 article Ferrara tries to adjust Vancil's "borrowing opportunity rate method." As argued in 3.4.2, when applying this method it may very well be that the sum of the equivalent depreciations as calculated by Vancil is unequal to the cash purchase price of the asset to be leased. Both factors will be equal only if the implicit interest rate of the lease equals the borrowing opportunity rate. Assuming the asset's useful life to be two years, according to Jenkins the implicit interest rate of the operating lease, k^J_{o12} , can be derived from:[3]

$$\$5,000 - \frac{\$3,200}{(1+k^J_{o12})^1} - \frac{\$3,200}{(1+k^J_{o12})^2} = 0$$

Hence it appears that $k^J_{o12} \approx 18.16\%$. Employing the same method Ferrara uses, Jenkins would divide this rate into interest (11%) and "lessor's premium" (7.16%). He would then calculate the annual amounts of lease interest, lessor's premium, and lease repayment included in each annual lease payment (see Table 5.3).

Table 5.3
Jenkins's Calculation of Lease Interest, Lessor's Premium, and Lease Repayment (Asset's Service Life = 2 Years)

Year (1)	Lease Principal according to Jenkins (2)	Lease Interest (3)=0.11x(2)	Lessor's Premium (4)= 0.0716x(2)	Lease Payment (5)	Lease Repayment (6)= (5)-(3)-(4)
1	5,000	550	358	3,200	2,292
2	2,708	298	194	3,200	2,708

By "Lease Principal according to Jenkins" I mean the amount of the loan Jenkins assumes to be embodied in the operating lease.

Now we are able to determine the tax savings on the difference between the lease payments and the lease interest payments (see

---

3) This calculation parallels the one on p. 26 where the implicit financial lease rate was computed.

Table 5.4).

Table 5.4
Tax Savings on Differences between Lease Payments and Lease
Interest Payments as Calculated by Jenkins (Asset's Service Life
= 2 Years)

Year (1)	Lease Payment (2)	Lease Interest (3)=(3) in Table 5.3	Difference (4)=(2)-(3)	Tax Saving on Difference (5)=0.4x(4)
1	3,200	550	2,650	1,060
2	3,200	298	2,902	1,161

Starting from a two-year asset life, the present value of the
operating lease opportunity according to Jenkins, PV^J_{o12} , is:

$$PV^J_{o12} = (\frac{\$3,200}{1.11^1} + \frac{\$3,200}{1.11^2}) - (\frac{\$1,060}{1.14^1} + \frac{\$1,161}{1.14^2})$$

$$= \$5,480 - \$1,823 = \$3,657$$

Like Ferrara Jenkins capitalizes the first cash flow series at
the loan rate or the borrowing opportunity rate (in our example:
11%) and the second one at the firm's cost of capital (14%).
   Let us now assume the useful life of the capital asset to be
one year. First we have to recalculate the operating lease rate,
k^J_{o11}. As can easily be seen this rate is negative:

$$\$5,000 - \frac{\$3,200}{(1+k^J_{o11})^1} = 0$$

Solving this equation we obtain k^J_{o11} = -36%. Again the operating
lease rate k^J_{o11} has to be divided into interest (11%) and lessor's premium (-47%), enabling us to determine the annual amounts
of lease interest, lessor's premium, and lease repayment included

in the annual lease payment. This computation is performed in Table 5.5.

Table 5.5
Jenkins's Calculation of Lease Interest, Lessor's Premium, and Lease Repayment (Asset's Service Life = 1 Year)

Year (1)	Lease Principal according to Jenkins (2)	Lease Interest (3)=0.11x(2)	Lessor's Premium (4)= -0.47x(2)	Lease Payment (5)	Lease Repayment (6)= (5)-(3)-(4)
1	5,000	550	-2,350	3,200	5,000

Finally we shall calculate Jenkins's tax savings (see Table 5.6).

Table 5.6
Tax Saving on Difference between Lease Payment and Lease Interest Payment as Calculated by Jenkins (Asset's Service Life = 1 Year)

Year (1)	Lease Payment (2)	Lease Interest (3)=(3) in Table 5.3	Difference (4)=(2)-(3)	Tax Saving on Difference (5)=0.4x(4)
1	3,200	550	2,650	1,060

If the asset is operated for only one year, the present value of the operating lease according to Jenkins, PV_{oll}^{J} , is:

$$PV^J_{o11} = \frac{\$3,200}{1.11^1} - \frac{\$1,060}{1.14^1} = \$2,883 - \$930 = \$1,953$$

Subtracting PV^J_{o12} from PV^J_{p2} we obtain $\$3,331 - \$3,657 = -\$326$. Starting from a one-year useful life we get $PV^J_{p1} - PV^J_{o11} = \$2,719 - \$1,953 = \$766$. At this point Jenkins would introduce a probability distribution of the asset's useful service lives (p.30). Let us assume that the firm's management expects that the probability of it operating the asset for two years is 80%, and that there is a 20% probability that the asset will be utilized for only one year. Multiplying these probabilities with the differences between PV^J_p and PV^J_{o1} we obtain: 0.8 x $-\$326 + 0.2$ x $\$766 = -\$108$. Since this results turns out to be negative, indicating the expected present value of the operating lease to exceed the expected present value of the purchase option, Jenkins would recommend purchasing the asset.

Evaluation

I   In his article Jenkins pays attention to choosing between operating leasing and purchasing only. He ignores the interactions of corporate financing and investment decisions. Apart from that, it seems that Jenkins utilizes his numerical example to enlarge on the advantage of being able to cancel the operating lease, as he argues that: "It will be recalled that the data used in this article were either the same as used by Ferrara or were purposely made more favorable to the purchase alternative; yet the result, unlike Ferrara's illustration, is favorable to leasing" (p. 31). However, it is easy to account for Jenkins preferring the operating lease arrangement to the purchase opportunity. In his illustrative example, the author observes that the salvage value of the asset having become "technologically obsolete," "is likely to be relatively small" (p. 30). In order to simplify this example he assumes the asset's salvage value to be zero, which results in a rather high "net cost of purchase" (see Jenkins's Table 5 on p. 30). In my opinion Jenkins's assumption need not be generally true in reality: even if the present user of an asset considers it to be obsolete, it may still be useful and valuable to another user. Another expla-

nation for Jenkins preferring the operating lease to the
purchase alternative may be found in the probability distributions he employs (p. 30). Starting from a different probability distribution quickly results in preference being given
to purchasing the asset.

II When capitalizing the relevant cash flows, Jenkins, without
due consideration, applies the discount rates Ferrara also
utilizes in his 1968 article. A few years later, however,
Ferrara recommends the use of a totally different approach to
resolve the lease valuation problem. He then pictures his
former model, which Jenkins utilizes to make the operating
lease-versus-borrow decision, as being "overly complex"
(Ferrara 1974, p. 21).

III Jenkins's model has been developed to value operating leases,
as he explicitly observes.

IV As was explained in the above, the results of this model are
expressed in present values.

V   Just like Ferrara Jenkins assumes a loan with a specific repayment schedule to be embodied in the operating lease (see
Table 5.3 and Table 5.5). Their approach can only be applied
in those situations where this loan has indeed been incorporated in the operating lease arrangement. Besides, although
Jenkins tries to quantify the advantage of being able to
cancel an operating lease, he does not explain how in a real-
world situation management should gather the necessary information to establish the probability distribution of the
future asset service lives.

5.6 Hax

Just like Jenkins Hax pays attention to the probabilities of
possible asset service lives when solving the operational lease-
or-purchase problem. Unlike this author, however, Hax does not
assume that the future useful service life of a purchased capital
asset will always be equal to the asset's future useful service
life in the case of leasing. If an asset is purchased, Hax
argues, management will be operating it as long as it generates
positive cash inflows. On the other hand, if the asset is leased

the lease will be cancelled as soon as the lease payments can no longer be made from the cash inflows the asset generates (Hax 1977, p. 28).

In order to compute the net present value of purchasing an asset, Hax employs the following cash flow series:
. the net cash inflows expected from asset operation,
. the cash purchase price of the asset (p. 29).
In his article, however, this German author completely ignores the corporate income taxes ("Körperschaftsteuer" in Germany). Apart from this, it is not clear to me what capitalization rate Hax is using. In his illustrative examples, Hax capitalizes the various cash flows at a minimum required rate of return of 9% ("geforderte Mindestverzinsung von 9%," p. 25) without giving a more exact definition of this rate. That is why, when illustrating Hax's analysis, I too shall discount the cash flows at 9%. Consequently, the net present value of purchasing the asset of our numerical example according to the Hax model, NPV_p^H, is:

$$NPV_p^H = \frac{\$4,000}{1.09^1} + \frac{\$3,800}{1.09^2} - \$5,000$$

$$= \$3,670 + \$3,198 - \$5,000 = \$1,868$$

In Hax's opinion, as long as the operating lease is not cancelled the relevant cash flows are:
. the net cash inflows the leased asset generates,
. the lease payments (p. 29).
In order to determine whether the operating lease will be cancelled or not, we need more information concerning the cash inflows. Let us assume that the expected values of these cash inflows utilized when calculating NPV_p^H were computed from Figure 5.1.

Figure 5.1

Cash Inflows Generated by the Capital Asset

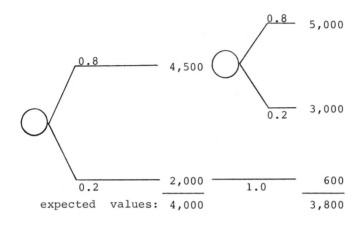

expected values: 4,000   3,800

According to Figure 5.1 the probability of the asset generating a cash inflow of $4,500 at the end of the first year is 80% (0.8), and the probability that the cash inflow at the end of this year will be only $2,000 equals 20% (0.2). If the asset turns out to have generated a cash inflow of $4,500 at the end of the first year, then there is a probability of 80% that it will generate a cash inflow of $5,000 and a probability of 20% that it will generate a cash inflow of $3,000 at the end of the second year. If, on the other hand, the asset generates $2,000 at the end of the first year, then it is certain that it will generate a cash inflow of $600 at the end of the second year. Therefore, the expected value of the cash inflow at the end of the first year of asset operation is 0.8 x $4,500 + 0.2 x $2,000 = $4,000. At the end of the second year, the expected value of the cash inflow equals 0.8 x 0.8 x $5,000 + 0.8 x 0.2 x $3,000 + 0.2 x $600 = $3,800. When we calculated NPV_p^H to be $1,868, we employed these two expected values.

Applying the Hax model, we find that if at the end of the first year the asset generates a cash inflow of $4,500, the operating lease is not cancelled. If, however, at the end of this year the cash inflow is only \$2,000, the lease will be cancelled, and therefore the cash inflow of \$600 at the end of the second year becomes irrelevant. Capitalizing the relevant cash flows (consisting of the cash inflows and the lease payments arising as long as the operating lease is not cancelled) at 9% we obtain the expected net present value of the operating lease as calculated by Hax, $E(NPV_{ol}^{H})$:

$$E(NPV_{ol}^{H}) = 0.8 \times 0.8 \times (\frac{\$4,500 - \$3,200}{1.09^1} + \frac{\$5,000 - \$3,200}{1.09^2})$$

$$+ 0.8 \times 0.2 \times (\frac{\$4,500 - \$3,200}{1.09^1} + \frac{\$3,000 - \$3,200}{1.09^2})$$

$$+ 0.2 \times \frac{\$2,000 - \$3,200}{1.09^1}$$

$$= 0.8 \times 0.8 \times \$2,708 + 0.8 \times 0.2 \times \$1,024$$

$$+ 0.2 \times -\$1,101 = \$1,733 + \$164 - \$220 = \$1,677$$

Comparing the buy-versus-lease alternatives, Hax would opt for the first arrangement because $NPV_p^{H} = \$1,868$ exceeds $E(NPV_{ol}^{H}) = \$1,677$.

Evaluation

I   Hax argues that choosing from an operating lease and a purchase opportunity is like making a capital budgeting decision and that this decision can be made using a number of procedures (p. 24). He then continues by discussing a number of capital budgeting procedures: net present values, uniform annual series, internal rates of return, benefit/cost ratios, and break-even economic lives (pp. 24-27). The last of these methods is almost identical to Vancil's model examined in section 5.2 (pp. 155-156) except that Hax completely omits the corporate income tax factor. However, Hax maintains that if a firm's management blindly applies these capital budgeting rules to solve the operating lease-versus-purchase problem, then the lease's flexible nature, caused by management being able to cancel such a lease, would be ignored

(p. 27). That is why he has developed his model. Although the author contends that the operating lease-versus-purchase decision is merely an investment decision, it is the advantage of being able to cancel the lease that turns the scale in his illustrative example (p. 29). This advantage can be realized only if the required capital asset is financed by entering into an operating lease. Consequently, the financing method is also of importance when making an investment decision.

II As observed in the above, Hax capitalizes the relevant cash flows at a minimum required rate of return of 9% without defining this rate in a more exact way. The author argues that capital rationing may prohibit investing funds in a project even though it generates the minimum required rate of return (p. 25). He observes that in a situation of capital rationing frequently the utilization of the internal rate of return method is recommended. Hax does not show this statement to be correct nor does he address the dangers of applying this method to compare alternative strategies. In order to compare such strategies if capital rationing is involved, the author prefers to make use of benefit/cost ratios ("Kapitalwertrate", p. 25). He does not state the grounds for this preference.

III At the beginning of his article, Hax states that his model has been developed to value operating leases.

IV As was explained earlier, employing this model results in net present values without considering the corporate income tax factor.

V   It is true that Hax tries to quantify the advantage of being able to cancel an operating lease, but he also simplifies his approach to such an extent that applying it in reality is very difficult. This is because in his article Hax ignores the corporate income tax factor, the depreciation schedule, the regulations concerning tax deductible losses, the asset's salvage value, and the way the cash purchase price of the asset is financed. The asset's financing method may be relevant for computing the tax savings as well as for determining whether purchasing the asset is to be preferred. As explained

before, Hax holds that an operating lease should be cancelled
as soon as the lease payments can no longer be made from the
cash inflows the asset generates. I think that the same
notion should be applied to the purchase opportunity: if the
cash inflows a purchased asset generates are becoming insufficient to make the loan payments, if any, then management
should stop operating the asset. This is all the more reason
not to depict the operating lease-or-purchase issue as merely
an investment decision (see requirement I). In addition to
this, I would like to observe that if the asset's residual
value becomes part of the analysis, management may decide to
stop operating the asset before the moment the cash inflows
drop to zero (see for instance the discussion on abandonment
value and capital budgeting in Weston and Brigham 1981, pp.
526-532). To conclude, no more than Jenkins does Hax explain
how to determine the probabilities that are required to employ his model. This may make it rather difficult to apply
this model in reality. Regarding the required probabilities,
Hax merely observes that in order to make the operating
lease-or-purchase decision management should be able to
quantify its expectations as to future developments and that
the resulting subjective probabilities may affect this choice
in a decisive way (p. 29). In his illustrative example, the
author assumes that in managment's view the probability of
the more favorable future developments exceed the probability
of the less attractive results, without explaining how management has gathered this information.

5.7 Beckman and Joosen

In their 1980 book on leasing, Beckman and Joosen (hereafter BJ)
value financial leases as well as operating leases. Section 3.4.8
discussed their financial lease evaluation model. Here I shall
look into their operating lease-or-buy methodology. When developing this model, the authors pay attention to the possible future
service lives of a capital asset, just as Jenkins does. In contrast with Jenkins's method, BJ do consider the cash inflows an

asset is expected to generate.

According to BJ the expected net present value of the purchase option should be calculated from:
. the net cash inflows after taxes,
. the depreciation deductions,
. the cash purchase price of the asset,
. its residual value,
. the tax effect of a possible difference between the asset's book value and its residual value (BJ 1980, p. 83).

Discounting these cash flows at the firm's cost of capital (in our example: 14%) and taking into account the probabilities of future service lives (two years with a probability of 0.8 and one year with a probability of 0.2), we obtain the expected net present value of purchasing as computed by BJ, $E(NPV_p^{BJ})$:

$$E(NPV_p^{BJ}) = 0.8 \times \{ \frac{(1-0.4) \times \$4,000 + 0.4 \times \$3,000}{1.14^1}$$

$$+ \frac{(1-0.4) \times \$3,800 + 0.4 \times \$2,000}{1.14^2} - \$5,000 \}$$

$$+ 0.2 \times \{ \frac{(1-0.4) \times \$4,000 + 0.4 \times \$3,000}{1.14^1} + \frac{\$1,000}{1.14^1}$$

$$+ 0.4 \times \frac{(\$5,000 - \$3,000) - \$1,000}{1.14^1} - \$5,000 \}$$

$$= 0.8 \times (\$3,158 + \$2,370 - \$5,000)$$

$$+ 0.2 \times (\$3,158 + \$877 + \$351 - \$5,000)$$

$$= 0.8 \times \$528 + 0.2 \times -\$614 = \$300$$

As can be seen from the above calculation, if the capital asset is utilized for two years, then we need the after-tax cash inflows, the depreciation deductions, and the asset's purchase price to determine the net present value of the purchase arrangement. If, on the other hand, the asset is operated for only one year, we also need its salvage value and the tax effect of the difference between the asset's book value ($5,000 - $3,000 = $2,000) and its salvage value ($1,000). The net present value of using the asset for two years ($528) is then multiplied by its probability (0.8) and added to the net present value of utilizing it for one year (-$614) multiplied by its probability (0.2) to arrive at the expected net present value of purchasing the capital asset as calculated by BJ ($300).

In order to compute the expected net present value of the operating lease alternative, BJ make use of the following cash flow series:

. the net cash inflows after taxes,

. the lease payments after taxes.

Applying the same probabilities as when calculating $E(NPV_p^{BJ})$, we obtain the expected net present value of the operating lease according to BJ, $E(NPV_{ol}^{BJ})$:

$$E(NPV_{ol}^{BJ}) = 0.8 \times \{ \frac{(1-0.4) \times (\$4,000 - \$3,200)}{1.14^1}$$

$$+ \frac{(1-0.4) \times (\$3,800 - \$3,200)}{1.14^2} \}$$

$$+ 0.2 \times \{ \frac{(1-0.4) \times (\$4,000 - \$3,200)}{1.14^1} \}$$

$$= 0.8 \times (\$421 + \$277) + 0.2 \times (\$421) = \$643$$

Setting $E(NPV_{ol}^{BJ})$ against $E(NPV_p^{BJ})$, BJ would opt for leasing the asset because the former expected value ($643) exceeds the latter ($300).

Evaluation

I   As can be inferred from the above calculations, BJ compute the net present value of the purchase and the operating lease arrangement. They make use of the net cash inflows the capital asset generates as well. Later on in their book, however, they state that in order to gain insight into the difference between these alternatives management had better leave common elements out of consideration (p. 84). I do not agree with this statement because if for instance the cash inflow series (a common element in the purchase and the lease alternative) is left out of account, then management knows which alternative to prefer but it does not know whether the preferred alternative is profitable.

II When capitalizing the relevant cash flows, BJ make use of the firm's cost of capital. They argue that utilizing this rate is acceptable, as the cash flows are subject to the firm's normal operating risks (pp. 82-83). As Myers has shown, however, there are many more conditions to be fulfilled for the firm's cost of capital to give the correct project hurdle rate (see 2.3).

III The BJ model examined here has been developed to resolve the operating lease-versus-purchase problem. BJ are of the opinion that in order to make a financial lease-versus-purchase decision management has to utilize another model. I discussed this model in 3.4.8.

IV The authors use net present values to choose from leasing and purchasing (see also the above discussion of requirement I).

V BJ do not explain how to finance the asset's purchase price. Their failure to address the tax advantages of debt financing affects the purchase option in that it becomes less attractive. This may have caused BJ to opt for leasing the asset instead of purchasing it when demonstrating their approach by way of a numerical example (p. 85). The same may also hold for applying the BJ model to our illustrative example, in which the operating lease is also preferred. Moreover, before employing this model management has to check whether Myers's necessary and sufficient conditions for utilizing the firm's cost of capital as the project hurdle rate have been met.

5.8 Toward a Model Meeting the Requirements I-V

The evaluations of the models discussed in the above can be summarized as follows:

I In the majority of the operating lease-or-purchase models, the interactions of investment and financing decisions are being ignored. Generally speaking, the authors involved do not pay attention to the cash inflows the capital asset is

expected to generate, and they confine themselves to choosing
between operating leasing and purchasing. They do not check
whether the chosen alternative is profitable. Only Hax and
Beckman and Joosen compute the net present value of the lease
and the purchase arrangement taking into consideration the
cash inflow series the asset generates. Unfortunately Hax
ignores the corporate income tax factor without explaining
this omission. On the other hand, Beckman and Joosen purport
that cash flows that are incorporated both in the operating
lease and in the purchase option, such as the cash inflows
generated by the asset, can be left out of account. On pp.
181-182 I objected to this approach.

II For discounting purposes most authors utilize the firm's cost
of capital: Vancil, Peirson and Bird, Goudsmit and Keijser,
Jenkins, and Beckman and Joosen use this rate. Many times
valid arguments for utilizing the firm's cost of capital are
absent. On imitation of Ferrara, Jenkins makes use of both
the firm's cost of capital and the firm's borrowing rate. Hax
does not explain which discount rate he is employing. That is
why, when illustrating his approach, I utilized the same 9%
discount rate he applies.

III The authors whose models were reviewed in Sections 5.2
through 5.7 explicitly state that their models have been
developed to value operating leases.

IV With the exception of Vancil's approaches, each of the evaluation models discussed earlier results in present values or
net present values. Vancil develops three criteria: the
return on investment, the break-even economic life, and the
break-even residual value. As explained in 5.2, I hold that
management had better start from net present values when
trying to solve the lease-versus-purchase problem.

V   In many of the above evaluation methods, making the ultimate
decision to purchase or to enter into an operating lease is
left to the firm's management. Management has to attach value
to the advantage of being able to transfer a major part of
the risk of early obsolescence to the lessor. Depending on
the results of this valuation process, it will opt for
leasing or for purchasing. Then there are authors such as

Jenkins, Hax, and Beckman and Joosen who try to help the firm's management by developing models whereby this advantage is being quantified. For this purpose both Jenkins and Beckman and Joosen start from probability distributions of possible future service lives of the capital asset. In doing so these authors use identical distributions for the lease and the purchase alternative. On the other hand, Hax makes use of a probability distribution of the cash inflows generated in any of the possible future situations. Contrary to Jenkins and to Beckman and Joosen, he feels it is possible for the future service life of a leased asset to differ from that of a purchased asset. None of the authors, however, discusses how, in a real-world situation, management is to determine the probabilities of the asset's service lives or of the cash inflows the asset is expected to generate. Apart from that, applying the approaches of Goudsmit and Keijser and of Jenkins in actuality may be very difficult or even impossible because these writers assume the asset's purchase price to be financed with a particular loan. Another restricting factor in applying the valuation models may be that before management is able to utilize the firm's after-tax weighted average cost of capital for discounting purposes several conditions have to be met.

Many times it is easier to point out shortcomings of models developed by others than it is to develop a new model. Nonetheless, I shall try to make a positive contribution toward modelling in the field of operating lease valuation. First, I am of the opinion that it is essential that management form a notion of the possible future service lives of a capital asset as well as of the cash inflow series generated by a leased and by a purchased asset and that it try to determine the probabilities of the various possible outcomes. In this way management can obtain insight into the advantage of being able to cancel an operating lease. Hence my evaluation method belongs to the second group of models discussed in 5.1. Not only management's own experiences and expectations play an important part when determining these probabilities but also those of other users of the capital asset involved. The lessor, being a specialist in this field, may be able to give information about this issue too. Management may also find a starting point for estimating the asset's future service life in its tax depreciation life. Gaumnitz and Ford argue that "when selecting a useful life for depreciation purposes, taxpayers may use guidelines or the Class Life Asset Depreciation Range System, which allows taxpayers to select depreciation lives that may be 20% shorter or 20% longer than life provided by the guidelines" (Gaumnitz and Ford 1978, p. 70). If, in spite of the above, the firm's management is unable to determine the probabilities of the possible future asset service lives, it can always apply the so-called Laplace Insufficient-Reason Criterion. Philippatos describes this approach by pointing out: "The Laplace criterion is based on the proposition that since in uncertainty we do not know the probabilities of future outcomes, we must consider each outcome to be equiprobable" (Philippatos 1973, p. 188).

Regarding the five requirements a lease evaluation model has to meet, I would like to stress that I shall not try to divorce the capital budgeting decision form the financing decision (requirement I). Also I would like to point out that with my model I intend to value operating leases (requirement III) and that applying it results in net present values (requirement IV). Just as I did in Chapter 4, I shall be paying more attention to the remaining two requirements beginning with requirement II: stating the grounds for the capitalization rates to be used.

Again the cash flows I am going to capitalize are cash flows to equity, and again I assume that operating a capital asset will result in the same cash inflow series, whether it is leased or purchased. On pp. 126-127 I argued that, although many authors start from the same assumption, it may be that the cash inflow a leased asset is expected to generate differs from the one generated by a purchased capital asset. As we did in Chapter 4, I shall capitalize these cash inflows at the appropriate project hurdle rate assuming perfect capital markets and all-equity financing. This rate may very well differ from the one used in Chapter 4, as a different capital project is involved. Regarding this issue I refer to Haley and Schall who argue: "It is also probable that each discount rate will be different for different

assets of the firm, since not all firm assets are of the same
risk" (Haley and Schall 1979, p. 462). I assume that, because of
the higher risk, the firm's management in this example considers
it appropriate to capitalize the project's cash inflow series at
a higher rate: 16% (rather than 15% as employed in 4.3).

Determining the discount rate to be applied to the various tax
deductions (resulting from the tax deductibility of lease payments, depreciation, any interest payments, and a possible tax
loss when selling the capital asset) does not seem to be much of
a problem now. In determining this rate the same procedure can be
applied as utilized when making the financial lease-versus-purchase decision: a capitalization rate that partly follows from
the regulations concerning tax deductible losses (see pp. 130-
131). There is one difference between making this decision and
choosing from operating leasing and purchasing a capital asset.
Since there is a possibility that an operating lease will be
cancelled, the tax savings on the operating lease payments are
not completely certain and should therefore not be discounted at
the risk-free rate, even if the fiscal authorities provide for
immediate and full loss offset provisions.

In order to compute the present value of the lease payments
and the present value of any loan payments (principal plus interest), I shall again make use of the lower of two interest rates
- the one implicit in the lease agreement and the interest rate
of a financing method that is comparable to the operating lease
and that, in view of applying the model in practice, can actually
be obtained. It is rather difficult, however, to determine this
rate. The first problem is calculating the operating lease rate.
Unlike the term of a financial lease, the operating lease term
has not been laid down in the operating lease contract. This term
corresponds with the useful service life of the capital asset to
be leased, for as soon as the lessee considers the asset's life
to be at an end it cancels the lease. Thus, in order to establish
the operating lease rate one must utilize a probability distribution of the possible future service lives of the asset. In our
numerical example, we assumed that the probability of the asset
being operated for two years is 80%, and that the probability of
it being operated for only one year is 20%. One also has to take

into account the asset's salvage value, which goes to the lessor.
If the firm's management decided to purchase the asset, selling
it may result in a cash inflow. In the case of leasing, this cash
inflow (i.e., the asset's salvage value) goes to the lessor.
Consequently this cash flow can be looked upon as an opportunity
cost to be added to the other costs: the lease payments. In the
same vein Dopuch, Birnberg, and Demski argue: "When a firm buys
an asset, it receives the right to any cash salvage value of that
asset when it is abandoned. This right does not usually extend to
the firm under a leasing contract, and any salvage value foregone
(sic.) under the lease contract must be treated as an additional
implicit cash payment to the lessor - a payment that is not tax
deductible" (Dopuch, Birnberg, and Demski 1982, p. 633). In our
example, we assumed the asset's residual value at the end of the
first year of asset operation to be $1,000, whereas at the end of
the second year the residual value is zero. The $1,000 residual
value has to be added to the first-year lease payment of $3,200.
Hence, the interest rate implicit in the operating lease, k_{ol},
can be derived from the following equations:

$$\$5,000 - 0.8 \times \left(\frac{\$3,200}{(1+k_{ol})^1} + \frac{\$3,200}{(1+k_{ol})^2}\right) - 0.2 \times \frac{\$3,200 + \$1,000}{(1+k_{ol})^1} = 0$$

$$\$5,000 - \frac{\$3,400}{(1+k_{ol})^1} - \frac{\$2,560}{(1+k_{ol})^2} = 0$$

From the former equation it can be seen that if the leased asset
will be used for two years (the probability of which is 80%) the
lessee has to make two lease payments of $3,200. If, on the other
hand, the asset will be operated for only one year (with a probability of 20%) the lessee's cost consist of the lease payment at
the end of this year plus the salvage value, which goes to the
lessor and therefore is lost by the lessee: $1,000. However, by
leasing the lessee saves itself paying the asset's cash purchase
price of $5,000. Solving the latter equation we obtain $k_{ol} \approx$
13.23%.

Now that the problem of calculating the operating lease rate
has been solved we are confronted with another problem: that of
determining the financing method that can be compared with an
operating lease. Although by entering into an operating lease the

greater part of the risk of obsolescence is transferred to the lessor, such a lease can be looked upon as debt (which is furnished in kind) and not as equity. First, this is because the lessee has to make the promised lease payments as long as the lease is not cancelled. Secondly, the amount of these payments is independent of the profits generated by the lessee's firm, and thirdly, the lessor has no voting rights in this firm. As seen from the viewpoint of business finance, there are other features that characterize an operating lease:

1. the asset's purchase price is entirely financed by the lessor (except for cases where the first lease payment is made at the beginning of the lease term),
2. the lessor (usually) remains the legal owner of the asset,
3. the lease term is not laid down in the lease contract but corresponds with the useful life of the asset,
4. the lessee expects to make the lease payments from the net cash inflows the leased asset generates.

In view of these characteristic features, one may set that kind of loan against an operating lease whereby:

1. the asset's purchase price is entirely financed by the lender (making a reservation for any payments made at the beginning of the loan term),
2. the loan is secured by the asset,
3. the loan is not determined in the loan contract but corresponds with the asset's useful life; as soon as this useful life comes to an end the remaining loan principal can be repaid without paying a call premium,
4. the borrower expects to meet the loan payments from the cash inflows the asset generates.

Characteristic 4 may give rise to some problems: management may decide to stop operating a capital asset if the results it generates fall behind management's expectations and if no change for the better is expected to occur. It would be rather unrealistic to assume that the remaining loan principal can be repaid from the disappointing cash inflows the asset generates. These problems may endanger the comparability of the operating lease and the loan. The fact is that cancelling an operating lease does not give rise to these cash flow problems: if such a lease is can-

celled the lessee has only to return the asset to the lessor
without making any additional payments. If, on the other hand,
management had purchased the asset and had financed its purchase
price by raising a loan, then, upon terminating the asset's operation, management has to repay the remaining loan balance, it
realizes the residual value of the asset, and it has to cope with
the tax effect if the asset's residual value differs from the
book value. These cash flow consequences can be illustrated with
the help of our numerical example. Let us assume that the asset's
purchase price ($5,000) has been entirely financed with a loan to
be repaid in two equal installments: $2,500 at the end of the
first year and $2,500 at the end of the second year. However,
management has the option to repay the entire loan at the end of
the first year if the asset's cash inflows turn out to be lower
than expected. Let us also assume that, because of disappointing
cash inflows generated by the purchased asset, the firm's management decides to stop operating it at the end of the first year.
Management then has to repay an additional $2,500. On the other
hand, it receives the residual value of the asset: $1,000.
Finally, since the asset's residual value at the end of the first
year ($1,000) differs from its book value (the cash purchase
price of the asset minus the first year depreciation = $5,000 -
$3,000 = $2,000), a tax effect may arise. If the tax authorities
provide for instantaneous and full loss offset provisions, the
firm's management immediately receives the corporate income tax
rate times loss from selling the asset at a price that is lower
than its book value: $0.4 \times (\$2,000 - \$1,000) = \$400$. If, however,
the fiscal authorities do not provide for any loss protection at
all, management receives nothing. Assuming there is no loss
protection, the cash flow consequences of stopping asset operation at the end of the first year are: -$2,500 (additional loan
repayment) + $1,000 (residual value of the asset) + $0 (the tax
effect is zero) = -$1,500. It may be imagined, at least in
theory, that management effects an insurance to protect its firm
against these cash flow consequences. Of course the firm's
management has to pay an insurance premium. Let us assume that
the annual insurance premium is $400. The interest rate of the
combination of the loan introduced on p. 188 and the insurance

contract, k_{11}, starting from the same probability distribution utilized when computing k_{o1} on p. 187, can be calculated from the following equation:

$$\$5,000 - 0.8 \times (\frac{\$2,500 + 0.11 \times \$5,000 + \$400}{(1+k_{11})^1}$$

$$+ \frac{\$2,500 + 0.11 \times \$2,500 + \$400}{(1+k_{11})^2})$$

$$- 0.2 \times (\frac{\$2,500 + 0.11 \times \$5,000 + \$400}{(1+k_{11})^1}) = 0$$

As apparent in this equation, there is a probability of 80% that the firm's management will be able to employ the capital asset for a period of two years. At the end of the first year it has to repay a part of the loan ($2,500) as well as interest (0.11 x $5,000) and the insurance premium ($400). At the end of the second year management has to repay the remaining loan balance ($2,500), interest (0.11 x $2,500), plus the insurance premium ($400). On the other hand, there is a probability of 20% that the asset can be operated for only one year. At the end of this year management has to pay principal reduction ($2,500), interest (0.11 x $5,000), plus the insurance premium ($400). The insurance company then makes a payment to the firm to prevent it from suffering losses upon terminating the asset's operation. In other words, the payment made by the insurance company and the firm's losses resulting from terminating the asset's operation cancel out. Setting the present value of the above payments against the loan principal ($5,000), i.e., solving the above equation, we obtain $k_{11} \approx 13.68\%$. This combination of a loan plus an insurance contract can be compared with an operating lease, because in fact such a lease is a contract whereby the lessor provides a loan (in kind) and takes the risk of obsolescence from the lessee. The lessor requires payment for both services. The latter service, however, can be looked upon as insuring the lessee against the cash flow consequences of early obsolescence of the leased asset. Therefore, an operating lease itself is a combination of a loan and an insurance contract. In our illustrative example this combination is somewhat cheaper than the former combination: $k_{o1} \approx 13.23\%$ whereas $k_{11} \approx 13.68\%$. Again we shall use the lower of these two rates to determine the present value of the operating lease payments, just as we did when computing the present value of the financial lease payments in Chapter 4 (see p. 129).

Before going on I would like to point out that I have been assuming that the asset's service life if leased equals its service life if it is purchased. In both cases I started from the same probability distribution, assuming that there is a probability of 80% that the asset will be operated for two years and a probability of 20% that it will be utilized for only one year. In my opinion, however, the asset's technical service life as well as its economic life may be affected by the way the right to operate the asset has been acquired. One of the factors influencing the technical service life of an asset is the manner in which it is utilized. It may be that a leased asset is operated in a different way, maybe somewhat less carefully, than a purchased asset. This may result in the leased asset's technical service life being shorter than the technical service life in the case of purchasing the capital asset. The economic life of a capital asset is affected by the cash inflows and the cash outflows it generates. Since operating a leased asset usually results in cash flows that differ from the ones generated by a purchased asset, a leased asset's economic life may differ from the economic life of a purchased asset. As observed in 5.6, Hax already stressed this problem. Another author, Wytzes, argues that there is a relationship between the economic life of a leased asset and the size of the operating lease payments: the higher the lease payments, the sooner the lessee will consider the asset to be obsolete. This is why Wytzes states that by demanding higher lease payments the lessor encourages the lessee to cancel the operating lease contract (Wytzes 1981, pp. 452-453). Also I would like to stress that there may be another way for the firm's management to avoid the obsolescence risk inherent in purchasing a capital asset. It may conclude a contract with the asset's seller whereby the seller buys back the asset paying such a price that the cash flows consequences of stopping asset operation are eliminated.

Now I shall turn to the calculation of the expected net

present value of leasing and of purchasing the capital asset of
our numerical example. In order to compute the net present value
of the operating lease agreement, we have to capitalize the
following cash flows:

. the net cash inflows after taxes,

. the tax savings on the lease payments,

. the lease payments.

As in 4.3, I shall apply the value-additivity principle to
determine the present value of this cash flow series, since in
reality it may be very difficult to compute the required rate of
return on equity necessary to calculate the present value of the
balance of the above cash flows, i.e., the cash flow to equity.
In fact, Copeland and Weston very properly observe that determining "the cost of equity capital, unfortunately, is still more an
art than a science" (Copeland and Weston 1983 p. 466).

The cash inflows generated by the capital asset will be
capitalized at the appropriate project hurdle rate (16%). When
discounting the tax savings on the lease payments, we assume that
the ·tax authorities do not provide for any compensation for
losses at all. Furthermore we assume that the total cash inflow
generated by the firm in a given year is the only source of funds
from which lease and loan payments can be made and that in the
future no changes as to the corporate income tax rate, the
regulations concerning tax deductible losses, and the tax
deductible costs are expected to occur. As was explained in 4.3,
because of these assumptions the tax savings can be capitalized
at the lower of the lease rate and the loan rate.[4] The rate
implicit in the operating lease has been calculated on p. 187,
$k_{ol} \approx 13.23\%$, and turned out to be somewhat lower than the rate
of the combined loan and insurance contract computed on pp. 189-
190: $k_{ll} \approx 13.68\%$. Consequently the tax savings can be capitalized
at the rate implicit in the operating lease contract. The same
goes for the lease payments. Now we have gathered the necessary
information to calculate the expected net present value of

---

[4] If these assumptions do not hold, other methods have to be
applied. See Section 4.3.

leasing the capital asset: $E(NPV_{ol})$. Starting from the same probability distribution as when applying the Hax model (see p. 176) we obtain:

$$E(NPV_{ol}) = 0.8 \times 0.8 \times [\{\frac{(1-0.4) \times \$4,500}{1.16^1} + \frac{(1-0.4) \times \$5,000}{1.16^2}\}$$

$$+ 0.4 \times (\frac{\$3,200}{1.1323^1} + \frac{\$3,200}{1.1323^2}) - (\frac{\$3,200}{1.1323^1} + \frac{\$3,200}{1.1323^2})]$$

$$+ 0.8 \times 0.2 \times [\{\frac{(1-0.4) \times \$4,500}{1.16^1} + \frac{(1-0.4) \times \$3,000}{1.16^2}\}$$

$$+ 0.4 \times (\frac{\$3,200}{1.1323^1} + \frac{\$3,200}{1.1323^2}) - (\frac{\$3,200}{1.1323^1} + \frac{\$3,200}{1.1323^2})]$$

$$+ 0.2 \times [\frac{(1-0.4) \times \$2,000}{1.16^1} + 0.4 \times \frac{\$3,200}{1.1323^1} - \frac{\$3,200}{1.1323^1}]$$

$$= 0.8 \times 0.8 \times \$1,364 + 0.8 \times 0.2 \times \$472 + 0.2 \times -\$661$$

$$= \$816$$

Next we shall determine the expected net present value of the purchase option. In order to compute this net present value, we assume that the asset's cash purchase price is financed by raising a callable loan and that the firm's management effects the insurance contract discussed on pp. 189-190. The cash flows necessary to calculate the expected net present value of purchasing under this first set of assumptions, or $E(NPV_{p,1})$, are:
. the net cash inflows after taxes,
. the tax savings on depreciation,
. the tax savings on interest,
. the tax savings on the insurance premiums,
. the cash purchase price of the asset,
. the principal of the loan used to finance this purchase price,
. the principal and interest payments of this loan and the insurance premiums.
Applying the value-additivity principle, the same discount rates

will be utilized as when determining $E(NPV_{ol})$. Therefore, the cash inflows expected from asset operation are discounted at the appropriate project hurdle rate (16%), whereas the various tax deductions and the principal and interest payments of the loan as well as the insurance premiums are discounted at the operating lease rate (13.23%). Hence,

$$E(NPV_{p,1}) = 0.8 \times 0.8 \times [\{\frac{(1-0.4) \times \$4,500}{1.16^1} + \frac{(1-0.4) \times \$5,000}{1.16^2}\}$$

$$0.4 \times (\frac{\$3,000}{1.1323^1} + \frac{\$2,000}{1.1323^2}) + 0.4 \times (\frac{\$550}{1.1323^1} + \frac{\$275}{1.1323^2})$$

$$+ 0.4 \times (\frac{\$400}{1.1323^1} + \frac{\$400}{1.1323^2}) - \$5,000 + \$5,000$$

$$- (\frac{\$2,500 + \$550 + \$400}{1.1323^1} + \frac{\$2,500 + \$275 + \$400}{1.1323^2})]$$

$$+ 0.8 \times 0.2 \times [\{\frac{(1-0.4) \times \$4,500}{1.16^1} + \frac{(1-0.4) \times \$3,000}{1.16^2}\}$$

$$+ 0.4 \times (\frac{\$3,000}{1.1323^1} + \frac{\$2,000}{1.1323^2}) + 0.4 \times (\frac{\$550}{1.1323^1} + \frac{\$275}{1.1323^2})$$

$$+ 0.4 \times (\frac{\$400}{1.1323^1} + \frac{\$400}{1.1323^2}) - \$5,000 + \$5,000$$

$$- (\frac{\$2,500 + \$550 + \$400}{1.1323^1} + \frac{\$2,500 + \$275 + \$400}{1.1323^2})]$$

$$+ 0.2 \times [\frac{(1-0.4) \times \$2,000}{1.16^1} + 0.4 \times \frac{\$3,000}{1.1323^1}$$

$$+ 0.4 \times \frac{\$550}{1.1323^1} + 0.4 \times \frac{\$400}{1.1323^1} - \$5,000$$

$$+ \$5,000 - \frac{\$2,500 + \$550 + \$400}{1.1323^1}]$$

$$= 0.8 \times 0.8 \times \$1,264 + 0.8 \times 0.2 \times \$373 + 0.2 \times -\$618$$

$$= \$745$$

Since $E(NPV_{ol}) = \$816$ and $E(NPV_{p,1}) = \$745$, we should prefer to lease the asset. When computing $E(NPV_{p,1})$, however, we assumed that the firm's management effects the insurance contract introduced on p. 189. If this is not the case, then the expected net present value of the purchase alternative is to be calculated with the help of:

. the net cash inflows after taxes,
. the tax savings on depreciation,
. the tax savings on interest,
. the cash flow consequences of terminating asset operation,
. the cash purchase price of the asset,
. the principal of the loan used to finance this purchase price,
. the principal and interest payments of this loan.

Capitalizing at the same discount rates as used in the previous calculations, the expected net present value of purchasing under the second set of assumptions, $E(NPV_{p,2})$, can be computed as:

$$E(NPV_{p,2}) = 0.8 \times 0.8 \times \left[\left\{ \frac{(1-0.4) \times \$4,500}{1.16^1} + \frac{(1-0.4) \times \$5,000}{1.16^2} \right\} \right.$$

$$+ 0.4 \times \left(\frac{\$3,000}{1.1323^1} + \frac{\$2,000}{1.1323^2} \right) + 0.4 \times \left(\frac{\$550}{1.1323^1} + \frac{\$275}{1.1323^2} \right)$$

$$- \$5,000 + \$5,000 - \left(\frac{\$2,500 + \$550}{1.1323^1} + \frac{\$2,500 + \$275}{1.1323^1} \right) \right]$$

$$+ 0.8 \times 0.2 \times \left[\left\{ \frac{(1-0.4) \times \$4,500}{1.16^1} + \frac{(1-0.4) \times \$3,000}{1.16^2} \right\} \right.$$

$$+ 0.4 \times \left(\frac{\$3,000}{1.1323^1} + \frac{\$2,000}{1.1323^2} \right) + 0.4 \times \left(\frac{\$550}{1.1323^1} + \frac{\$275}{1.1323^2} \right)$$

$$- \$5{,}000 + \$5{,}000 - (\frac{\$2{,}500 + \$550}{1.1323^1} + \frac{\$2{,}500 + \$275}{1.1323^2})\ ]$$

$$+ 0.2 \times [\ \frac{(1-0.4) \times \$2{,}000}{1.16^1} + 0.4 \times \frac{\$3{,}000}{1.1323^1}$$

$$+ 0.4 \times \frac{\$550}{1.1323^1} - \frac{\$1{,}500}{1.16^1} - \$5{,}000$$

$$+ \$5{,}000 - \frac{\$2{,}500 + \$550}{1.1323^1}\ ]$$

$$= 0.8 \times 0.8 \times \$1{,}663 + 0.8 \times 0.2 \times \$772 + 0.2 \times -\$1{,}699$$

$$= \$848$$

In this calculation it is assumed that the cash flows of terminating asset operation at the end of the first year (-\$1,500) can be discounted at the same rate as the cash inflows expected from asset operation (16%). Comparing the three net present values, we find that $E(NPV_{ol}) = \$816$, $E(NPV_{p,1}) = \$745$ and $E(NPV_{p,2}) = \$848$, so purchasing the asset, without effecting the insurance contract, is to be preferred to leasing, whereas the latter arrangement is to be preferred to purchasing and insuring against the risks of early obsolescence. This sequence may be caused by the insurance contract being rather expensive, whereas the probability of negative cash flows resulting from early obsolescence is rather small (20%).

When computing $E(NPV_{p,1})$ and $E(NPV_{p,2})$ we have been assuming that the asset's purchase price was financed by means of a loan. Of course, the firm's management may also decide to finance this purchase price in another way. Regarding the effect the financing method may have on the resulting net present value of the purchase option, I refer to Section 4.3. As to different loss offset provisions, the performance of a sensitivity analysis, the effects a financing method may have upon the rates of return investors require, and any qualitative considerations that might influence the decision to lease or to purchase, I refer to this section too. No more than in that section do I advocate bluntly applying the same lease evaluation model in every conceivable situation. The model must be flexible enough to take into consideration the firm's goal(s), the position it is in (among other things, its income tax status), and the financing alternatives open to it.

Concerning the fifth requirement lease evaluation models should meet, one may wonder whether the insurance contract introduced on p. 189 can actually be effected. Koks, a Dutch author, points out that a firm has to cope with primary as well as secondary risks. According to Koks an example of the first group of risks is the risk that the products of a factory, which at the moment is under construction, may in the future be produced at higher cost, whereas the product's sales may fall behind the estimated sales and the actual selling prices may be lower than expected (Koks 1978, p. 41). He then observes that a firm also has to face secondary risks, for example, the risk that its factory or its products may be damaged by fire. Regarding the possibilities of the firm's management insuring against these risks, Koks holds that primary risks are not insurable, whereas secondary risks in principle can be insured against. To my thinking the risk that a capital asset may become obsolete can be looked upon as a primary risk and therefore, according to Koks, management cannot insure against it. As was explained in 5.1 however, by entering into an operating lease the lessee transfers the greater part of the risk of early obsolescence to the lessor and pays the lessor for performing this service. In other words, the lessor insures the lessee against a primary risk: the risk a capital asset may become obsolete earlier than expected. Lessors sometimes reinsure against this risk. In the past lessors of computers reinsured against the cash flows consequences of their lessees cancelling operating lease contracts (Lloyd's so-called J-policy, see Beckman and Joosen 1980, p. 19). As observed on p. 191, another possibility to cope with the risk of early obsolescence of a capital asset is a contract with the asset's seller whereby the seller buys back the asset paying such a price that any cash flow consequences of terminating the asset's operation because of its having become obsolete are eliminated. In the

Netherlands captive leasing companies usually conclude such a contract. The seller of the leased object commits itself to buy back the object at a predetermined price if the lessee stops making the lease payments (Beckman and Joosen 1980, p. 7). A similar solution to the obsolescence problem "is to buy insurance where a terminal value is guaranted by the insurance company" (Bierman 1982, p. 87; see also Leasing Digest, July 1982, p. 4 and p. 8). From the foregoing I conclude that in practice there indeed are possibilities of insuring against the risk of a capital asset's early obsolescence.[5] There are parallels of such insurances for private persons, for example, a special clause in a life insurance contract called the "accidental death benefit," or "double indemnity," which "provides that an additional sum, equal to the face of the policy, will be paid if death occurs by accidental means" (Cohen 1979, p. 177).

---

[5] Lee, Martin, and Senchak observe that "the [lease] rentals can be insured so as to eliminate the risk of default on the lease receipt" (Lee, Martin, and Senchak 1982, p. 35).

6 EMPIRICAL EVIDENCE

6.1 Introduction

As far as I know very few studies have been done on the methods applied in reality to make the lease-versus-purchase decision. One of the few that have been done is the one conducted by Anderson and Martin that I shall discuss in 6.3. That section will also go into my own experiences regarding lease-versus-purchase models as applied by Dutch companies. Extensive surveys have been made into the reasons that may result in preference being given to leasing. In 6.2 I shall take stock of these considerations. It is interesting to notice that during the fifties and the sixties these surveys were mainly done in the United States, whereas during the seventies European countries like England and West Germany also became involved in this kind of research. Probably these differences result from leasing having become an important means of raising capital in the United States at an earlier stage than in any other country.

6.2 Reasons for Leasing

One of the first surveys into the reasons for leasing was conducted by Vancil and Anthony in the beginning of 1959. These authors questioned financial analysts of the major financial institutions in the United States and in Canada, as well as treasurers and controllers of the major companies in the United States (Vancil and Anthony 1959, p. 113). They made use of direct-mail surveys in order to obtain an answer to the question of whether a long-term lease is considered to be equivalent to debt financing (p. 130). Vancil and Anthony conducted their surveys because of Gant's article "Illusion in Lease Financing." In his article Gant argues that, although a lease may not be shown on the lessee's balance sheet, "institutional investors, investment bankers, financial analysts, investment advisers, and bond-rating services ... are fully aware that lease commitments represent a form of indebtness." Therefore, he expects "these same investors to take lease commitments into consideration when making investment decisions." The author then describes some methods for the evaluation of leases (Gant 1959, p. 139). Nonetheless, it appeared from the surveys of Vancil and Anthony that a lessee might be willing to pay a higher interest rate in order to avoid showing the lease obligation on its balance sheet.[1] Other reasons turned out to be:

. "the tax advantages of being able to deduct 100% of the lease payments as an expense,
. the advantage of not having to invest any equity or working capital in the new building,
. the advantage of avoiding any restrictive covenants that might be written into a debt agreement,
. the saving of the financing cost that would be incurred if debenture financing were used,
. the advantage of using leasing to avoid piecemeal debt financing through a series of debenture issues" (Vancil and Anthony 1959, p. 129).

According to Vancil and Anthony: "Many of these reasons are among the frequently cited advantages of lease financing, and even

---

[1] In the meantime the Financial Accounting Standards Board has issued Statement No. 13 according to which "capital leases" ought to be shown on the balance sheet of the lessee (see "Accounting for Leases", FASB Statement No. 13 as amended and interpreted through May 1980). On p. 206 I shall return to this issue.

though they were not listed on the questionnaire many analysts believed in their realness and importance enough to go to the trouble to write them in" (p.129).

In 1968 Marrah conducted a survey into the advantages and the disadvantages of leasing. He mailed a questionnaire to "60 manufacturers to evaluate leasing as a source of capital" (Marrah 1968, p. 96). Advantages of leasing appeared to be:

. "conserves working capital,
. shifts the risk of obsolescence from user to buyer,
. eliminates the problem of asset disposal,
. preserves credit capacity,
. encourages trying new equipment,
. permits greater flexibility in use,
. avoids restrictive covenants in bank loans,
. eliminates maintenance problems,
. low cost,
. tax advantage."

Disadvantages of leasing were mentioned, too:

. "high cost,
. increases fixed obligations,
. does not build an equity,
. objectionable clauses and limitations,
. reluctance to absorb loss if equipment becomes obsolete,
. tax disadvantages,
. curtails freedom of the lessee in use of equipment,
. difficult to get improvements on leased equipment,
. difficult to finance improvements on leased equipment,
. forced to use inferior supply items in leased equipment" (p. 96).

Apart from gathering these advantages and disadvantages, Marrah also pays attention to the lease-or-purchase problem. When resolving this issue, Marrah recommends separating the investment decision from the financing decision: the latter decision should

be made only after the firm has decided to invest in a capital
asset (p. 91). At the end of his article Marrah repeats his ideas
concerning this sequence of decisions (p. 104). Moreover, the
numerical example with which he illustrates the way management
should choose between financial leasing and purchasing may give
rise to some confusion. This is because Marrah capitalizes the
relevant cash flows at "an assumed cost of capital," which he
describes as "the highest rate of return had the funds been
invested in other assets of the business" (p. 92). This definition may be more appropriate when defining the firm's investment
opportunity rate than its cost of capital.

A third survey into was set up by Fawthrop and Terry. In 1974
they addressed "senior financial executives of 54 major corporations in the United Kingdom" by way of a questionnaire and
interviews (Fawthrop and Terry 1975, p. 296). They found that
more than 60% of these corporations try to make the lease-versus-
purchase decision after it has been decided to invest in the
capital asset. Concerning the remaining firms, these authors
observe "that any integrated decision process was carried out at
a very superficial level or by routines which were frankly highly
suspect as to their validity" (p. 307). So, hardly any attention
was paid to the interactions of investment and financing decisions. Apart from this it became clear that frequently a lease
was being set against some kind of debt. Usually this lease-or-
borrow issue was resolved by comparing the interest rate of the
lease with the debt rate (p. 308). From their interviews Fawthrop
and Terry concluded that reasons to lease were that "it leaves
conventional credit lines clear," "it relieves a shortage of
borrowing power," and "it meets a desire to have a better balance
sheet" (p. 304). On the other hand, the majority of the executives participating in the Fawthrop and Terry survey felt that
leasing can be considered to be "an expensive form of finance"
(p. 304).

In 1976 the Deutsche Leasing AG (a German leasing company)
gathered information concerning the motives for leasing of 576
large German firms. Ranked in order of importance these motives
were:

- leasing permits 100% financing,
- the amounts of the lease payments are known in advance,
- avoiding restrictive covenants in debt agreements,
- leasing conserves working capital,
- leasing facilitates modernization of equipment,
- tax advantages,
- the lease payments are made out of the cash inflows the leased capital asset generates,
- the lease term corresponds with the asset's useful life,
- leasing is relatively inexpensive,
- off-balance-sheet financing,
- leasing serves as a hedge against inflation (Spittler 1977, p. 47).

In the same year Sykes undertook a study in England mailing a questionnaire to 202 British firms. According to the respondents "advantages of leasing as a source of funds" are:

- "provides source of funds which does not use existing working capital,
- permits 100% financing,
- no dilution of equity, no dependence on solvency,
- off-balance sheet financing,
- maximum loss potential reduced" (Sykes 1976, pp. 19-20).

In his postal survey, Dietz concentrated on West German and Swiss firms. It is interesting to observe that the firms in these two countries provided about the same set of reasons for leasing but that the sequence of these reasons was different. In order of importance, respondents in West Germany mentioned the following considerations:

- "100% finance,
- fixed costs,
- credit links remain open,
- capital freed,

. tax advantages,
. parallel between costs and return,
. protection against obsolescence,
. cheaper than other credit,
. balance sheet neutrality,
. effect as regard inflation" (Dietz 1977, p. 97).

Comparing these results with the ones from his Swiss study, Dietz found that "100% finance," "fixed costs," and "tax advantages" were considered to be less relevant in Switzerland. In addition, "capital freed" and "cheaper than other credit" appeared to be of no account in this country. On the other hand, "matching of terms" and "parallel between costs and return" turned out to be more important in Switzerland than in West Germany. These deviations between the reasons for leasing in the two countries may be explained from differences in the price structure of the German and Swiss capital markets as well as from differences in the tax regulations.

By postal survey Anderson and Martin asked executives of 180 American companies to score forty possible reasons for leasing. The results are:[2]

. "leasing provides 100 per cent deductibility of costs,
. leasing provides long term finance without diluting control,
. leasing frees working capital for other uses,
. leasing avoids problems of disposing of second-hand equipment,
. leasing allows piecemeal financing of small items of equipment,
. leasing protects company against obsolescence,
. leasing has a lower after-tax cost than equity finance,
. leasing enables the lessor to pass on tax credits,
. the tax deductibility of lease payments improves the cash flow,

----

[2] Information obtained from Tomkins, Lowe, and Morgan, "Leasing: the Gulf between Theory and Practice," a paper presented to the Nijenrode Conference on Financial Management of Corporate Resource Allocations, The Netherlands, August 7-10, 1979.

. leasing leaves normal lines of credit undisturbed."

Next I shall look into the survey Tomkins, Lowe, and Morgan conducted in England. They addressed seventeen leasing companies and
found, among other things, "that the leasing market is not homogeneous in terms of all lessors operating across all types of
lease" (Tomkins, Lowe, and Morgan 1979, p.14). In 1974 McGugan
and Caves arrived at the same conclusion. Starting from their
U.S. study, these authors concluded that "equipment leasing takes
place not in a homogeneous national market but in one slightly
fractured into regional and equipment-class submarkets" (McGugan
and Caves 1974, p. 389). According to Tomkins, Lowe, and Morgan
there are several ways to segment the leasing market. They then
argue that "the most clear segmentation occurred with companies
classified according to average lease size" (p. 16). Based on
this criterion, the authors distinguish between (p. 12): "Group I
(4 lessors with average lease size written in 1976 of £ 834,000),
Group II (7 lessors with average lease size £ 45,000), Group III
(3 lessors with average lease size £ 853)." Tomkins, Lowe, and
Morgan are of the opinion that the differences between the first
and the third group are very obvious and that this may very well
be an indication of differences in lessee motivation to lease (p.
18). They attach little value to studies in which the leasing
market has not been segmented (p. 23). To my thinking however,
Tomkins, Lowe, and Morgan have not yet adequately shown that the
reasons for leasing really differ according to the market segment
and that this would apply to countries other than England as
well. Also, the three authors set little value upon surveys
conducted with the help of a postal questionnaire. They argue
that the possibility exists for such a questionnaire to be filled
out by executives not primarily involved in the lease-or-purchase
decision and long after having made the decision (p. 23). In my
opinion Anderson and Martin solved this problem when they conducted their survey on lease valuation practices. They sent their
questionnaires to the company's chief financial officer "asking
him to forward it to the person or department responsible for
lease-purchase analyses" (Anderson and Martin 1977, p. 46). Based

on interviews with three lessees and one lessor Tomkins, Lowe, and Morgan prepared a list of reasons for leasing:

- . "the tax benefit,
- . off-balance sheet financing,
- . avoid capital expenditure limits,
- . nullifying government and central bank regulations,
- . a unique source of finance,
- . handling political risks,
- . government risk insurance and subsidies,
- . economies of scale in purchasing and maintenance, specialised knowledge of secondhand equipment values,
- . learning to lease,
- . raising massive sums of money" (pp. 26-38).

The authors observe that, because of FASB Statement No. 13, the second reason can be discounted for American lessees (p. 26). This observation, however, is justified only insofar as capital leases are involved. Moreover, there are possibilities of avoiding a lease to be classified as a capital lease. Ecker, manager of a German leasing company, argues that a "Lloyds-Restwertversicherung" (an insurance contract effected with Lloyd's insuring lessors against disappointing salvage values, see also Chapter 5 p. 197) transfers "normal Leasingvertrage" (normal lease contracts) into operating leases (Ecker 1977, p. 28). Brealey and Myers also give an example of the manner in which management may make use of "this arbitrary boundary between operating and financial leases" (Brealey and Myers 1981, p. 526).

The "Survey of Company Car Schemes" was undertaken by the Tolley Publishing Company in England. "The survey ... was based on the analysis of the car schemes of over 1,000 companies operating a total of 95,000 cars" (see Martin 1982, p. 31). According to this 1981 study, the six most important reasons for leasing were:

. "saving of capital,

. simplified budgeting,

. taxation,

. inflation proof,

. saving in administrative cost,

. preferential car purchase at end of lease".

For illustrative purposes, Table 6.1 summarizes all of the above survey findings.

Table 6.1

Reasons for Leasing Found by Various Authors and Institutions

Reasons for Leasing:	Vancil and Anthony 1959 (U.S.)	Marrah 1968 (U.S.)	Fawthrop and Terry 1975 (England)	Deutsche Leasing AG 1976 (W. Germany)	Sykes 1976 (England)	Dietz 1977 (W. Germany)	Dietz 1977 (Switzerland)	Anderson and Martin 1979 (U.S.)	Tomkins, Lowe and Morgan 1979 (England)	Tolley Publishing Cy 1981 (England)
off-balance sheet financing	X		X	X	X	X		X		
tax advantages	X	X		X		X	X	X	X	
conserves working capital	X	X		X	X	X		X		X
avoids restrictive covenants and regulations	X	X	X					X		
low cost	X	X		X		X		X	X	X
flexibility	X	X					X	X	X	
transfers risk of obsolescence	X		X		X	X	X			
eliminates problems of asset disposal	X							X		
preserves debt capacity	X	X	X			X	X	X		
encourages trying new equipment	X	X								
lease payments are known in advance				X	X	X	X		X	
100% finance				X	X	X	X			
pay as you earn				X		X	X			
serves as a hedge against inflation				X		X	X			X
no dilution of equity					X			X		
unique source of finance									X	
handling political risks									X	
government risk insurance and subsidies									X	
learning to lease									X	
preferential car purchase at end of lease										X

Survey Conducted by:

As seen in Table 6.1, next to considerations that were mentioned only a few times by the respondents (such as "no dilution of equity" and "unique source of finance") there are reasons for leasing that were considered to be more important. The five most important reasons appear to be:

. tax advantages,
. off-balance sheet financing,
. conserves (working) capital,
. low cost,
. preserves debt capacity.

This does not imply that these positive aspects of leasing will be of importance in every conceivable situation. The advantages and the disadvantages of leasing are mainly determined by the conditions of a lease contract and by the financing alternatives open to a firm's management. This statement can be illustrated with the help of what proved to be the most frequently mentioned reason for leasing: the tax advantages it yields. This advantage was discovered in eight out of the ten studies summarized in Table 6.1. However, there are differences in the importance respondents attach to the tax advantage: in Marrah's analysis this advantage was mentioned in the last place, whereas according to the Anderson and Martin survey tax advantages were more important than any of the other reasons for leasing. Besides, the above statement can also be illustrated starting from the fourth consideration of the list compiled from Table 6.1: the low cost of leasing. A lease agreement's being cheaper than other sources of funds is a result of the conditions of the lease contract itself and of the conditions of the alternative financing methods. As appears from two studies in which attention was paid to possible disadvantages of leasing (the 1968 study of Marrah and the 1975 survey of Fawthrop and Terry), leasing was even pictured to be relatively expensive. Again, this results from the conditions of the pertinent lease contracts and those of the alternative financing arrangements.

Next I shall pay attention to the possibilities of quantifying the above five reasons for leasing. The tax advantages leasing brings along, its low cost, the fact that leasing conserves working capital, and the fact that it preserves debt capacity can be measured in percentages, sums of money, and the like. This does not seem to be the case with the second advantage of the above list: off-balance sheet financing. Maybe this reason for leasing, which was put forward in seven out of the ten studies, can be considered a cause for leasing to preserve a firm's debt capacity (number 5 of the list). This statement is based on one of the results of Fawthrop and Terry's analysis: the majority of the respondents to their survey regarded the "ratio of debt to equity in the balance sheet" as "very relevant" or "relevant" for the determination of the "limit to the amount of debt a company ought to use"[3] (Fawthrop and Terry 1975, p. 300). Hence, if a lease is not shown in a firm's balance sheet the ratio of debt to equity will not be affected, and consequently the firm's debt capacity will not be influenced.

It follows that in reality the choice between leasing and purchasing, at least according to the ten surveys summarized, is mainly based on quantitative considerations, and also that qualitative factors (such as "unique source of finance" and "learning to lease") are considered to be less relevant. Since the results of the lease-versus-purchase models discussed in earlier chapters are also expressed in quantitative terms (e.g., net present values), I feel that these models are useful instruments for making the lease-or-purchase decision in real-world situations. Nonetheless, continuing research on the reasons for leasing and on the methods used for attaching weight to these reasons when choosing between leasing and purchasing appears to be worthwhile. Building on the results of the analysis of McGugan and Caves as well as on those of the survey conducted by Tomkins,

----

[3] In the second and the third place, respondents mentioned as criteria for determining a firm's debt capacity the "prior charges cover in the profit and loss account" and the "prior charges cover afforded by a cash flow forecast of some kind."

Lowe, and Morgan, attention can be paid to the relevance of
market segmentation for determining the reasons preference is
given to leasing. Contrary to the majority of the surveys discussed in the above, to my thinking it is useful to look into the
advantages and the disadvantages of leasing as perceived by the
respondents. This is because positive as well as negative aspects
of leasing may play a part when choosing between a lease and a
purchase arrangement.

6.3 Lease Evaluation Models Used in Practice

In 1975 Anderson and Martin conducted a very interesting study on
lease evaluation practices among sixty-three large U.S. industrial firms. They asked executives of these firms to apply their
normal financial lease analysis method for solving a modified
version of the numerical example Johnson and Lewellen utilized to
illustrate their lease-or-purchase model (Anderson and Martin
1977, p. 42). Just as Fawthrop and Terry concluded from their
1974 analysis in England, Anderson and Martin observe that many
firms employ internal rates of return to choose between leasing
and purchasing. Anderson and Martin argue that this is because
practitioners prefer to express financing costs as a rate (p.
43). A second model that was frequently applied was the approach
Weston and Brigham developed in the 1966 edition of their textbook (see 3.4.3.2). The third place was occupied by Weston and
Brigham's 1969 model (see 3.4.3.3), whereas the remaining companies applied Vancil's borrowing opportunity rate method (as
discussed in 3.4.2), Weston and Brigham's 1972 model (3.4.3.4),
and the Bower, Herringer, and Williamson model (3.4.4). Qualitative considerations did not seem to be very relevant, for only
some firms stated that in a real-world situation these factors
should be considered along with the results of the numerical
analysis.

Anderson and Martin were surprised to notice that the respondents made many computational errors as well as "fundamental
errors of financial analysis" (p. 42). Besides, it appeared that

many respondents were "unaware of the academic source of their
lease-purchase models": being unable to cite a source, refer-
encing the comptroller's manual of their firm, or even citing a
wrong academic source. This kind of mistake can be avoided for
the most part if managers would be willing to pay more attention
to theoretical achievements in this field. Apart from this
Anderson and Martin observe that many firms make use of evaluation models "which may be biased in favor of the purchase
alternative" (p. 43). They argue that this may be caused by,
first, the "failure to adjust for risk differences in the cash
flows," and second, because according to the majority of the
models employed management should first be able to justify purchasing the required capital assets before addressing the lease-
versus-purchase issue. In their recent survey, O'Brien and
Nunnally also discovered that "many decision-makers incorrectly
omit lease analyses if projects have not already been recommended
on a purchase basis" (O'Brien and Nunnally 1983, p. 33). Section
4.3 addressed the risk differences in the cash flows of the lease
and the purchase alternative and the effects of these differences
upon the discount rates to be utilized. Regarding the second
cause Anderson and Martin mention, I have stressed the importance
of considering the interactions of the firm's financing and
investment decisions (requirement I), thus enabling an original
negative purchase decision to be reversed by an attractive lease
proposal.

Finally, I shall give an account of my findings regarding some
Dutch lease-or-purchase practices. The first case studied involved a firm's management considering whether to purchase or to
lease a building. From the information provided to me (including
detailed computations for a forty-year period), I inferred that
the Bower, Herringer, and Williamson model, discussed in 3.4.4,
had been applied. Two issues, however, attracted my attention. In
the first place the interest rate of the loan used to finance the
building's purchase price exceeded the financial lease rate, so
that (using the terminology of Bower, Herringer, and Williamson)
the lease showed a "financial advantage." Secondly, the first
lease payment had to be made five years after the lease contract

was concluded. Just as Bower, Herringer, and Williamson would recommend to do, during these years the interest payments on the so-called equivalent loan were not considered to be made (nor were the loan principal payments) but were added to the principal of the equivalent loan.

In the second case I am about to discuss, the question of whether a computer should be purchased or leased was at issue. The method employed to make this decision does not correspond with any of the models discussed in Chapters 3, 4, and 5. Instead, the firm's management grounded its decision on the sum total of the costs of each of the alternatives. For this purpose, the sum of the lease payments was set against the sum of depreciation and interest of the purchase alternative. Management opted for the arrangement with the lower total costs. This is a remarkable approach to the lease-or-purchase problem: not only were costs rather than cash flows used to solve this problem but also adding instead of capitalizing was involved. Neither the time value of money nor the risk premium expressed in the capitalization rate were taken into consideration. Besides, the tax effects of both arrangements were ignored completely.

In the next case once more leasing or purchasing a computer was at issue. Contrary to the decision process just examined, capitalizing instead of adding was made use of, employing the firm's cost of capital as the capitalization rate. Strangely enough, the question to be answered was depicted as "lease-or-borrow," whereas the borrowing rate was assumed to be zero. Because of this the interest factor is of no importance at all. This approach was not explained. From the calculations management made, it can be inferred that the valuation model Weston introduced in the appendix to his chapter on leasing in the first edition of Managerial Finance was applied (see 3.5.1.1).

The last case I would like to discuss does not so much involve an actual decision but the directives a firm's headquarters issued concerning the method to be employed when choosing between financial leasing and purchasing. According to these directives, a situation where the financial lease-or-purchase decision can be considered a separate decision should be distinguished from a situation in which this issue has to be resolved as a part of the firm's total capital budgeting and financing plan. Contrary to the first situation, capital rationing would be involved in the second situation. If no capital rationing is involved, the implicit financial lease rate is compared with the borrowing rate. According to the firm's headquarters, management should choose the arrangement with the lower interest rate.[4] The tax factor should be ignored when calculating the lease and the loan rate because, as maintained in the directives, leasing should not be aimed at saving taxes but at generating profits. In my opinion this approach is not correct; in situations in which taxes are levied management should strive to maximize the firm's after-tax profits. Consequently, I feel that the tax factor is relevant in these situations. Further on in the directives issued by the firm's headquarters this problem is addressed once more. Then the tax factor does, however, form a part of the computations. This is because the directives then dictate employing the evaluation model Mitchell developed more than ten years ago (Mitchell 1970, pp. 308-314). Applying this model, the after-tax financial lease rate is set against the after-tax loan rate. The arrangement with the lower interest rate should be chosen. It has not become clear to me which evaluation method the firm's headquarters prefer to utilize: ignoring the tax factor or making it a part of the calculations. If both approaches result in the same decision being made, then the tax issue is rather irrelevant. If on the other hand applying both approaches results in preferring different arrangements, which is most likely if the tax factor has a different impact on leasing and purchasing, then confusion may be caused. For the rest, I fail to see that in practice a financial lease-versus-purchase decision can be regarded as a separate decision, independent of the firm's other activities.

If the firm is confronted with capital rationing constraints, then, according to the headquarters' directives, the before-tax

----

[4] The examination of Vancil's borrowing opportunity rate method in 3.4.2 also discussed this approach.

financial lease rate should be compared with the rate of return generated if purchasing the asset were possible. If the before-tax financial lease rate turns out to be lower than this rate of return, then operating the leased capital asset is acceptable. According to the directives, this rate of return should be computed using the method McEachron introduced (see 3.4.1). It is rather remarkable that, when determining this rate, the tax factor is of relevance (as explained on pp. 20-23, the rate of return McEachron calculates is an after-tax rate).

From the above it can be concluded that some lease-versus-purchase analysis models as developed by academics are in fact being applied by practitioners. In addition, I am under the impression that in real-world situations more extensive calculations are being made if larger sums of money are involved. If, however, relatively small sums of money are at stake, then the lease-purchase decision seems to be grounded on qualitative considerations. An example of these considerations is the fact that if an asset is leased, obtaining the right to operate it and acquiring the necessary funds are combined, which is easier to accomplish than effecting two separate transactions. Another example is the possibility of transferring the risk of early obsolescence to the lessor by concluding an operating lease contract. Sometimes such arguments are supplemented with a comparison of the before-tax lease and loan rates.[5] Although at first sight it appears to be efficient not to deal at great length with decisions that seem to be less important, one should not underestimate the adverse effects of making a number of these decisions badly. That is why management should try to state its starting points as explicitly as possible and should also try to quantify the considerations that result in the decision to lease or to purchase.

---

[5] When conducting their survey, Fawthrop and Terry discovered this to be the most frequently used lease-versus-purchase decision model (Fawthrop and Terry 1975, p. 308).

7 LEASING IN SOME WESTERN EUROPEAN COUNTRIES

7.1 Introduction

The previous chapter concluded from the surveys conducted by various authors and institutions that tax advantages as well as the advantage of off-balance sheet financing are the most frequently mentioned reasons for leasing. However, there are great differences between the corporate income tax systems and the accounting regulations of various countries, especially in Western Europe. That is why I shall discuss the principal corporate income tax and accounting aspects of leasing in some of the more prominent European countries: England, France, The Netherlands, the Northern European countries (Denmark, Finland, Norway, and Sweden), Switzerland, and West Germany (see Sections 7.3 and 7.4). In all of these countries, financial leasing of movables was introduced in the beginning of the sixties. Since in some cases the regulations issued by the tax authorities and the accounting profession are connected with the legal provisions, I shall first look into the legal aspects of leasing (Section 7.2). Paying attention to these issues is justified all the more as the above aspects are in fact part of the information required for making the lease-or-purchase decision in one of the Western European countries I shall be discussing.

The following sections draw upon Chapter 9 of the book by Beckman and Joosen, two Dutch authors, who provide an excellent overall picture of the aspects that will be discussed below.

7.2 General and Legal Aspects

England is the first European country where leasing was introduced. In fact, leasing of real estate has been known since the
Middle Ages. "In 1980 leasing accounted for 12.4 per cent of all
new capital investment in plant and equipment in the United Kingdom compared with 10.6 per cent in 1979" (Exposure Draft No. 29,
"Accounting for Leases and Hire Purchase Contracts," 1981, Preface, paragraph 1). It is estimated that leasing accounts for
about 7% of total English investments. Most leasing companies are
members of the Equipment Leasing Association (E.L.A.). As Franks
and Broyles observe, "the majority of lessors fall into one of
the following five categories:
(a) Subsidiaries of the Clearing Banks (e.g., Lloyds Bank),
(b) Merchant Banks (e.g., Brandts),
(c) Finance Houses (e.g., Mercantile Credit),
(d) Other financial institutions (e.g., I.C.F.C.),
(e) U.S. leasing companies (e.g., Citicorp Leasing)."
Along with to leasing transactions conducted in England, the
volume of cross-border leasing has increased too (Franks and
Broyles 1979, p. 318). In addition to leasing of capital assets
(mainly ships, aircraft, and computers), leasing of consumer
durables (especially television sets) has been applied on a
larger scale than in any other European country. There are no
separate legal provisions for leasing, which is considered to be
a special form of renting whereby the lessee selects the specific
equipment it requires. The lease should not give the lessee the
option to purchase the equipment, otherwise it is regarded as a
hire purchase arrangement. However, "in most U.K. lease agreements, there is a clause which stipulates that a specified
proportion of the proceeds from the sale of the asset will accrue
to the lessee at the end of the lease. The proportion typically
ranges from 85 to 95 per cent" (Franks and Broyles 1979, p. 326).
The English legislator does not distinguish between financial and
operational leasing. Leases of personal property are subject to
common law and to more specific regulations such as the Consumer
Credit Act 1974 and the Consumer Safety Act 1978. Some more

specific regulations regarding leasing of real estate by business firms are contained in the Landlord and Tenant Act 1954.

In France financial leasing (especially of real estate) has become an important source of business financing, mainly because other sources of intermediate-term financing were considered to be inadequate. Operational leasing, particularly of automobiles, is becoming rather popular too. There are special laws regarding financial leasing ("crédit-bail") and regarding the leasing companies that are engaged in this form of leasing. On the other hand, operating lease contracts are looked upon as ordinary renting arrangements. The French laws contain a definition of the term "crédit-bail." Important elements of this definition are the fact that capital assets are involved, that these assets have been purchased by the leasing company for the sole purpose of leasing them, and that the lessee has an option to purchase the leased capital asset at a price that is determined in advance. In the definition of "crédit-bail" there is no mention of the risk of early obsolescence being borne by the lessee. However, "crédit-bail" contracts concluded in reality turn out to be fully amortized. Hence, the risk of obsolescence is borne by the lessee. As observed in the above, there are also special laws concerning leasing companies that offer "crédit-bail" arrangements that, among other things, dictate the minimum capital requirements these companies should meet. Furthermore, these leasing companies are subject to general directions that other financial institutions have to meet as well. On the whole, these guidelines are more stringent for personal property than for real estate. Besides, there are regulations concerning the disclosure of certain information about the leasing agreements "crédit-bail" companies conclude, such as information regarding the parties and the leased objects involved in the agreements.

After being introduced in 1963, leasing has become an important financing method in the Netherlands. It is estimated that about 5% of the total capital expenditures of Dutch firms is financed by entering into financial lease contracts (Goudsmit 1981, p. 5). Moreover, Dutch firms are also becoming interested in operating leases, notably of computers, automobiles, and real estate. Important reasons for these developments may be that many firms lack the ability to retain sufficient earnings and that raising equity funds has turned out to be rather difficult. Lease contracts are offered by specialized leasing companies, by dealers of the objects to be leased, and by various financial institutions, such as banks and insurance companies. There are no specific legal provisions regarding lease contracts. Operating leases are usually considered to be ordinary rental arrangements whereas, depending on the conditions of the contract, financial leases of movables may be looked upon as a rental agreement, a conditional sales contract, a secured loan, or an installment purchase. Some authors prefer to consider a financial lease of movables to be a separate type of contract, a so-called contractus sui generis (see Beckman and Joosen 1980, p. 160, and Goudsmit and Keijser 1972, p. 87). On the other hand, financial leasing of immovables is usually looked upon as renting.

"From time immemorial, Swedish land has been leased out by its owners." Besides, in Sweden ship and plant leasing have been known since the Middle Ages (see 5000 Years of Leasing, Livijn 1969, pp. 7-10). In view of the many similarities of modern leasing in the Northern European countries of Denmark, Finland, Norway, and Sweden, I shall give a joint description of leasing in these countries. Financial leasing of personal property was introduced in 1963-1965. After that other types of leases were also introduced. In Norway leasing companies are normally financed with equity and short-term loans because it is very difficult to raise intermediate-term loans. The interest rates of lease contracts are usually variable, just like in the other Northern European countries. There are no specific laws for leasing in Denmark, Finland, Norway, and Sweden; leases are regarded as ordinary rental arrangements. There are, however, special regulations for leasing companies containing the conditions such a company has to meet, for example, minimum capital requirements.

Lüem, a Swiss author, argues that there are some factors that may hamper the growth of leasing in his country: the fact that Swiss firms tend to finance a major part of their assets with equity, that leasing hardly yields tax advantages, and that as a result of pride-of-ownership considerations Swiss entrepreneurs prefer purchasing to leasing (Lüem 1967). Operational leasing of automobiles and computers was introduced in the beginning of the sixties. After that financial leasing was introduced, and at the moment the volume of this type of leasing (particularly of real estate) is increasing. As in England, leasing of consumer durables (even of ships and airplanes) is practised. There are no specific legal provisions for lease contracts. An operating lease is usually identified with rent, whereas a financial lease is often considered to be a "contractus sui generis," containing elements of, among other things, rent and installment purchase.

Leasing was introduced in West Germany in 1962. Since that year, financial leasing has become an important financing method especially for real estate. In addition to financing the object, the lessor frequently provides for other services as well, for example, supervising the construction of the buildings (see Krumbholz and Streitferdt 1975, p. 79, and Graf von Westphalen 1979, p. 157). It is hard to determine which legal provisions apply to financial leases in Germany. Depending on the terms of the contract, a financial lease may even be considered to be a hire purchase arrangement or an installment loan. There are also German writers who advocate considering a financial lease of personal property to be a contractus sui generis (e.g., Graf von Westphalen 1979, p. 25 and p. 43). On the other hand, financial leases of real estate and operating leases are subject to the regulations that apply to rental agreements.

7.3 Tax Aspects

In England the U.K. Inland Revenue allows many movable assets to be fully depreciated in the first year of operation. Different regulations apply to ships and buildings. In the case of leasing, the lessor, who is considered to be the asset's owner, is granted the right to depreciate the leased assets in the first year. If the lessor's profits are insufficient to benefit fully by these tax advantages, it is allowed to depreciate the remaining amount in the following years. Another possibility for the lessor would be to cooperate with other institutions to gain the full benefits of the English tax provisions. These provisions have stimulated the growth of leasing, especially the leasing of automobiles (see Leasing Digest, August 1982, pp. 31-32).

As was explained on p. 219, the French authorities distinguish between "crédit-bail" contracts and other lease contracts. If the "crédit-bail" arrangement concerns movables, then the common tax laws are applicable. The lessor is considered to be the owner of the leased assets and is allowed to depreciate the objects, whereas for the lessee the lease payments, if they correspond with the depreciation allowances, are deductible costs. There are, however, special laws for "crédit-bail" of real property. Leasing companies that offer this kind of contract do not have to pay corporate income taxes if they fulfill certain conditions (for example, minimum capital requirements). If the lease arrangement does not meet the definition of "crédit-bail" as given by the French legislature, then the lease is regarded as an operating lease, whereby the leased asset is owned by the lessor.

Before 1978 the Dutch tax authorities tried to stimulate capital budgeting plans with the help of accelerated tax depreciation allowances and with investment tax credits. In order to benefit from these facilities, a firm had to have sufficient taxable capacity. If this was not the case, the necessary capital assets could be leased, enabling the lessor to benefit from the tax provisions and to transfer them (in part) to the lessee. Since 1978 the Dutch tax authorities have provided for tax-free grants according to the so-called Wet Investeringsrekening to firms that make investments meeting the conditions laid down by this law, even if those firms are incurring losses. Nonetheless, before concluding a lease contract it is still sensible to establish which part of the tax advantages the lessor (if regarded as the asset's owner) passes on to the lessee. In the case of leasing, an important question to be answered is: who do the tax authorities consider to be the owner of the leased assets? Generally, according to these authorities that party is looked upon as the asset's owner that bears the major part of the risks of the changes in the asset's value (e.g., the risk of early obsolescence). If the lease agreement is a financial lease, the Dutch tax authorities consider the lessee to be the owner of the asset. The lessee then has to record the financial lease as an asset as well as a liability on its balance sheet, is allowed to depreciate the asset, and benefits from the tax regulations intended to stimulate investments. The lessor then has to pay corporate income taxes on its profits (which mainly consist of interest implicit in the financial lease payments). If on the other hand an operating lease, which the tax authorities consider to be an ordinary rental arrangement, is involved, the lessor is looked upon as the owner of the leased asset, has to record the asset on its balance sheet, depreciates the asset, and is allowed to make use of the tax advantages. For the lessee the full amount of the lease payments is deductible for income tax purposes. There is, however, a peculiarity in the Dutch tax system. If a firm that operates capital assets does not pay the taxes due, the tax authorities have the right to recover these taxes from all the movable assets being on the firm's premises, even if these assets belong to other firms, for instance, to leasing companies. This is the "fiscale bodembeslag" that the tax authorities apply more and more. More and more voices are heard demanding that this right is getting out of date and should be abolished (see, among others, Van der Lande 1983, pp. 31-36).

In the Northern European countries - Denmark, Finland, Norway, and Sweden - there are no special tax laws for leasing. Leases are considered to be ordinary rental arrangements. Consequently, the tax authorities regard the lessor as the owner of the leased objects, and the lessee is allowed to deduct the lease payments when determining its profits.

There are no special laws and taxes concerning leases in Switzerland. Lease contracts are treated like ordinary rental contracts: the lessor is considered to be the owner of the leased objects and for the lessee the full amount of the annual lease payments is deductible for income tax purposes. Limitations regarding tax deductibility may exist in some cases. Apart from that, there are differences between the tax regulations of the various cantons in Switzerland. Therefore, a firm's management trying to choose between leasing and purchasing should first acquaint itself with these limitations and differences.

In West Germany there are detailed tax regulations concerning leases. An important question to be answered is: who is the leased asset's beneficial owner, the lessor or the lessee? This owner has to record the leased asset on its balance sheet, depreciates the asset, and is entitled to measures introduced by the German tax authorities to stimulate investments. In the case of a special lease object, which can only be operated by the lessee ("Spezial-Leasing"), the lessee is regarded as the object's owner. This is also the case if the lease arrangement contains a bargain purchase option entitling the lessee to buy the asset at a price that is substantially lower than its fair value. Moreover, there are detailed regulations based on the possible ratios of the lease term and the leased object's useful life. Starting from these ratios and from the regulations of the German tax authorities, one is able to determine whether the lessee or the lessor is the leased object's owner. If, however, the lease is a non-payout lease the lessor is regarded as the object's owner (Beckman 1982, p. 103). In fact, as a result of the detailed German tax regulations many leases are being drafted in such a way that the lessor is considered to be the owner of the leased object.

7.4 Accounting Aspects

In England if a lease contract contains a purchase option, then it is looked upon as a hire purchase contract and not as a true lease. Such a hire purchase arrangement ought to be recorded in the balance sheet of the hire purchaser. If the contract is considered to be a true lease, then the lessee is allowed to show the leased asset and the lease obligation on its balance sheet. The lessee is not, however, obliged to record the lease, and in practice the lessor usually shows the lease on its balance sheet.

In October 1981 Exposure Draft 29, <u>Accounting for Leases and Hire Purchase Contracts</u>, was published, describing the situations in which the lessee has to record the lease in its balance sheet. In general, in these situations a "finance lease" is involved. "A finance lease is a lease that transfers substantially all the risks and rewards of ownership of an asset to the lessee" (ED 29, Definition of Terms, paragraph 12). A matter for consideration for recording finance leases in the lessee's balance sheet is that "in substance a finance lease and a hire purchase agreement are very similar" (ED 29, Preface, paragraph 10) and, as observed above, assets as well as liabilities connected with hire purchase agreements are to be shown in the balance sheet of the user firm.

In France the lessee is not allowed to show the lease on its balance sheet; the lessor, being the legal owner of the leased asset, has to record the lease. If the lease is a "crédit-bail" contract, then the lessee must show the lease payments separately from the other payments in its income statement. The lessee should also indicate whether the lease payments result from "crédit-bail" of personal property or of real estate. In addition to this requirement, footnote disclosures are required concerning the future obligations arising from "crédit-bail" of these two types of assets.

In the Netherlands the accounting regulations concerning leases in part parallel the regulations issued by the Dutch tax authorities: the party that bears the majority of the risks of changes in the value of the leased asset has to show this asset in its balance sheet. The lessee must record the leased asset in the balance sheet if the lease term equals the asset's useful life, if there is a bargain purchase option, or if the lessee is allowed to continue leasing the asset at a very low price. As well as recording the leased asset, the lessee has to show the lease obligation. The lessee should depreciate the leased asset in the same way as in the case of purchasing it and should also amortize the lease obligation. The lessor, on the other hand, has to show the lease payments to be received in the future on its balance sheet and has to record the profits in its income statement. However, if an operating lease is involved the lessee has to show the lease payments in its income statement. If the operating lease involves payments that have to be made during several years, the lessee should also provide additional information, such as the amounts of the future payments to be made. In the case of an operating lease, the lessor has to record the leased asset in its balance sheet, depreciates this asset, and has to show the lease payments received in its profit and loss account.

Although the Ministers of Justice have decided to harmonize the general corporation laws, differences between the Northern European countries still exist in this area. In Denmark and Sweden in some situations the lessee is allowed to account for financial leases in the balance sheet, but in Finland and Norway it is forbidden to do so. Let us look into this issue a little further. If it is agreed that on expiry of the lease term a Swedish lessee is becoming the legal owner of the leased asset, then Swedish auditors recommend recording the leased asset as well as the lease obligation in the lessee's balance sheet. If such an agreement does not exist, the lessee is not allowed to show the lease in its balance sheet. In Denmark a lessee is in some cases also allowed to show a financial lease on the balance sheet, but in reality the lessor usually accounts for the leased asset. However, it is demanded that the lessee disclose material information concerning leases, such as the amount of the future lease payments to be made. In Norway the lessee is not allowed to record a financial or an operating lease in its balance sheet. Leased assets appear in the lessor's balance sheet, and it is the lessor that depreciates these assets. If material, a Norwegian lessee ought to give footnote information concerning the future lease payments to be made, any purchase options, and so forth. To conclude, in Finland it is also forbidden for a lessee to account for a lease in its balance sheet. If, however, the lease in fact is an installment purchase and the lessee is becoming the asset's legal owner, then it is allowed to show the lease in the balance sheet.

In Switzerland a lessee is allowed to account for financial and operating leases in its balance sheet, but it is not required to do so. Swiss auditors recommend providing footnote disclosure regarding the assets leased, but again the lessee is not required to do so. If the lessee nevertheless choses to record a lease in its balance sheet, it can apply the U.S. regulations as issued by the Financial Accounting Standards Board (see FASB Statement No. 13, as amended and interpreted through May 1980).

There are detailed regulations concerning accounting for leases in West Germany. Many a time this fact results in lease contracts being drawn up in such a way that the lessor shows the leased asset in its balance sheet. The regulations for lease accounting largely agree with the regulations issued by the German tax authorities. When accounting for leases, German firms are allowed to apply the tax regulations unless applying these rules is at variance with the accounting regulations. Just as the tax authorites dictate, the leased asset's beneficial owner has to show this asset in the balance sheet together with the accompanying liability. That party is considered to be the beneficial owner of the leased asset that has the right to operate, to sell, to exchange, even to destroy the asset and is also expected to make use of these rights. A lease is regarded as a financial lease if, among other things, the lessee is unable to cancel the contract. If a financial lease is involved and the lessee is the leased asset's beneficial owner, the lease has to be recorded in the lessee's balance sheet. If a financial lease is involved but the lessee is not the beneficial owner of the asset, then the lessee is allowed to choose either to account for the financial lease in its balance sheet or to utilize footnote disclosure showing, among other things, the present value of the lease payments to be made in the next four years.

8 SUMMARY OF MAIN CONCLUSIONS

Chapter 1 introduced the problem dealt with in this study and the firm's goal assumed in trying to solve this problem. Chapter 2 states that leases have four characteristic features in common. First, any lease can be looked upon as a loan providing (almost) 100% financing of the leased asset's purchase price. Second, the lessee obtains the right only to use the asset. Third, the lessor usually remains the asset's owner, and fourth, the lease term corresponds with the expected service life of the capital asset. Because of these common features, I first defined the word leasing as such and then looked into the various types of leases. I thereby distinguished between financial and operating leases. With a financial lease, the risk of early obsolescence is largely borne by the lessee, whereas by entering into an operating lease this risk is transferred to the lessor. This is because after having concluded a financial lease contract the financial lessee is irrevocably committed to making the lease payments until at least the leased asset's purchase price has been repaid to the lessor. On the other hand, an operating lease does not involve such a fixed future commitment, since the operating lessee is allowed to continue leasing the asset if its operation turns out to be profitable (in some cases it is even allowed to purchase the asset) or to cancel the lease if the leased asset's service life is considered to be at an end. After having defined the concepts of leasing, financial leasing, and operating leasing, I discussed the five requirements financial and operating lease-versus-purchase models should meet. With the help of these requirements, I evaluated a number of financial lease-versus-purchase decision models in Chapter 3. Each of these models can be categorized as either a lease-or-borrow or a lease-or-buy

model. The criterion for this classification is the way the
purchase price of the asset would be financed if it were purchased rather than leased. The majority of the financial lease
valuation models reviewed in Chapter 3 turned out to be lease-or-
borrow models. Since none of the models examined appeared to meet
all five requirements discussed in Chapter 2, I introduced a
financial lease valuation model of my own (Chapter 4). Starting
from the cash flows to equity and making use of the value-
additivity principle, I applied the risk-adjusted discount rate
approach to value the various cash flow streams. I argued that
the present value of the lease payments is to be calculated by
capitalizing these payments at the lower of the implicit financial lease rate and the interest rate of an equivalent loan. This
loan has some characteristic features in common with the financial lease option. If the loan is utilized to finance the asset's
purchase price, then the lower of the two interest rates should
be used to compute the present value of the loan principal and
interest payments. I also argued that the rate to be employed for
capitalizing the tax savings of the financial lease and the purchase arrangement depends to a large extent on the tax system in
force, notably on regulations as to tax deductible losses. In
practice it may be necessary to perform a sensitivity analysis in
order to value the various tax savings. In my opinion a financial
and an operating lease valuation model must be flexible enough to
take into consideration factors as the firm's goal(s), the
position it is in (among other things, its income tax status),
and the financing alternatives open to it. When choosing between
leasing and purchasing, management should pay attention both to
any influence that entering into a financial lease or purchase
contract might have upon the rates of return investors require
and to any qualitative considerations (such as pride-of-ownership). This also applies to the choice between an operating lease
and a purchase arrangement. In Chapter 5 I observed that the
number of operating lease valuation models is much smaller than
the number of models designed for valuing financial leases. A
distinction can be made between operating lease valuation models
where the flexibility of such a lease is not quantified and

models in which this advantage is quantified. Since none of the operating lease-versus-purchase models turned out to meet all five requirements introduced in Chapter 2, I developed my own operating lease evaluation model. Applying this model, management has to assign probabilities to the various possible future asset lives and to the possible cash inflows the asset generates. According to the model, management should again start from the cash flows to equity and, employing the value-additivity principle, should apply the risk-adjusted discount rate approach. As for the risk-adjusted discount rates to be utilized, I refer to Chapter 4. I demonstrated that an operating lease can be regarded as a combination of a callable loan and an insurance contract, insuring the operating lessee against the cash flow consequences of the leased asset's early obsolescence. Next, in Chapter 6, I gathered empirical evidence concerning the reasons for leasing in real-world situations, based on surveys conducted by various authors and institutions. It appeared that there is a relatively small number of reasons for leasing that were mentioned in almost every survey and that the majority of these motives can be quantified. Besides, it turned out that a few lease valuation methods as developed in literature are in fact being applied in practice. From Chapter 7 we learned that with regard to leasing there are considerable differences between the legal provisions, the corporate income tax systems, and the accounting regulations of various countries, notably in Western Europe. It is sensible to investigate these aspects of leasing because they form part of the information that is required to make the lease-or-purchase decision in any of the countries discussed. Finally, Appendices 1 and 2 summarize the various financial and operating lease valuation models by use of mathematical notation. I find that this approach increases the possibilities for comparing these models, especially if a standardized method of mathematical notation is employed.

APPENDIX 1: FINANCIAL LEASES

This appendix summarizes the financial lease evaluation models discussed in Chapters 3 and 4 utilizing mathematical notation. Appendix 2 summarizes the operating lease evaluation models of Chapter 5. The notation will be as follows:

X_t = net cash inflow (cash revenues less cash expenses) before corporate income taxes at time t expected from operating a capital asset,

I_0 = cash purchase price of the asset to be paid at time t=0,

DP_t = economic and tax depreciation charge at time t,

S_t = salvage value of the asset at time t,

$D_{1,t}$ = loan principal at time t,

$D_{fl,t}$ = financial lease principal at time t, i.e., amount of debt implicit in the financial lease contract at time t,

E_t = equity funds invested in the capital asset at time t,

$R_{1,t}$ = promised loan repayment at time t,

L_t = promised lease payment at time t,

$R_{fl,t}$ = promised financial lease repayment at time t, i.e., principal payment contained in the promised financial lease payment at time t,

t_c = corporate income tax rate,

n = economic and tax life of the asset,

k_1 = interest rate of the loan,

k_{fl} = interest rate implicit in the financial lease,

k_{ol} = interest rate implicit in the operating lease,

k_x = appropriate project hurdle rate assuming perfect capital markets and all-equity financing,

k_o = after-tax weighted average cost of capital of the firm,

k_e = required rate of return on the firm's equity.

Any terms not indicated above will be defined when introduced. Like Schall, I assume that the tax rate on gains and losses from disposing of the asset equals t_c, the tax rate on ordinary firm income (see Schall 1974, p. 1210).

3.4.1 McEachron

McEachron calculates the "discounted cash flows rate of return" of purchasing a capital asset and of leasing that asset. The former rate, r_p^{Mc}, can be computed from:

$$\sum_{t=1}^{n} \{(1-t_c)X_t + t_c DP_t\}(1+r_p^{Mc})^{-t} - I_0 = 0 \qquad (3.4.1.1)$$

The discounted cash flow rate of return of financial leasing, r_{fl}^{Mc}, can be determined as follows:

$$\sum_{t=1}^{n} \{(1-t_c)X_t + t_c L_t - t_c k_1 D_{1,t-1}^{Mc}\}(1+r_{fl}^{Mc})^{-t} - \sum_{t=1}^{n} L_t(1+k_1)^{-t} = 0$$

$$(3.4.1.2)$$

where:

$$D_{1,0}^{Mc} = \sum_{t=1}^{n} L_t(1+k_1)^{-t} \text{ and } D_{1,t}^{Mc} = D_{1,t-1}^{Mc} - (L_t - k_1 D_{1,t-1}^{Mc}) \qquad (3.4.1.3)$$

3.4.2 Vancil

One of the first calculations Vancil performs concerns k_{fl}:

$$I_0 - \sum_{t=1}^{n} L_t(1+k_{fl})^{-t} = 0 \qquad (3.4.2.1)$$

Then Vancil criticizes the lease evaluation model used by, among others, Weston and Brigham in 1966 (see equations 3.4.3.6 and 3.4.3.7 below). Some years later a Swiss author, Bender, shows that starting from this model the difference between PV_p^{WB66} and PV_{fl}^{WB66} can be explained from effects of differences in the amount of funds provided by leasing and by borrowing, effects of differences between the after-tax borrowing rate and the after-tax lease rate, and effects of differences in noninterest tax deductions (see pp. 28-31), or:

$$PV_p^{WB66} - PV_{fl}^{WB66} = \sum_{t=1}^{n} (D_{fl,t-1} - D_{1,t-1}^{W62})\{k_o-(1-t_c)k_1\}(1+k_o)^{-t}$$

$$+ (1-t_c) \sum_{t=1}^{n} D_{fl,t-1}(k_1-k_{fl})(1+k_o)^{-t}$$

$$+ t_c \sum_{t=1}^{n} (DP_t-R_{fl,t})(1+k_o)^{-t} \qquad (3.4.2.2)$$

where:

$$D_{fl,0} = I_0 \text{ and } D_{fl,t} = D_{fl,t-1} - R_{fl,t} \quad \text{where:}$$
$$R_{fl,t} = L_t - k_{fl}D_{fl,t-1} \qquad (3.4.2.3)$$

$$D_{1,0}^{W62} = I_0 \text{ and } D_{1,t}^{W62} = D_{1,t-1}^{W62} - R_{1,t}^{W62} \qquad (3.4.3.1)$$

In equation form Vancil's so-called borrowing opportunity rate method looks like:

$$PV_p^V = I_0 - t_c \sum_{t=1}^{n} DP_t(1+k_o)^{-t} \qquad (3.4.2.4)$$

$$PV_{fl}^V = \sum_{t=1}^{n} L_t(1+k_1)^{-t} - t_c \sum_{t=1}^{n} (L_t-k_1D_{1,t-1}^V)(1+k_o)^{-t} \qquad (3.4.2.5)$$

where:

$$D_{1,0}^V = I_0 \text{ and } D_{1,t}^V = D_{1,t-1}^V - (L_t-k_1D_{1,t-1}^V) \qquad (3.4.2.6)$$

3.4.3 Weston and Brigham

In the successive editions of Managerial Finance, Weston and Brigham develop several lease valuation models, both lease-or-borrow and lease-or-buy models. The latter group of models will be discussed in Section 3.5.1. We now look into the lease-or-borrow models these authors utilize.

3.4.3.1 Weston 1962 (First Edition)

Equation 3.4.3.1 defined the loan Weston employs to finance the cash purchase price of the capital asset. This loan is used in calculating:

$$PV_p^{W62} = \sum_{t=1}^{n} \{R_{1,t}^{W62} + (1-t_c)k_1 D_{1,t-1}^{W62} - t_c DP_t\} (1+k_1)^{-t} \qquad (3.4.3.2)$$

On p. 38, while illustrating Weston's 1962 model with the help of our numerical example, we assumed that the loan raised to finance the asset's purchase price is repaid in two equal installments, each consisting of loan repayment and interest: $R_{1,t}^{W62} + k_1 D_{1,t-1}^{W62}$. Since:

$$\sum_{t=1}^{n} \{R_{1,t}^{W62} + k_1 D_{1,t-1}^{W62}\}(1+k_1)^{-t} = D_{1,0}^{W62} = I_0 \qquad (3.4.3.3)$$

PV_p^{W62} can also be computed as:

$$PV_p^{W62} = I_0 - t_c \sum_{t=1}^{n} (DP_t + k_1 D_{1,t-1}^{W62})(1+k_1)^{-t} \qquad (3.4.3.4)$$

According to Weston the present value of the financial lease agreement can be determined as:

$$PV_{fl}^{W62} = (1-t_c) \sum_{t=1}^{n} L_t (1+k_1)^{-t} \qquad (3.4.3.5)$$

3.4.3.2 Weston and Brigham 1966 (Second Edition)
The 1966 model of Weston and Brigham was already discussed in 3.4.2 as this type of lease valuation model has been criticized by Vancil. In the 1966 edition of Managerial Finance, Weston and Brigham hold that:

$$PV_p^{WB66} = \sum_{t=1}^{n} \{R_{1,t}^{W62} + (1-t_c)k_1 D_{1,t-1}^{W62} - t_c DP_t\}(1+k_o)^{-t} \qquad (3.4.3.6)$$

$$PV_{fl}^{WB66} = (1-t_c) \sum_{t=1}^{n} L_t (1+k_o)^{-t} \qquad (3.4.3.7)$$

3.4.3.3 Weston and Brigham 1969 (Third Edition)
The authors now determine the present value of purchasing as:

$$PV_p^{WB69} = \sum_{t=1}^{n} \{R_{1,t}^{W62} + (1-t_c)k_1 D_{1,t-1}^{W62} - t_c DP_t\}\{1+(1-t_c)k_1\}^{-t} \qquad (3.4.3.8)$$

On pp. 38-39 I demonstrated that since:

$$\sum_{t=1}^{n} \{R_{1,t}^{W62} + (1-t_c)k_1 D_{1,t-1}^{W62}\}\{1+(1-t_c)k_1\}^{-t} = D_{1,0}^{W62} = I_0 \qquad (3.4.3.9)$$

this present value can also be computed from:

$$PV_p^{WB69} = I_0 - t_c \sum_{t=1}^{n} DP_t\{1+(1-t_c)k_1\}^{-t} \qquad (3.4.3.10)$$

The present value of the financial lease is calculated from:

$$PV_{fl}^{WB69} = (1-t_c) \sum_{t=1}^{n} L_t\{1+(1-t_c)k_1\}^{-t} \qquad (3.4.3.11)$$

3.4.3.4 Weston and Brigham 1972 (Fourth Edition)

In the 1972 edition of their textbook, Weston and Brigham in essence apply the lease evaluation procedure they introduced in the 1969 edition.

3.4.3.5 Weston and Brigham 1975 (Fifth Edition)

As observed on p. 47, the lease-or-borrow model of the fifth edition of Managerial Finance equals the one the authors employ in the second edition of 1966.

3.4.3.6 Weston and Brigham 1975 Appendix (Fifth Edition)

The 1975 appendix model differs from the model Weston and Brigham apply in their chapter on leasing. In that appendix the authors introduce the "Net Advantage to Lease," i.e., the difference between PV_p^{WB75a} and PV_{fl}^{WB75a}, to choose between purchasing and financial leasing. This difference can be expressed as:

$$PV_p^{WB75a} - PV_{fl}^{WB75a} = I_0 - \sum_{t=1}^{n} L_t(1+k_1)^{-t}$$

$$- t_c \sum_{t=1}^{n} (DP_t + k_1 D_{1,t-1}^{WB75a} - L_t)\{1+(1-t_c)k_1\}^{-t}$$

$$(3.4.3.12)$$

where:

$$D_{1,0}^{WB75a} = I_0 \text{ and } D_{1,t}^{WB75a} = D_{1,t-1}^{WB75a} - R_{1,t}^{WB75a} \qquad (3.4.3.13)$$

Weston and Brigham argue that "if NAL is positive, the lease should be accepted, but the loan should be used if NAL is negative" (Weston and Brigham 1975, p. 492).

3.4.4 Bower, Herringer, and Williamson

These writers also use the difference between the present value of purchasing, PV_p^{BHW}, and the present value of financial leasing, PV_{fl}^{BHW}, to choose between the alternatives:

$$PV_p^{BHW} - PV_{fl}^{BHW} = I_0 - \sum_{t=1}^{n} L_t(1+k_1)^{-t} - t_c \sum_{t=1}^{n} (DP_t + k_1 D_{1,t-1}^{BHW} - L_t)(1+k_o)^{-t}$$
$$(3.4.4.1)$$

where:

$$R_{1,t}^{BHW} + k_1 D_{1,t-1}^{BHW} = L_t \times \frac{I_0}{\sum\limits_{t=1}^{n} L_t(1+k_1)^{-t}} \qquad (3.4.4.2)$$

$$D_{1,0}^{BHW} = I_0 \text{ and } D_{1,t}^{BHW} = D_{1,t-1}^{BHW} - R_{1,t}^{BHW} \qquad (3.4.4.3)$$

Bower, Herringer, and Williamson call the difference between I_0 and $\sum_{t=1}^{n} L_t(1+k_1)^{-t}$ the financial advantage of the lease, whereas the remaining part of 3.4.4.1 is the lease's operating advantage.

3.4.5 Bower

To make a long story short:

$$PV_p^B = I_0 - t_c \sum_{t=1}^{n} DP_t(1+k)^{-t} \qquad (3.4.5.1)$$

$$PV_{fl}^B = \sum_{t=1}^{n} L_t(1+k_1)^{-t} - t_c \sum_{t=1}^{n} (L_t - k_1 D_{1,t-1}^{Mc})(1+k)^{-t} \qquad (3.4.5.2)$$

Bower employs McEachron's loan to finance the asset's purchase price. He then performs a sensitivity analysis using various rates to determine the present value of the tax savings. In his illustrative example, k ranges from 0% up to 14%, inclusive.

3.4.6 Gordon

Gordon calculates the net present value of financial leasing and of purchasing, taking into consideration the net cash inflows expected from asset operation:

$$NPV_{fl}^G = (1-t_c) \sum_{t=1}^{n} X_t(1+k_x)^{-t} - (1-t_c) \sum_{t=1}^{n} L_t(1+k_1)^{-t} \qquad (3.4.6.1)$$

$$NPV_p^G = (1-t_c) \sum_{t=1}^{n} X_t(1+k_x)^{-t} - \sum_{t=1}^{n} \{R_{1,t}^G + (1-t_c)k_1 D_{1,t-1}^G - t_c DP_t\}(1+k_1)^{-t}$$
$$(3.4.6.2)$$

where:

$$R_{1,t}^G + k_1 D_{1,t-1}^G = \frac{I_0}{\displaystyle\sum_{t=1}^{n}(1+k_1)^{-t}} \qquad (3.4.6.3)$$

$$D_{1,0}^G = I_0 \text{ and } D_{1,t}^G = D_{1,t-1}^G - R_{1,t}^G \qquad (3.4.6.4)$$

3.4.7 Myers, Dill, and Bautista

In order to determine the value of the lease, these authors start from the following equation (Myers, Dill, and Bautista 1976, p. 802):

$$PV_p^{MDB} - PV_{fl}^{MDB} = I_0 - \sum_{t=1}^{n} \{(1-t_c)L_t + t_c DP_t + t_c k_1 D_{1,t-1}^{MDB}\}(1+k_1)^{-t}$$
$$(3.4.7.1)$$

Since $D_{1,t}^{MDB}$ would depend on the value of the lease, Myers, Dill, and Bautista simplify the above equation obtaining (p. 805):

$$PV_p^{MDB} - PV_{fl}^{MDB} = I_0 - \sum_{t=1}^{n} \{(1-t_c)L_t + t_c DP_t\}\{1+(1-t_c)k_1\}^{-t}$$

(3.4.7.2)

If the value of the lease is positive, the firm's management should lease the asset, but if this value turns out to be negative purchasing ought to be preferred.

3.4.8 Beckman and Joosen

The first evaluation method Beckman and Joosen apply is comparing the before-tax rates of leasing and of borrowing, so k_{fl} (calculated from equation 3.4.2.1) is set against k_1. Then they compare $(1-t_c)k_{fl}$ with $(1-t_c)k_1$, and finally the authors calculate the present value of the alternatives. The present value of the purchase alternative is:

$$PV_p^{BJ} = \sum_{t=1}^{n} \{R_{1,t}^{BJ} + (1-t_c)k_1 D_{1,t-1}^{BJ}\}\{1+(1-t_c)k_1\}^{-t} = I_0 \qquad (3.4.8.1)$$

Beckman and Joosen assume that the loan used to finance the asset's purchase price is to be repaid in a lump-sum at the end of the loan term. Consequently:

$$D_{1,0}^{BJ} = D_{1,t}^{BJ} = R_{1,n}^{BJ} = I_0 \qquad (3.4.8.2)$$

The present value of the financial lease is computed as:

$$PV_{fl}^{BJ} = \sum_{t=1}^{n} \{L_t - t_c k_{fl} D_{fl,t-1}\}\{1+(1-t_c)k_1\}^{-t} \qquad (3.4.8.3)$$

3.5.1 Weston and Brigham

After having expressed in mathematical form the lease-or-borrow models of section 3.4, I shall now go into the lease-or-buy models of 3.5 starting with the various Weston and Brigham lease-or-buy methods.

3.5.1.1 Weston 1962 Appendix (First Edition)

In his appendix model Weston computes the differences between the present values of purchasing and of financial leasing:

$$PV_p^{W62a} - PV_{fl}^{W62a} = I_0 - \sum_{t=1}^{n} \{(1-t_c)L_t + t_c DP_t\}(1+k_o)^{-t} \qquad (3.5.1.1)$$

3.5.1.2 Weston and Brigham 1978 (Sixth Edition)

In this edition Weston and Brigham compute the net present value of the alternatives incorporating the net cash inflows in their analysis:

$$NPV_{fl}^{WB78} = (1-t_c) \sum_{t=1}^{n} (X_t - L_t)(1+k_o)^{-t} \qquad (3.5.1.2)$$

$$NPV_p^{WB78} = \sum_{t=1}^{n} \{(1-t_c)X_t + t_c DP_t\}(1+k_o)^{-t} - I_0 \qquad (3.5.1.3)$$

3.5.1.3 Weston and Brigham 1981 (Seventh Edition)

Now the two authors are again ignoring the cash inflow series expected to be generated by the asset; again they calculate the present value of purchasing and of financial leasing:

$$PV_p^{WB81} = I_0 - t_c \sum_{t=1}^{n} DP_t(1+k_o)^{-t} \qquad (3.5.1.4)$$

$$PV_{fl}^{WB81} = (1-t_c) \sum_{t=1}^{n} L_t(1+k_o)^{-t} \qquad (3.5.1.5)$$

3.5.2 Johnson and Lewellen: Article, Comments, and Reply

In the following I shall analyze the lease-or-buy model of Johnson and Lewellen and some comments on their article.

3.5.2.1 Johnson and Lewellen

Like Gordon and Weston and Brigham in 1978, Johnson and Lewellen compute the net present value of purchasing and of financial leasing taking into account the net cash inflows:

$$NPV_{fl}^{JL} = (1-t_c) \sum_{t=1}^{n} X_t (1+k_o)^{-t} - (1-t_c) \sum_{t=1}^{n} L_t \{1+(1-t_c)k_1\}^{-t}$$

$$(3.5.2.1)$$

$$NPV_p^{JL} =$$

$$NPV_p^{WB78} = \sum_{t=1}^{n} \{(1-t_c)X_t + t_c DP_t\}(1+k_o)^{-t} - I_0 \qquad (3.5.1.3)$$

3.5.2.3 Lusztig

In the first instance Lusztig holds that the net present value of purchasing and of financial leasing ought to be calculated as:

$$NPV_p^L = (1-t_c) \sum_{t=1}^{n} X_t (1+k_o)^{-t} + t_c \sum_{t=1}^{n} DP_t \{1+(1-t_c)k_1\}^{-t} - I_0$$

$$(3.5.2.2)$$

$$NPV_{fl}^L = (1-t_c) \sum_{t=1}^{n} X_t(1+k_o)^{-t} - (1-t_c) \sum_{t=1}^{n} (L_t - k_{fl}D_{fl,t-1})\{1+(1-t_c)k_1\}^{-t}$$

$$(3.5.2.3)$$

However, the author then argues that there must be a mistake somewhere, because NPV_{fl}^L would always exceed NPV_p^L. As can readily be proven, Lusztig is correct. Subtracting equation 3.5.2.2 from equation 3.5.2.3 yields:

$$NPV_{fl}^L - NPV_p^L = I_0 - \sum_{t=1}^{n} \{t_c DP_t + (1-t_c)(L_t - k_{fl}D_{fl,t-1})\}\{1+(1-t_c)k_1\}$$

$$(3.5.2.4)$$

The result of this equation must always be positive, since:

$$I_0 = t_c \sum_{t=1}^{n} DP_t + (1-t_c) \sum_{t=1}^{n} (L_t - k_{fl}D_{fl,t-1}) \qquad (3.5.2.5)$$

which equation is based upon:

$$I_0 = \sum_{t=1}^{n} DP_t = \sum_{t=1}^{n} (L_t - k_{fl}D_{fl,t-1}) \qquad (3.5.2.6)$$

3.5.2.4 Bierman

Bierman introduces four lease evaluation models summarized below.

Bierman 1

$$NPV_{fl}^{B1} = (1-t_c) \sum_{t=1}^{n} (X_t - L_t)\{1+(1-t_c)k_1\}^{-t} \qquad (3.5.2.7)$$

$$NPV_p^{B1} = \sum_{t=1}^{n} \{(1-t_c)X_t + t_c DP_t\}\{1+(1-t_c)k_1\}^{-t} - I_0 \qquad (3.5.2.8)$$

Bierman 2

$$NPV_{fl}^{B2} = (1-t_c) \sum_{t=1}^{n} X_t \{1+(1-t_c)k_1\}^{-t} - \sum_{t=1}^{n} L_t(1+k_1)^{-t}$$

$$+ t_c \sum_{t=1}^{n} (L_t - k_1 D_{1,t-1}^{Mc})\{1+(1-t_c)k_1\}^{-t} \qquad (3.5.2.9)$$

$$NPV_p^{B2} =$$

$$NPV_p^{B1} = \sum_{t=1}^{n} \{(1-t_c)X_t + t_c DP_t\}\{1+(1-t_c)k_1\}^{-t} - I_0 \qquad (3.5.2.8)$$

Bierman 3

$$NPV_{fl}^{B3} =$$

$$NPV_{fl}^{B1} = (1-t_c) \sum_{t=1}^{n} (X_t - L_t)\{1+(1-t_c)k_1\}^{-t} \qquad (3.5.2.7)$$

$$NPV_p^{B3} = \sum_{t=1}^{n} \{(1-t_c)X_t + t_c DP_t - R_{1,t}^{B3} - (1-t_c)k_1 D_{1,t-1}^{B3}\}\{1+(1-t_c)k_1\}^{-t}$$

$$(3.5.2.10)$$

where:

$$D_{1,0}^{B3} = I_0 \quad \text{and} \quad D_{1,t}^{B3} = D_{1,t-1}^{B3} - R_{1,t}^{B3} \qquad (3.5.2.11)$$

Bierman 4

$$PV^{B4}_{fl} = (1-t_c) \sum_{t=1}^{n} L_t \{1+(1-t_c)k_1\}^{-t} \qquad (3.5.2.12)$$

$$PV^{B4}_{p} = I_0 - t_c \sum_{t=1}^{n} DP_t \{1+(1-t_c)k_1\}^{-t} \qquad (3.5.2.13)$$

Bierman argues that his four models "are equivalent to each other" (Bierman 1973, p. 1019). This can easily be proven by calculating the difference between the net present values of all four alternatives:

$$NPV^{B1}_{fl} - NPV^{B1}_{p} = I_0 - \sum_{t=1}^{n} \{(1-t_c)L_t + t_cDP_t\}\{1+(1-t_c)k_1\}^{-t}$$
$$(3.5.2.14)$$

$$NPV^{B2}_{fl} - NPV^{B2}_{p} = I_0 - \sum_{t=1}^{n} L_t(1+k_1)^{-t}$$
$$t_c \sum_{t=1}^{n} (DP_t - L_t + k_1 D^{Mc}_{1,t-1})\{1+(1-t_c)k_1\}^{-t}$$
$$(3.5.2.15)$$

$$NPV^{B3}_{fl} - NPV^{B3}_{p}$$

$$= \sum_{t=1}^{n} \{R^{B3}_{1,t}+(1-t_c)k_1D^{B3}_{1,t-1}-(1-t_c)L_t-t_cDP_t\} \{1+(1-t_c)k_1\}^{-t}$$
$$(3.5.2.16)$$

$$PV^{B4}_{p} - PV^{B4}_{fl} = I_0 - \sum_{t=1}^{n} \{(1-t_c)L_t + t_cDP_t\}\{1+(1-t_c)k_1\}^{-t}$$
$$(3.5.2.17)$$

Comparing equations 3.5.2.14 and 3.5.2.17, we find that $NPV^{B1}_{fl} - NPV^{B1}_{p} = PV^{B4}_{p} - PV^{B4}_{fl}$. Furthermore, since:

$$\sum_{t=1}^{n} \{R^{B3}_{1,t} + (1-t_c)k_1D^{B3}_{1,t-1}\}\{1+(1-t_c)k_1\}^{-t} = I_0 \qquad (3.5.2.18)$$

equation 3.5.2.16 can be rewritten as:

$$NPV^{B3}_{fl} - NPV^{B3}_{p} = I_0 - \sum_{t=1}^{n} \{(1-t_c)L_t + t_cDP_t\}\{1+(1-t_c)k_1\}^{-t}$$
$$(3.5.2.19)$$

Consequently, $NPV_{fl}^{B3} - NPV_p^{B3} = NPV_{fl}^{B1} - NPV_p^{B1} = PV_p^{B4} - PV_{fl}^{B4}$. Moreover, as Bower has shown that (Bower 1973, pp. 33-34):

$$\sum_{t=1}^{n} L_t(1+k_1)^{-t} + t_c \sum_{t=1}^{n} k_1 D_{1,t-1}^{Mc} \{1+(1-t_c)k_1\}^{-t} = \sum_{t=1}^{n} L_t \{1+(1-t_c)k_1\}^{-t}$$

$$(3.5.2.20)$$

equation 3.5.2.15 can also be written as:

$$NPV_{fl}^{B2} - NPV_p^{B2} = I_0 - \sum_{t=1}^{n} \{(1-t_c)L_t + t_c DP_t\}\{1+(1-t_c)k_1\}^{-t}$$

$$(3.5.2.21)$$

Therefore, $NPV_{fl}^{B2} - NPV_p^{B2} = NPV_{fl}^{B3} - NPV_p^{B3} = NPV_{fl}^{B1} - NPV_p^{B1} = PV_p^{B4} - PV_{fl}^{B4}$. In fact the four Bierman models are not only equivalent to each other but also equivalent to the lease-or-borrow model Weston and Brigham introduce in the third edition of _Managerial Finance_. This can be demonstrated in the following way. Subtracting equation 3.4.3.11 from 3.4.3.10 (see p. 237) and rearranging terms we find that:

$$PV_p^{WB69} - PV_{fl}^{WB69} = I_0 - \sum_{t=1}^{n} \{(1-t_c)L_t + t_c DP_t\}\{1+(1-t_c)k_1\}^{-t}$$

$$(3.5.2.22)$$

and consequently that: $PV_p^{WB69} - PV_{fl}^{WB69} = NPV_{fl}^{B1} - NPV_p^{B1} =$

$NPV_{fl}^{B2} - NPV_p^{B2} = NPV_{fl}^{B3} - NPV_p^{B3} = PV_p^{B4} - PV_{fl}^{B4}$.

3.5.3 _Vial_

Like Weston and Brigham in 1978 Vial computes the net present values of the alternatives:

$$NPV_{fl}^{V} = \sum_{t=1}^{n} \{(1-t_c)X_t + t_c DP_t\}(1+k_0)^{-t}$$

$$- \sum_{t=1}^{n} \{(1-t_c)L_t + t_c DP_t\} \{1+(1-t_c)k_1\}^{-t} \qquad (3.5.3.1)$$

$$NPV_p^V =$$

$$NPV_p^{WB78} = \sum_{t=1}^{n} \{(1-t_c)X_t + t_c DP_t\}(1+k_o)^{-t} - I_0 \qquad (3.5.1.3)$$

3.5.4 Krumbholz and Streitferdt

These German authors assume that 70% of the asset's cash purchase price is financed with a loan and the remaining 30% with equity funds. They capitalize the relevant cash flows at k_e:

$$PV_p^{KS} = I_0 - D_{1,0}^{KS} + \sum_{t=1}^{n} \{R_{1,t}^{KS} + (1-t_c)k_1 D_{1,t-1}^{KS} - t_c DP_t\}(1+k_e)^{-t} \qquad (3.5.4.1)$$

where:

$$D_{1,0}^{KS} = 0.7\ I_0 \quad \text{and} \quad D_{1,t}^{KS} = D_{1,t-1}^{KS} - R_{1,t}^{KS} \qquad (3.5.4.2)$$

$$PV_{fl}^{KS} = (1-t_c) \sum_{t=1}^{n} L_t (1+k_e)^{-t} \qquad (3.5.4.3)$$

3.5.5 Spittler

Just like his countrymen Krumbholz and Streitferdt, Spittler assumes that 70% of the purchase price of the capital asset is financed with debt and 30% with equity. He also utilizes k_e for discounting purposes. Unlike these two authors, however, Spittler calculates the net present values of financial leasing and of purchasing incorporating the cash inflow series:

$$NPV_{fl}^S = (1-t_c) \sum_{t=1}^{n} (X_t - L_t)(1+k_e)^{-t} \qquad (3.5.5.1)$$

$$NPV_p^S = \sum_{t=1}^{n} \{(1-t_c)(X_t - DP_t - k_1 D_{1,t-1}^S) - k_e E_{t-1}^S\}(1+k_e)^{-t} \qquad (3.5.5.2)$$

where:

$$D_{1,t}^S = 0.7\ (I_0 - \sum_{i=1}^{t} DP_i) \qquad (3.5.5.3)$$

$$E_t^S = 0.3 \ (I_0 - \sum_{i=1}^{t} DP_i) \tag{3.5.5.4}$$

In order to determine $D_{1,t}^S$ and E_t^S Spittler takes the sum of the depreciation amounts DP_i from I_0 and multiplies these amounts by 70% and 30%, respectively.

3.5.6 Haley and Schall

As observed on p. 108, Haley and Schall capitalize the expected values of all relevant cash flows. In the following equations, I shall place a bar over these cash flows indicating that their expected values are involved. Note that I already defined X_t as an expected value. Also, I shall use the same capitalization rates as Haley and Schall.

$$NPV_{fl}^{HS} = (1-t_c) \sum_{t=1}^{n} X_t (1+k_X)^{-t} - (1-t_c) \sum_{t=1}^{n} \overline{L}_t (1+k_L)^{-t} \tag{3.5.6.1}$$

$$NPV_p^{HS} = \sum_{t=1}^{n} \{(1-t_c)X_t + t_c \overline{DP}_t\}(1+k_G)^{-t} + t_c \sum_{t=1}^{n} k_1 \overline{D}_{1,t-1}^{HS}(1+k_R)^{-t} - I_0 \tag{3.5.6.2}$$

where:

$$\overline{D}_{1,0}^{HS} = \overline{D}_{1,t}^{HS} = 0.8 \ I_0 \tag{3.5.6.3}$$

3.5.7 Schall and Haley

Again the authors compute the net present values of financial leasing and purchasing, but (presumably) they do not utilize the expected values of all the relevant cash flows to arrive at these net present values. For example, the authors (probably) capitalize the promised lease payments rather than their expected values. Furthermore, they employ two capitalization rates only.

$$NPV_{fl}^{SH} = (1-t_c) \sum_{t=1}^{n} (X_t - L_t)(1+k_L)^{-t} \tag{3.5.7.1}$$

When illustrating this net present value calculation on p. 112, I assumed that Schall and Haley's k_L equals our k_e (see also pp.

113-114). As for purchasing:

$$NPV_p^{SH} =$$

$$NPV_p^{WB78} = \sum_{t=1}^{n} \{(1-t_c)X_t + t_cDP_t\}(1+k_o)^{-t} - I_0 \qquad (3.5.1.3)$$

3.5.8 Theunissen

Theunissen does not take into consideration the cash inflows generated by the capital asset. In his illustrative example, the author assumes that 80% of the asset's purchase price is financed with debt and 20% with equity:

$$PV_p^T = I_0 - D_{1,0}^T + \sum_{t=1}^{n} (R_{1,t}^T + (1-t_c)k_1D_{1,t-1}^T - t_cDP_t\}\{1+(1-t_c)k_1\}^{-t}$$
$$(3.5.8.1)$$

where:

$$D_{1,0}^T = 0.8 \, I_0 \quad \text{and} \quad D_{1,t}^T = D_{1,t-1}^T - R_{1,t}^T \qquad (3.5.8.2)$$

As shown on p. 117, this equation can be simplified to the present value of purchasing as calculated according to Weston and Brigham 1969:

$$PV_p^T =$$

$$PV_p^{WB69} = I_0 - t_c \sum_{t=1}^{n} DP_t\{1+(1-t_c)k_1\}^{-t} \qquad (3.4.3.10)$$

As for the financial lease agreement:

$$PV_{fl}^T =$$

$$PV_{fl}^{WB69} = (1-t_c) \sum_{t=1}^{n} L_t\{1+(1-t_c)k_1\}^{-t} \qquad (3.4.3.11)$$

As can easily be seen from the above, utilizing mathematical
notation in order to represent the various financial lease evaluation models discussed in Chapter 3 is an appropriate method to
provide a summary of these models. Nonetheless, using mathematics
results in a rather comprehensive survey. I shall therefore summarize this survey employing a standardized method of notation.
According to this method, the difference between the present
value of purchasing and the present value of leasing, or the
difference between the net present value of leasing and the net
present value of purchasing, is explained from:
. the present value of the before-tax cash flows of purchasing,
. the present value of the before-tax cash flows of leasing,
. the present value of the differences in tax savings resulting
  from both alternatives.
I have found that this method of standardization improves the
comparability of the various lease-or-borrow and lease-or-buy
models. Any differences between the first two present values may
be relevant if a company is in a non-taxpaying position. Myers,
Dill, and Bautista discuss such a situation when analyzing the
lease contract Anaconda considered concluding in 1973 (Myers,
Dill, and Bautista 1976, p. 807). Although the first two present
values are based upon cash flows before taxes, the corporate
income tax rate may still be of relevance. For example, tax
effects might have played a part in determining the size and the
time pattern of the lease payments (see Myers, Dill, and Bautista
1976, pp. 808-809). To conclude, by means of the third present
value the differences between the tax savings resulting from
depreciation plus any interest payments in the case of purchasing
and the tax savings due to the tax deductibility of the lease
payments are quantified.

There are, however, some financial lease evaluation models
that cannot readily be represented with the help of this standardized method of notation, e.g., the models of McEachron, of
Haley and Schall, and of Schall and Haley. This is because these
authors capitalize the cash inflows generated in the case of
purchasing at a different rate than the cash inflows arising from
operating the leased capital asset. I therefore added two present

values to the following equations: the present value of the
after-tax cash inflows when purchasing and the present value of
the after-tax cash inflows when leasing:

McEachron

$$I_0 - \sum_{t=1}^{n} L_t(1+k_1)^{-t} - t_c\{\sum_{t=1}^{n} DP_t(1+r_p^{Mc})^{-t} + \sum_{t=1}^{n} (k_1 D_{1,t-1}^{Mc} - L_t)(1+r_{f1}^{Mc})\}^{-t}$$

$$- (1-t_c)\{\sum_{t=1}^{n} X_t(1+r_p^{Mc})^{-t} - \sum_{t=1}^{n} X_t(1+r_{f1}^{Mc})^{-t}\} = 0 \qquad (3.4.1.4)$$

Haley and Schall

$$NPV_{f1}^{HS} - NPV_p^{HS} = I_0 - \sum_{t=1}^{n} \overline{L_t}(1+k_L)^{-t} - t_c\{\sum_{t=1}^{n} \overline{DP_t}(1+k_G)^{-t}$$

$$+ \sum_{t=1}^{n} k_1 \overline{D_{1,t-1}^{HS}}(1+k_R)^{-t} - \sum_{t=1}^{n} \overline{L_t}(1+k_L)^{-t}\}$$

$$- (1-t_c)\{\sum_{t=1}^{n} X_t(1+k_G)^{-t} - \sum_{t=1}^{n} X_t(1+k_X)^{-t}\}$$

$$\qquad (3.5.6.4)$$

Schall and Haley

$$NPV_{f1}^{SH} - NPV_p^{SH} = I_0 - \sum_{t=1}^{n} L_t(1+k_L)^{-t} - t_c\{\sum_{t=1}^{n} DP_t(1+k_o)^{-t}$$

$$- \sum_{t=1}^{n} L_t(1+k_L)^{-t}\} - (1-t_c)\{\sum_{t=1}^{n} X_t(1+k_o)^{-t}$$

$$- \sum_{t=1}^{n} X_t(1+k_L)^{-t}\} \qquad (3.5.7.2)$$

The models developed for valuing financial leases that can be
represented by means of this standardized notation method are
represented below:

Vancil

$$PV_p^V - PV_{f1}^V = I_0 - \sum_{t=1}^{n} L_t(1+k_1)^{-t} - t_c \sum_{t=1}^{n} (DP_t + k_1 D_{1,t-1}^V - L_t)(1+k_o)^{-t}$$

$$\qquad (3.4.2.7)$$

Weston 1962

$$PV_p^{W62} - PV_{fl}^{W62} = I_0 - \sum_{t=1}^{n} L_t(1+k_1)^{-t} - t_c \sum_{t=1}^{n} (DP_t + k_1 D_{1,t-1}^{W62} - L_t)(1+k_1)^{-t}$$

$$(3.4.3.14)$$

Weston and Brigham 1966

$$PV_p^{WB66} - PV_{fl}^{WB66} = \sum_{t=1}^{n} (R_{1,t}^{W62} + k_1 D_{1,t-1}^{W62})(1+k_o)^{-t} - \sum_{t=1}^{n} L_t(1+k_o)^{-t}$$

$$- t_c \sum_{t=1}^{n} (DP_t + k_1 D_{1,t-1}^{W62} - L_t)(1+k_o)^{-t}$$

$$(3.4.3.15)$$

Weston and Brigham 1969

$$PV_p^{WB69} - PV_{fl}^{WB69} = I_0 - \sum_{t=1}^{n} L_t\{1+(1-t_c)k_1\}^{-t} - t_c \sum_{t=1}^{n} (DP_t - L_t)\{1+(1-t_c)k_1\}^{-t}$$

$$(3.4.3.16)$$

Weston and Brigham 1975 Appendix

$$PV_p^{WB75a} - PV_{fl}^{WB75a} = I_0 - \sum_{t=1}^{n} L_t(1+k_1)^{-t}$$

$$- t_c \sum_{t=1}^{n} (DP_t + k_1 D_{1,t-1}^{WB75a} - L_t)\{1+(1-t_c)k_1\}^{-t}$$

$$(3.4.3.12)$$

Bower, Herringer, and Williamson

$$PV_p^{BHW} - PV_{fl}^{BHW} = I_0 - \sum_{t=1}^{n} L_t(1+k_1)^{-t} - t_c \sum_{t=1}^{n} (DP_t + k_1 D_{1,t-1}^{BHW} - L_t)(1+k_o)^{-t}$$

$$(3.4.4.1)$$

Bower

$$PV_p^{B} - PV_{fl}^{B} = I_0 - \sum_{t=1}^{n} L_t(1+k_1)^{-t} - t_c \sum_{t=1}^{n} (DP_t + k_1 D_{1,t-1}^{Mc} - L_t)(1+k)^{-t}$$

$$(3.4.5.3)$$

Gordon

$$NPV_{fl}^G - NPV_p^G = \sum_{t=1}^{n} (R_{1,t}^G + k_1 D_{1,t-1}^G)(1+k_1)^{-t} - \sum_{t=1}^{n} L_t(1+k_1)^{-t}$$
$$- t_c \sum_{t=1}^{n} (DP_t + k_1 D_{1,t-1}^G - L_t)(1+k_1)^{-t} \qquad (3.4.6.5)$$

This equation can be simplified as:

$$NPV_{fl}^G - NPV_p^G = I_0 - \sum_{t=1}^{n} L_t(1+k_1)^{-t} - t_c \sum_{t=1}^{n} (DP_t + k_1 D_{1,t-1}^G - L_t)(1+k_1)^{-t}$$
$$(3.4.6.6)$$

Myers, Dill, and Bautista

As explained on p. 65, if $\lambda = 1$ then $PV_p^{MDB} - PV_{fl}^{MDB} =$

$$PV_p^{WB69} - PV_{fl}^{WB69} = I_0 - \sum_{t=1}^{n} L_t \{1+(1-t_c)k_1\}^{-t}$$
$$- t_c \sum_{t=1}^{n} (DP_t - L_t)\{1+(1-t_c)k_1\}^{-t} \qquad (3.4.3.16)$$

Beckman and Joosen

$$PV_p^{BJ} - PV_{fl}^{BJ} = \sum_{t=1}^{n} (R_{1,t}^{BJ} + k_1 D_{1,t-1}^{BJ})\{1+(1-t_c)k_1\}^{-t} - \sum_{t=1}^{n} L_t \{1+(1-t_c)k_1\}^{-t}$$
$$- t_c \sum_{t=1}^{n} (k_1 D_{1,t-1}^{BJ} - k_{fl} D_{fl,t-1})\{1+(1-t_c)k_1\}^{-t}$$
$$(3.4.8.4)$$

Alternatively:

$$PV_p^{BJ} - PV_{fl}^{BJ} = I_0 - \sum_{t=1}^{n} L_t \{1+(1-t_c)k_1\}^{-t} + t_c \sum_{t=1}^{n} k_{fl} D_{fl,t-1} \{1+(1-t_c)k_1\}^{-t}$$
$$(3.4.8.5)$$

Weston 1962 Appendix

$$PV_p^{W62a} - PV_{fl}^{W62a} = I_0 - \sum_{t=1}^{n} L_t(1+k_o)^{-t} - t_c \sum_{t=1}^{n} (DP_t - L_t)(1+k_o)^{-t}$$
$$(3.5.1.6)$$

Weston and Brigham 1978

$$NPV_{fl}^{WB78} - NPV_p^{WB78} =$$

$$PV_p^{W62a} - PV_{fl}^{W62a} = I_0 - \sum_{t=1}^{n} L_t(1+k_o)^{-t} - t_c \sum_{t=1}^{n} (DP_t - L_t)(1+k_o)^{-t}$$

$$(3.5.1.6)$$

Weston and Brigham 1981

$$PV_p^{WB81} - PV_{fl}^{WB81} =$$

$$PV_p^{W62a} - PV_{fl}^{WB62a} = I_0 - \sum_{t=1}^{n} L_t(1+k_o)^{-t} - t_c \sum_{t=1}^{n} (DP_t - L_t)(1+k_o)^{-t}$$

$$(3.5.1.6)$$

Johnson and Lewellen

$$NPV_{fl}^{JL} - NPV_p^{JL} = I_0 - \sum_{t=1}^{n} L_t\{1+(1-t_c)k_1\}^{-t}$$

$$- t_c[\sum_{t=1}^{n} DP_t(1+k_o)^{-t} - \sum_{t=1}^{n} L_t\{1+(1-t_c)k_1\}^{-t}]$$

$$(3.5.2.23)$$

Lusztig

$$NPV_{fl}^{L} - NPV_p^{L} = I_0 - \sum_{t=1}^{n} (L_t - k_{fl}D_{fl,t-1})\{1+(1-t_c)k_1\}^{-t}$$

$$- t_c \sum_{t=1}^{n} (DP_t + k_{fl}D_{fl,t-1} - L_t)\{1+(1-t_c)k_1\}^{-t}$$

$$(3.5.2.24)$$

Bierman

$$NPV_{fl}^{B1} - NPV_p^{B1} = NPV_{fl}^{B2} - NPV_p^{B2} = NPV_{fl}^{B3} - NPV_p^{B3} = PV_p^{B4} - PV_{fl}^{B4} =$$

$$PV_p^{WB69} - PV_{fl}^{WB69} = I_0 - \sum_{t=1}^{n} L_t\{1+(1-t_c)k_1\}^{-t} - t_c \sum_{t=1}^{n} (DP_t - L_t)\{1+(1-t_c)k_1\}^{-t}$$

$$(3.4.3.16)$$

Vial

$$NPV_{fl}^{V} - NPV_{p}^{V} =$$

$$PV_{p}^{WB69} - PV_{fl}^{WB69} = I_0 - \sum_{t=1}^{n} L_t \{1+(1-t_c)k_1\}^{-t} - t_c \sum_{t=1}^{n} (DP_t - L_t)\{1+(1-t_c)k_1\}^{-}$$

$$(3.4.3.16)$$

Krumbholz and Streitferdt

$$PV_{p}^{KS} - PV_{fl}^{KS} = I_0 - D_{1,0}^{KS} + \sum_{t=1}^{n} (R_{1,t}^{KS} + k_1 D_{1,t-1}^{KS})(1+k_e)^{-t} - \sum_{t=1}^{n} L_t (1+k_e)^{-t}$$

$$- t_c \sum_{t=1}^{n} (DP_t + k_1 D_{1,t-1}^{KS} - L_t)(1+k_e)^{-t} \qquad (3.5.4.4)$$

Spittler

$$NPV_{fl}^{Sp} - NPV_{p}^{Sp} = \sum_{t=1}^{n} (DP_t + k_1 D_{1,t-1}^{S} + k_e E_{t-1}^{S})(1+k_e)^{-t} - \sum_{t=1}^{n} L_t (1+k_e)^{-t}$$

$$- t_c \sum_{t=1}^{n} (DP_t + k_1 D_{1,t-1}^{S} - L_t)(1+k_e)^{-t} \qquad (3.5.5.5)$$

Theunissen

$$PV_{p}^{T} - PV_{fl}^{T} = I_0 - D_{1,0}^{T} + \sum_{t=1}^{n} (R_{1,t}^{T} + k_1 D_{1,t-1}^{T})\{1+(1-t_c)k_1\}^{-t}$$

$$- \sum_{t=1}^{n} L_t \{1+(1-t_c)k_1\}^{-t} - t_c \sum_{t=1}^{n} (DP_t + k_1 D_{1,t-1}^{T} - L_t)\{1+(1-t_c)k_1\}^{-t}$$

$$(3.5.8.3)$$

On p. 248 it was explained that:

$$PV_{p}^{T} - PV_{fl}^{T} =$$

$$PV_{p}^{WB69} - PV_{fl}^{WB69} = I_0 - \sum_{t=1}^{n} L_t \{1+(1-t_c)k_1\}^{-t} - t_c \sum_{t=1}^{n} (DP_t - L_t)\{1+(1-t_c)k_1$$

$$(3.4.3.16)$$

Having applied the standardized method of notation, we may conclude that:
. except for the evaluation models of Weston and Brigham 1966,

Krumbholz and Streitferdt, Spittler, and Theunissen, the present value of the before-tax cash flows of purchasing equals I_0 (the capital asset's cash purchase price at time t=0),

. in more than half of the models discussed the present value of the before-tax cash flows of financial leasing is calculated by capitalizing the lease payments at the (after-tax) borrowing rate,

. there are significant differences of opinion regarding the computation of the present values of the tax savings of purchasing and financial leasing. Except for the lease-or-borrow model of Beckman and Joosen (who start from the fact that the Dutch fiscal authorities look upon a financial lessee as the owner of the leased asset so that this lessee is allowed to deduct depreciation as well as interest charges when determining its taxable income), in any of the evaluation models reviewed the depreciation charges and the lease payments are considered to be relevant for the calculation of the present values of the tax savings. In some models these are the only items considered to be of relevance for this calculation, namely in the models of Schall and Haley, of Weston and Brigham 1969,[1] of Weston 1962 appendix,[2] and of Johnson and Lewellen. Other authors argue that the loan interest charges are relevant as well. There exists, however, a considerable disagreement concerning the determination of these interest charges. This is because there are differences of opinion as to the amount and the repayment schedule of the loan to be used for financing a part of the asset's purchase price. These differences find expression in the superscripts added to $D_{1,t-1}$ (e.g., $D_{1,t-1}^V$ and $D_{1,t-1}^S$). Besides, there is considerable disagreement regarding

----

[1] Whose model, if represented according to the standardized method of notation, is equivalent to the model of Myers, Dill, and Bautista (if their $\lambda = 1$), of Bierman, of Vial, and of Theunissen.

[2] Whose model, applying the standardized notation method, is equivalent to the models of Weston and Brigham 1978 and 1981.

the discount rates to be employed in order to capitalize the various tax savings. That is why Bower, who already looked into this issue in his 1973 article on leasing, advocated performing a sensitivity analysis based on "different tax shelter discount rates" (Bower 1973, p. 31; see also 3.4.5).

Next I shall present my own financial lease evaluation model, as developed in 4.3, using mathematical notation:

$$NPV_{fl} = (1-t_c) \sum_{t=1}^{n} X_t (1+k_x)^{-t} + t_c \sum_{t=1}^{n} L_t (1+\ldots)^{-t} - \sum_{t=1}^{n} L_t (1+\ldots)^{-t}$$

$$(4.3.1)$$

$$NPV_p = (1-t_c) \sum_{t=1}^{n} X_t (1+k_x)^{-t} + t_c \sum_{t=1}^{n} DP_t (1+\ldots)^{-t}$$

$$+ t_c \sum_{t=1}^{n} k_1 D_{1,t-1} (1+\ldots)^{-t} - I_0 + D_{1,0} - \sum_{t=1}^{n} (R_{1,t}+k_1 D_{1,t-1})(1+\ldots)^{-t}$$

$$(4.3.2)$$

As explained in 4.3, in order to calculate these net present values we have to gather information concerning the tax system (particularly the regulations regarding tax deductible losses), the financial lease rate in proportion to the loan rate, the way the asset's purchase price is to be financed in the case of buying, and so forth. We are then able to determine which discount rates to use (see pp. 124-131). Applying the standardized notation method we obtain:

$$NPV_{fl} - NPV_p = I_0 - D_{1,0} + \sum_{t=1}^{n} (R_{1,t}+k_1 D_{1,t-1})(1+\ldots)^{-t}$$

$$- \sum_{t=1}^{n} L_t (1+\ldots)^{-t} - t_c \sum_{t=1}^{n} (DP_t+k_1 D_{1,t-1}-L_t)(1+\ldots)^{-t}$$

$$(4.3.3)$$

If in the case of buying the asset the firm's management is going to finance its entire purchase price by means of equity, equation 4.3.2 can be rewritten as:

$$NPV_p = (1-t_c) \sum_{t=1}^{n} X_t (1+k_x)^{-t} + t_c \sum_{t=1}^{n} DP_t (1+\ldots)^{-t} - I_0 \qquad (4.3.4)$$

Employing the standardized method of notation we now get:

$$NPV_{fl} - NPV_p = I_0 - \sum_{t=1}^{n} X_t(1+k_x)^{-t} + t_c \sum_{t=1}^{n} (DP_t - L_t)(1+\ldots)^{-t}$$

$$(4.3.5)$$

Section 4.3 also explained that if the tax authorities regard the financial lessee as the owner of the leased asset (for instance, as in the Netherlands), this lessee has to deduct depreciation and financial lease interest charges rather than the lease payments when computing its taxable income. The net present value of the leasing arrangement should then be calculated from:

$$NPV_{fl} = (1-t_c) \sum_{t=1}^{n} X_t(1+k_x)^{-t} + t_c \sum_{t=1}^{n} (DP_t + k_{fl}D_{fl,t-1})(1+\ldots)^{-t}$$

$$- \sum_{t=1}^{n} L_t(1+\ldots)^{-t} \qquad\qquad (4.3.6)$$

Again using the standardized method of notation and starting from equations 4.3.2 and 4.3.6 we obtain:

$$NPV_{fl} - NPV_p = I_0 - D_{1,0} + \sum_{t=1}^{n} (R_{1,t} + k_1 D_{1,t-1})(1+\ldots)^{-t}$$

$$- \sum_{t=1}^{n} L_t(1+\ldots)^{-t} - t_c \sum_{t=1}^{n} (k_1 D_{1,t-1} - k_{fl}D_{fl,t-1})(1+\ldots)^{-t}$$

$$(4.3.7)$$

APPENDIX 2 : OPERATING LEASES

I shall now analyze the operating lease evaluation models discussed in Chapter 5, employing the notation of Appendix 1.

5.2 Vancil

In order to choose between an operating lease and a purchase arrangement, Vancil uses two evaluation methods: "return on investment" and "profitability measured in present-value dollars." As
shown on p. 152, when applying the first method we have to calculate k_{ol}^V from:

$$I_0 - \sum_{t=1}^{n} \{(1-t_c)L_t + t_c DP_t\}(1+k_{ol}^V)^{-t} = 0 \qquad (5.2.1)$$

As we observed in Section 5.2, Vancil does not explain with which
rate to compare k_{ol}^V. His second evaluation method involves performing two break-even analyses: the "break-even economic life"
and the "break-even residual value." The first measure, t^*, can
be derived from the following equation:

$$I_0 - \sum_{t=1}^{t^*} \{(1-t_c)L_t + t_c DP_t\}(1+k_o)^{-t} - S_{t^*}(1+k_o)^{-t^*}$$

$$- t_c\{(I_0 - \sum_{t=1}^{t^*} DP_t)-S_{t^*}\}(1+k_o)^{-t^*} = 0 \qquad (5.2.2)$$

where:
t^* = break-even economic life.

A similar equation can be used for determining the break-even
residual value:

$$I_0 - \sum_{t=1}^{n} \{(1-t_c)L_t + t_c DP_t\}(1+k_o)^{-t} - S_n^*(1+k_o)^{-n}$$

$$- t_c\{I_0 - \sum_{t=1}^{n} DP_t) - S_n^* \}(1+k_o)^{-n} = 0 \qquad (5.2.3)$$

where:

S_n^* = break-even residual value at time n.

5.3 Peirson and Bird

These authors compute the present value of purchasing and the present value of the operating lease from:

$$PV_p^{PB} = I_0 - t_c \sum_{t=1}^{j} DP_t(1+k_o)^{-t} - S_j(1+k_o)^{-j} - t_c\{I_0 - \sum_{t=1}^{j} DP_t) - S_j\}(1+k_o)^{-j}$$

$$(5.3.1)$$

$$PV_{ol}^{PB} = (1-t_c) \sum_{t=1}^{j} L_t(1+k_o)^{-t} \qquad (5.3.2)$$

where:

j = useful service life of the asset.

In our illustrative example, we first assumed j=1 year and then j=2 years.

5.4 Goudsmit and Keijser

Goudsmit and Keijser also compute the present value of the purchase and the operating lease option. The present value of the former option is:

$$PV_p^{GK} = \sum_{t=1}^{n} \{R_{1,t}^{GK} + (1-t_c)k_1 D_{1,t-1}^{GK} - t_c DP_t\}(1+k_o)^{-t} \qquad (5.4.1)$$

where:

$$D_{1,0}^{GK} = I_0 \quad \text{and} \quad D_{1,t}^{GK} = D_{1,t-1}^{GK} - R_{1,t}^{GK} \qquad (5.4.2)$$

The present value of the operating lease is calculated from:

$$PV_{ol}^{GK} = (1-t_c) \sum_{t=1}^{n} L_t(1+k_o)^{-t} \qquad (5.4.3)$$

5.5 Jenkins

As observed on p. 168, Jenkins starts from Ferrara's 1968 financial lease-or-borrow model to solve the operating lease-versus-
purchase problem. This model has partly been based on the
"borrowing opportunity rate method" developed by Vancil. I use
the word "partly" since Ferrara employs Vancil's model to calculate the present values of purchasing and of leasing, but he
holds that the loan that has been incorporated in the lease has a
repayment schedule that differs from the one Vancil uses. Therefore: $PV_p^F =$

$$PV_p^V = I_0 - t_c \sum_{t=1}^{n} DP_t (1+k_o)^{-t} \qquad (3.4.2.4)$$

$$PV_{f1}^F = \sum_{t=1}^{n} L_t (1+k_1)^{-t} - t_c \sum_{t=1}^{n} (L_t - k_1 D_{1,t-1}^F)(1+k_o)^{-t} \qquad (5.5.1)$$

where:

$$D_{1,0}^F = I_0 \quad \text{and} \quad D_{1,t}^F = D_{1,t-1}^F - (L_t - k_{f1} D_{1,t-1}^F) \qquad (5.5.2)$$

In order to apply this model (as described in Ferrara 1968, pp.
55-63) to the operating lease-or-purchase issue, Jenkins adds two
items: "the total cost of leasing for various lengths of time"
and "the probability distribution of various possible holding
periods" (Jenkins 1970, p. 31). The "various lengths of time" are
the possible useful service lives of the asset (j) already utilized in 5.3. Starting from any of the possible asset service
lives, Jenkins computes the present values of purchasing and of
the operating lease. In the case of purchasing it may be that
upon termination of asset operation the asset's salvage value
differs from its book value:

$$PV_p^J = I_0 - t_c \sum_{t=1}^{j} DP_t (1+k_o)^{-t} - S_j (1+k_o)^{-j}$$

$$- t_c \{I_0 - \sum_{t=1}^{j} DP_t) - S_j\}(1+k_o)^{-j} \qquad (5.5.3)$$

$$PV_{o1}^J = \sum_{t=1}^{j} L_t (1+k_1)^{-t} - t_c \sum_{t=1}^{j} (L_t - k_1 D_{1,t-1}^F)(1+k_o)^{-t} \qquad (5.5.4)$$

Next Jenkins subtracts PV_{o1}^J from PV_p^J (p. 30):

$$PV_p^J - PV_{ol}^J = I_0 - \sum_{t=1}^{j} L_t(1+k_1)^{-t} - t_c \sum_{t=1}^{j} (DP_t + k_1 D_{1,t-1}^F - L_t)(1+k_o)^{-t}$$

$$- S_j(1+k_o)^{-j} - t_c\{(I_0 - \sum_{t=1}^{j} DP_t) - S_j\}(1+k_o)^{-j} \qquad (5.5.5)$$

Finally, he introduces "the probability distribution of various possible holding periods" resulting in the expected value of $PV_p^J - PV_{ol}^J$:

$$E(PV_p^J - PV_{ol}^J) = \sum_{j=1}^{m} p_j [I_0 - \sum_{t=1}^{j} L_t(1+k_1)^{-t} - t_c \sum_{t=1}^{j} (DP_t + k_1 D_{1,t-1}^F - L_t)(1+k_o)$$

$$- S_j(1+k_o)^{-j} - t_c\{(I_0 - \sum_{t=1}^{j} DP_t) - S_j\}(1+k_o)^{-j}] \qquad (5.5.6)$$

where:

p_j = probability of the asset's useful service life being j years
m = maximum useful service life of the asset.

5.6 Hax

When illustrating the Hax model by means of our numerical example, we observed that Hax does not pay attention to corporate income taxes and that it is not clear which capitalization rate he uses. We therefore made use of the same discount rate Hax utilizes: 9% (k_H). In his analysis Hax incorporates a probability distribution of possible future situations, where each situation is defined by the cash inflow the capital asset generates. Unlike Jenkins the author also takes into consideration the cash inflows resulting from asset operation. The expected net present value of the operating lease, applying Hax's methodology, can be deter-mined from:

$$E(NPV_{ol}^H) = \sum_{i=1}^{l} p_i \sum_{t=1}^{q} (X_{i,t} - L_t)(1+k_H)^{-t} \qquad (5.6.1)$$

where:

p_i = probability of situation i
$X_{i,t}$ = net cash inflow before corporate income taxes in situation i at time t.

Hax argues that the operating lease will be cancelled in a situation in which $(X_{1,t}-L_t) < 0$, consequently q is the first moment where $(X_{1,t}-L_t) < 0$. The expected net present value of the purchase option according to the Hax model is:

$$E(NPV_p^H) = \sum_{1=1}^{1} p_1 \sum_{t=1}^{m} X_{1,t}(1+k_H)^{-t} - I_0 \qquad (5.6.2)$$

Since in the numerical example Hax utilizes the capital asset will be operated until time m, equation 5.6.2 can be rewritten as follows:

$$NPV_p^H = \sum_{t=1}^{m} X_t(1+k_H)^{-t} - I_0 \qquad (5.6.3)$$

I used this equation when illustrating Hax's model with the help of our numerical example.

5.7 Beckman and Joosen

Just like Jenkins these authors make use of a probability distribution of possible future asset service lives. However, unlike Jenkins they take into account the cash inflow series resulting from asset operation:

$$E(NPV_{ol}^{BJ}) = \sum_{j=1}^{m} p_j\{(1-t_c) \sum_{t=1}^{j} (X_t-L_t)(1+k_o)^{-t}\} \qquad (5.7.1)$$

$$E(NPV_p^{BJ}) = \sum_{j=1}^{m} p_j[\sum_{t=1}^{j} \{(1-t_c)X_t + t_cDP_t\}(1+k_o)^{-t} + S_j(1+k_o)^{-j}$$
$$+ t_c\{(I_0 - \sum_{t=1}^{j} DP_t) - S_j\}(1+k_o)^{-j} - I_0] \qquad (5.7.2)$$

As in Appendix 1, I shall utilize the standardized method of notation to summarize the lease-versus-purchase models discussed above.

Vancil

Vancil applies three measures to resolve the operating lease-versus-purchase issue. The first measure involves computing k_{ol}^V from:

$$I_0 - \sum_{t=1}^{n} L_t(1+k_{ol}^V)^{-t} - t_c \sum_{t=1}^{n} (DP_t-L_t)(1+k_{ol}^V)^{-t} = 0 \qquad (5.2.4)$$

The second measure is the break-even economic life t*:

$$I_0 - S_{t*}(1+k_o)^{-t*} - \sum_{t=1}^{t*} L_t(1+k_o)^{-t} - t_c[\sum_{t=1}^{t*} (DP_t-L_t)(1+k_o)^{-t}$$

$$- \{(I_0 - \sum_{t=1}^{t*} DP_t)-S_{t*}\}(1+k_o)^{-t*}] = 0 \qquad (5.2.5)$$

The third measure is the break-even residual value S_n^* :

$$I_0 - S_n^*(1+k_o)^{-n} - \sum_{t=1}^{n} L_t(1+k_o)^{-t} - t_c[\sum_{t=1}^{n} (DP_t-L_t)(1+k_o)^{-t}$$

$$- \{(I_0 - \sum_{t=1}^{n} DP_t) - S_n^*\}(1+k_o)^{-n}] = 0 \qquad (5.2.6)$$

Peirson and Bird

$$PV_p^{PB} - PV_{ol}^{PB} = I_0 - S_j(1+k_o)^{-j} - \sum_{t=1}^{j} L_t(1+k_o)^{-t} - t_c[\sum_{t=1}^{j} (DP_t-L_t)(1+k_o)^{-t}$$

$$- \{(I_0 - \sum_{t=1}^{j} DP_t)-S_j\}(1+k_o)^{-j}] \qquad (5.3.3)$$

Goudsmit and Keijser

$$PV_p^{GK} - PV_{ol}^{GK} = \sum_{t=1}^{n} (R_{1,t}^{GK} + k_1 D_{1,t-1}^{GK})(1+k_o)^{-t} - \sum_{t=1}^{n} L_t(1+k_o)^{-t}$$

$$- t_c \sum_{t=1}^{n} (DP_t + k_1 D_{1,t-1}^{GK} - L_t)(1+k_o)^{-t} \qquad (5.4.4)$$

Jenkins

$$E(PV_p^J - PV_{ol}^J) = \sum_{j=1}^{m} p_j [I_0 - S_j(1+k_o)^{-j} - \sum_{t=1}^{j} L_t(1+k_1)^{-t}$$

$$- t_c\{\sum_{t=1}^{j} (DP_t + k_1 D_{1,t-1}^F - L_t)(1+k_o)^{-t}\}$$

$$- t_c\{(I_0 - \sum_{t=1}^{j} DP_t) - S_j\}(1+k_o)^{-j}] \qquad (5.5.7)$$

Hax

$$E(NPV^H_{ol}) - NPV^H_p = I_0 - \sum_{i=1}^{1} p_i \sum_{t=1}^{q} L_t(1+k_H)^{-t}$$
$$- \{ \sum_{t=1}^{m} X_t(1+k_H)^{-t} - \sum_{i=1}^{1} p_i \sum_{t=1}^{q} X_{1,t}(1+k_H)^{-t} \} \tag{5.6.4}$$

Note that Hax ignores the corporate income tax factor.

Beckman and Joosen

$$E(NPV^{BJ}_{ol}) - E(NPV^H_p) = \sum_{j=1}^{m} p_j[I_0 - S_j(1+k_o)^{-j} - \sum_{t=1}^{j} L_t(1+k_o)^{-t}$$
$$- t_c\{ \sum_{t=1}^{j} (DP_t - L_t)(1+k_o)^{-t} \}$$
$$- t_c\{ (I_0 - \sum_{t=1}^{j} DP_t) - S_j \}(1+k_o)^{-j}] \tag{5.7.3}$$

From the above we may conclude that:
- except for Goudsmit and Keijser all of the authors whose models were just summarized equate the present value of the before-tax cash flows of the purchase option with I_0 (minus the present value of the salvage value of the asset),
- in more than half of the models discussed, the present value of the before-tax cash flows of the operating lease is computed by discounting the lease payments at the firm's cost of capital,
- just as I concluded on p. 255, there are considerable differences of opinion as to the calculation of the present values of the tax savings of the purchase and the lease agreements. In most of the models reviewed, the tax consequences of a difference between the asset's book value and its residual value are taken into consideration. In any of the above models (except for the model of Hax, who completely ignores the corporate income tax factor), the depreciation charges and the lease payments are considered to be relevant for the calculation of the present values of the tax savings. According to Vancil, Peirson and Bird, and Beckman and Joosen, these are the only

two relevant cash flows items. On the other hand, Goudsmit and Keijser as well as Jenkins argue that the interest payments of a loan used to finance the asset's purchase price are to be taken into consideration too. However, they disagree as to repayment schedule of the loan. Quite remarkably, the authors whose evaluation methods were examined agree on the discount rate to be applied to the various tax savings: they all make use of the firm's cost of capital in order to capitalize these savings.

In addition to the above agreement I would like to point out that authors on operating lease evaluation agree on some other issues as well. Chapter 5 already stressed certain resemblances between the models of Peirson and Bird and of Vancil (see p. 162), between the models of Goudsmit and Keijser and of Peirson and Bird (see p. 165), and between the models of Jenkins and of Peirson and Bird (p. 169). Besides, if we compare equation 5.3.3 with equation 5.7.3, we find that in fact the model of Beckman and Joosen equals the Peirson and Bird model plus a probability distribution of the asset service lives.

Using mathematical notation I shall now explain the model introduced in section 5.8. As observed on pp. 186-187, we first have to compute the interest rate implicit in the operating lease, k_{ol}:

$$I_0 - \sum_{i=1}^{l} p_i \sum_{t=1}^{r} L_t (1+k_{ol})^{-t} = 0 \qquad (5.8.1)$$

The cash flow consequences of the firm's management deciding to terminate operating a purchased asset at time s, CF_s, are (see also pp. 188-189):

$$CF_s = - (D_{1,0} - \sum_{t=1}^{s} R_{1,t}) + S_s + t_c \{(I_0 - \sum_{t=1}^{s} DP_t) - S_s\} \qquad (5.8.2)$$

As it appears from this equation, CF_s consists of the repayment of the remaining balance of the loan used to finance the asset's purchase price, $- (D_{1,0} - \sum_{t=1}^{s} R_{1,t})$, the asset's salvage value at time s, S_s, and the tax effects of any differences between the book value of the asset, $I_0 - \sum_{t=1}^{s} DP_t$, and its salvage value. It may be that there are no tax effects at all, e.g., if the asset's book value exceeds its salvage value whereas the tax authorities do not provide for any loss protection (as assumed on p. 189). In Section 5.8 it was then argued that management may conclude an insurance contract to protect its firm against these cash flow consequences. The interest rate of the combination of the loan introduced on p. 188 and that insurance contract, k_{11}, can be determined as follows:

$$D_{1,0} - \sum_{i=1}^{1} p_i \sum_{t=1}^{s} (R_{1,t} + k_1 D_{1,t-1} + P_t)(1+k_{11})^{-t} = 0 \qquad (5.8.3)$$

where:

P_t = insurance premium at time t.

The expected net present value of the operating lease can now be computed from:

$$E(NPV_{ol}) = \sum_{i=1}^{1} p_i \{(1-t_c) \sum_{t=1}^{r} X_{1,t}(1+k_x)^{-t} + t_c \sum_{t=1}^{r} L_t(1+\ldots)^{-t}$$
$$- \sum_{t=1}^{r} L_t(1+\ldots)^{-t}\} \qquad (5.8.4)$$

In calculating the expected net present value of the purchase arrangement we assume, just as we did in Section 5.8, that the asset's purchase price is financed by raising the loan introduced on p. 188 and that the firm's management effects the insurance:

$$E(NPV_p) = \sum_{i=1}^{1} p_i \{(1-t_c) \sum_{t=1}^{s} X_{1,t}(1+k_x)^{-t} + t_c \sum_{t=1}^{s} DP_t(1+\ldots)^{-t}$$
$$+ t_c \sum_{t=1}^{s} k_1 D_{1,t-1}(1+\ldots)^{-t} + t_c \sum_{t=1}^{s} P_t(1+\ldots)^{-t}$$
$$- \sum_{t=1}^{s} (R_{1,t} + k_1 D_{1,t-1} + P_t)(1+\ldots)^{-t}\} - I_0 + D_{1,0} \qquad (5.8.5)$$

As explained in 5.8 it may be that the technical and economic service life of the capital asset if leased differs from its service life if purchased (see p. 191). I therefore used the symbols s (see equations 5.8.2, 5.8.3 and 5.8.5) and r (equation 5.8.1 and 5.8.4). In order to determine which discount rates to use, we have to gather information regarding, among other things, the tax system and the operating lease rate (k_{ol}) in proportion to the rate calculated according to equation 5.8.3 (k_{li}).

In equation 5.8.5 it was assumed that the insurance contract was concluded. If this is not the case then the expected net present value of purchasing can be determined from:

$$E(NPV_p) = \sum_{i=1}^{1} p_i \{(1-t_c) \sum_{t=1}^{s} X_{i,t}(1+k_x)^{-t} + t_c \sum_{t=1}^{s} DP_t(1+...)^{-t}$$

$$+ t_c \sum_{t=1}^{s} k_1 D_{1,t-1}(1+...)^{-t} - \sum_{t=1}^{s} (R_{1,t}+k_1 D_{1,t-1})(1+...)^{-t}$$

$$+ CF_s(1+...)^{-s}\} - I_0 + D_{1,0} \qquad (5.8.6)$$

It may be, of course, that the firm's management prefers to finance the cash purchase price of the asset (in part) with equity funds. As for the effects this method of financing may have upon $E(NPV_p)$, I refer to 4.3 and to Appendix 1. To conclude, I shall employ the standardized method of notation. Starting from equations 5.8.4 and 5.8.5 we obtain:

$$E(NPV_{ol}) - E(NPV_p) = I_0 - D_{1,0} + \sum_{i=1}^{1} p_i [\sum_{t=1}^{s} (R_{1,t}+k_1 D_{1,t-1}+P_t)(1+...)$$

$$- \sum_{t=1}^{r} L_t(1+...)^{-t} - t_c \{ \sum_{t=1}^{s} (DP_t+k_1 D_{1,t-1}+P_t)(1+...$$

$$- \sum_{t=1}^{r} L_t(1+...)^{-t} \} - (1-t_c) \{ \sum_{t=1}^{s} X_{i,t}(1+k_x)^{-t}$$

$$- \sum_{t=1}^{r} X_{i,t}(1+k_x)^{-t} \}] \qquad (5.8.7)$$

Applying the standardized notation method to equations 5.8.4 and 5.8.6 yields:

$$E(NPV_{o1}) - E(NPV_p) = I_0 - D_{1,0} + \sum_{i=1}^{1} p_1 [\sum_{t=1}^{s} (R_{1,t} + k_1 D_{1,t-1})(1+\ldots)^{-t}$$

$$- \sum_{t=1}^{r} L_t (1+\ldots)^{-t} - t_c \{ \sum_{t=1}^{s} (DP_t + k_1 D_{1,t-1})(1+\ldots)^{-t}$$

$$- \sum_{t=1}^{r} L_t (1+\ldots)^{-t} \} - CF_s (1+\ldots)^{-s}$$

$$- (1-t_c) \{ \sum_{t=1}^{s} X_{1,t}(1+k_x)^{-t} - \sum_{t=1}^{r} X_{1,t}(1+k_x)^{-t} \}]$$

$$(5.8.8)$$

BIBLIOGRAPHY

Anderson, P.F., and J.D. Martin, Lease versus Purchase Decisions: A Survey of Current Practice, Financial Management, Spring 1977, pp. 41-47.

Ashton, D.J., The Reasons for Leasing - a Mathematical Programming Framework, Journal of Business Finance and Accounting, Summer 1978, pp. 233-251.

Baker, C.R., and R.S. Hayes, A Guide to Lease Financing, An Alternative to Buying, Ronald Press, New York, 1981.

Beckman, H., Financiële Leasing in de Jaarrekening van Lessees, Bedrijfskunde, Tijdschrift voor Modern Management, 1982/2, pp. 99-109.

Beckman, H., and A.W.A. Joosen, Leasing van Roerend en Onroerend Goed, Stenfert Kroese, Leiden (The Netherlands), 1980.

Beechy, T.H., Quasi-Debt Analysis of Financial Leases, Accounting Review, April 1969, pp. 375-381.

___, The Cost of Leasing, Comment and Correction, Accounting Review, October 1970, pp. 769-773.

Bender, A., Le Financement par la Location, Analyse Quantitative de la Location Financière, Thèse No.224, Genève (Switzerland), 1973.

Bibot, P., Le Leasing, une Opération Financière, Voordrachten van het Studiecentrum voor Bank en Financiewezen, Brussels (Belgium), 1966.

Bierman, H., Analysis of the Lease-or-Buy Decision: Comment, Journal of Finance, September 1973, pp. 1019-1021.

___, The Lease versus Buy Decision, Prentice-Hall, Englewood Cliffs, New Jersey, 1982.

Bierman, H., and S. Smidt, The Capital Budgeting Decision, Econo-
mic Analysis of Investment Projects, Macmillan, New York,
1960.
___, The Capital Budgeting Decision, Economic Analysis of Invest-
ment Projects, Macmillan, New York, 1980.
Bloomfield, E.C., and R. Ma, The Lease Evaluation Solution,
Accounting and Business Research, Autumn 1974, pp. 297-302.
Bouma, J.L., Leerboek der Bedrijfseconomie, Deel II, De Theorie
van de Financiering van Ondernemingen, Delwel, Wassenaar (The
Netherlands), 1980.
Bower, R.S., Issues in Lease Financing, Financial Management,
Winter 1973, pp. 25-34.
Bower, R.S., F.C. Herringer, and J.P. Williamson, Lease Evalu-
ation, Accounting Review, April 1966, pp. 257-265.
Bowles, G.N., Some Thoughts on the Lease Evaluation Solution,
Accounting and Business Research, Spring 1977, pp. 124-126.
Brealey, R.A., and S.C. Myers, Principles of Corporate Finance,
McGraw-Hill, New York, 1981.
Brealey, R.A., and C.M. Young, Debt, Taxes and Leasing - A Note,
Journal of Finance, December 1980, pp. 1245-1250.
Brigham, E.F., Hurdle Rates for Screening Capital Expenditure
Proposals, Financial Management, Winter 1975, pp. 17-25.
Burrows, G., The Lease Evaluation Solution, a Further Comment,
Accounting and Business Research, Summer 1977, pp. 208-210.
Carsberg, B., and A. Hope, Business Investment Decisions under
Inflation, Theory and Practice, Institute of Chartered Ac-
countants in England and Wales, London, 1976.
Clark, T.M., Leasing, McGraw-Hill, London, 1978.
Clark, J.J., T.J. Hindelang, and R.E. Pritchard, Capital Budget-
ing: Planning and Control of Capital Expenditures, Prentice-
Hall, Englewood Cliffs, New Jersey, 1979.
Clark, R.A., J.M. Jantorni, and R.R. Gann, Analysis of the Lease-
or-Buy Decision: Comment, Journal of Finance, September 1973,
pp. 1015-1016.
Cohen, J.B., Personal Finance, Irwin, Homewood, Illinois, 1979.

Cooper, K., and R.H. Strawser, Evaluation of Capital Investment Projects Involving Asset Leases, Financial Management, Spring 1975, pp. 44-49.

Copeland, T.E., and J.F. Weston, A Note on the Evaluation of Cancellable Operating Leases, Financial Management, Summer 1982, pp. 60-67.

___, Financial Theory and Corporate Policy, Addison-Wesley, Reading, Massachusetts, 1983.

Crawford, P.J., C.P. Harper, and J.J. McConnell, Further Evidence on the Terms of Financial Leases, Financial Management, Autumn 1981, pp. 7-14.

Diepenhorst, A.I., A Multi-Period Cost of Capital Concept and Its Impact on the Formulation of Financial Policy, Centre for Research in Business Economics, Report 7813/F, Erasmus University Rotterdam (The Netherlands), 1978.

Dietz, A., Marketing and Commercial Policy, Paper Presented to Leaseurope Conference, Oslo (Norway), 1977.

Doenges, R.C., The Cost of Leasing, Engineering Economist, Winter 1971, pp. 31-44.

Dopuch, N., and J.G. Birnberg, Cost Accounting, Accounting Data for Management's Decisions, Harcourt, Brace & World, New York, 1969.

Dopuch, N., J.G. Birnberg, and J.S. Demski, Cost Accounting, Accounting Data for Management's Decisions, Harcourt Brace Jovanovich, New York, 1982.

Dyl, E.A., and S.A. Martin, Setting Terms for Leveraged Leases, Financial Management, Winter 1977, pp. 20-27.

Ecker, P., USA Rücken Capital Leases in die Balans des Nehmers, Handelsblatt, 27 October 1977, p. 28.

Elgers, P.T., and J.J. Clark, The Lease/Buy Decision, A Simplified Guide to Maximizing Financial and Tax Advantages in the 1980s, Macmillan, New York, 1980.

Exposure Draft No.29, Accounting for Leases and Hire Purchase Contracts, Accounting Standards Committee, Edinburgh, 1982.

Fawthrop, R.A., Underlying Problems in Discounted Cash Flow Appraisal, in R.J. Lister (ed.), Studies in Optimal Financing, Macmillan, London, 1973, pp. 106-129.

Fawthrop, R.A., and B. Terry, Debt Management and the Use of Leasing Finance in UK Corporate Financing Strategies, Journal of Business Finance and Accounting, Autumn 1975, pp. 295-314.

___, The Evaluation of an Integrated Investment and Lease-Financing Decision, Journal of Business Finance and Accounting, Autumn 1976, pp. 79-111.

___, The Evaluation of an Integrated Investment and Lease-Financing Decision: a Reply, Journal of Business Finance and Accounting, Spring 1979, pp. 89-93.

Ferrara, W.L., Should Investment and Financing Decisions Be Separated?, Accounting Review, January 1966, pp. 106-114.

___, Capital Budgeting and Financing or Leasing Decisions, Management Accounting, July 1968, pp. 55-63.

___, Lease versus Purchase: a Quasi-Financing Approach, Management Accounting, January 1974, pp. 21-26.

Financial Accounting Standards Board, Accounting for Leases, FASB Statement No.13 as Amended and Interpreted Through May 1980, Stamford, Connecticut.

Findlay, M.C., Financial Lease Evaluation: Survey and Synthesis, in D.E. Fisher (ed.), Proceedings of the 1973 Annual Meeting of the Eastern Finance Association, Storrs, Connecticut, 1973.

Finnerty, J.E., R.N. Fitzsimmons, and T.W. Oliver, Lease Capitalization and Systematic Risk, Accounting Review, October 1980, pp. 631-639.

Franks, J.R., and J.E. Broyles, Modern Managerial Finance, Wiley, Chichester, 1979.

Franks, J.R., and S.D. Hodges, Valuation of Financial Lease Contracts: a Note, Journal of Finance, May 1978, pp. 657-669.

Friedlander, G., Leitfaden für das Leasing Geschäft, Organisator, Zürich (Switzerland), 1964.

Gant, D.R., Illusion in Lease Financing, Harvard Business Review, March/April 1959, pp. 121-142.

Gaumnitz, J.E., and A. Ford, The Lease or Sell Decision, Financial Management, Winter 1978, pp. 69-74.

Gopal, P.G., D. Heller, and M.E. Barker, Lease or Sell-Calculating a Profitable Rental, Financial Executive, October 1973, pp. 40-45.

Gordon, M.J., A General Solution to the Buy or Lease Decision: a Pedagogical Note, Journal of Finance, March 1974, pp. 245-250.

Goslings, J.H.W., Vermogenskosten, Leasing en Marktimperfekties, Maandblad voor Accountancy en Bedrijfshuishoudkunde, June 1976, pp. 333-342.

Goudsmit, A.C., Operationele Leasing in Ontwikkeling, Kwartaalfacetten, December 1977, pp. 10-12.

___, Leasing in Ontwikkeling, Paper Presented to the Euroforum Seminar Leasing van Bedrijfsmiddelen, Amsterdam (The Netherlands), October 1981.

Goudsmit, A.C., and J.A.M.P. Keijser, Leasing van Bedrijfsmiddelen, VUGA, The Hague (The Netherlands), 1972.

Graf von Westphalen, F., Der Leasingvertrag, Finanzierungsleasing, Hersteller-Leasing, Operating-Leasing unter besonderer Berucksichtigung des AGB-Gesetzes, Otto Schmidt, Cologne (Germany), 1979.

Green, D.E.W., The Evaluation of an Integrated Investment and Lease - Financing Decision: a Comment, Journal of Business Finance and Accounting, Spring 1979, pp. 71-88.

Griffiths, P., Leasing, the Forgotten Dimension, Australian Accountant, July 1980, pp. 376-377.

Grinyer, J.R., The Lease Evaluation Solution: a Comment and Alternative, Accounting and Business Research, Summer 1975, pp. 231-235.

Haley, C.W., and L.D. Schall, The Theory of Financial Decisions, McGraw-Hill, New York, 1979.

Hamel, H.G., Leasing in Industry, Studies in Business Policy, No. 127, National Industrial Conference Board Inc., New York, 1968.

Hax, H., Die Entscheidung zwischen Kauf und Miete (Leasing) von Anlagen, Zeitschrift für Betriebswirtschaftliche Forschung, Kontaktstudium, 1977, pp. 23-30.

Henderson, G.V., A General Solution to the Buy or Lease Decision: a Pedagogical Note: Comment, Journal of Finance, March 1976, pp. 147-151.

Herbst, A.F., Capital Budgeting Theory, Quantitative Methods, and Applications, Harper & Row, New York, 1982.

Herst, A.C.C., De Lease/Koop-Beslissing, Beoordelingsmaatstaven in Theorie en Praktijk, Stenfert Kroese, Leiden (The Netherlands), 1981.

Hetz, R.W., Residual Values and Vendors, Leasing Digest, July 1982, p. 4 and p. 8.

Hirshleifer, J., On the Theory of Optimal Investment Decision, Journal of Political Economy, August 1958, pp. 329-352.

___, Investment, Interest and Capital, Prentice-Hall, Englewood Cliffs, New Jersey, 1970.

Honig, L.E., and S.C. Coley, An After-tax Equivalent Payment Approach to Conventional Lease Analysis, Financial Management, Winter 1975, pp. 28-35.

Hubbard, G., Leasing: the Cash Flow Myth, Management Accountant, February 1980, pp. 24-26.

Idol, C.R., A Note on Specifying Debt Displacement and Tax Shield Borrowing Opportunities in Financial Lease Valuation Models, Financial Management, Summer 1980, pp. 24-29.

Isom, T.A., and S.P. Amembal, The Handbook of Leasing: Theory and Techniques, Petrocelli, New York, 1982.

Jenkins, D.O., Purchase or Cancellable Lease: Which Is the Better?, Financial Executive, April 1970, pp. 26-31.

Johnson, R.W., and W.G. Lewellen, Analysis of the Lease-or-Buy Decision, Journal of Finance, September 1972, pp. 815-823.

___, Reply, Journal of Finance, September 1973, pp. 1024-1028.

Joosen, A.W.A., Internationale Leasing, Intermediair, 18 February 1977, pp. 29-33.

___, Over de Voordelen van Financiële Leasing, Bank- en Effectenbedrijf, August 1978, pp. 278-282.

___, Leasing versus Eigen Beheer van Personenauto's, Management Team, March 1982, pp. 62-69.

___, Autoleasing en Wagenparkbeheer, Vormen van Externe Dienstverlening, Stenfert Kroese, Leiden (The Netherlands), 1983.

Kaminsky, S., Mietweise Nutzungsüberlassung in der modernen Wirtschaft, in K.F. Hagenmüller (ed.), Leasing-Handbuch, Knapp, Frankfurt am Main (Germany), 1968, pp. 63-90.

Kaspar, L.J., Evaluating the Cost of Financial Leases, Management Accounting, May 1977, pp. 43-51.

Kim, E.H., A Mean-Variance Theory of Optimal Capital Structure and Corporate Debt Capacity, Journal of Finance, March 1978, pp. 45-63.

Koch, J., and H.J. Ploog, Leasing - eine Finanzierungsalternative auch für die Landwirtschaft?, in H. Pruns (ed.), Berichte über Landwirtschaft, Parey, Hamburg and Berlin (Germany), 1978, pp. 96-118.

Koks, C.J.M., Verzekeren tegen Schade?, in M.J.L. Jonkhart, J.W.R. Schuit and J. Spronk (eds.), Financiering en Belegging, Stand van Zaken anno 1978, Stenfert Kroese, Leiden (The Netherlands), 1978, pp. 39-50.

Krumbholz, S., and L. Streitferdt, Leasing oder Kreditfinanzierung ?, Ein Vergleich des Leasing mit anderen Arten der Kreditfinanzierung, Hanstein, Cologne (Germany), 1975.

Lee, W.Y., J.D. Martin, and A.J. Senchak, The Case for Using Options to Evaluate Salvage Values in Financial Leases, Financial Management, Autumn 1982, pp. 33-41.

Lev, B.E., and Y.E. Orgler, Analysis of the Lease-or-Buy Decision: Comment, Journal of Finance, September 1973, pp. 1022-1023.

Levy, H., and Y. Landskroner, Lease Financing: Cost versus Liquidity, Engineering Economist, Fall 1981, pp. 59-69.

Levy, H., and M. Sarnat, Leasing, Borrowing, and Financial Risk, Financial Management, Winter 1979, pp. 47-54.

____, Capital Investments and Financial Decisions, Prentice-Hall, Englewood Cliffs, New Jersey, 1982.

Lewellen, W.G., M.S. Long, and J.J. McConnell, Asset Leasing in Competitive Capital Markets, Journal of Finance, June 1976, pp. 787-797.

Livijn, C.O., 5000 Years of Leasing, Svensk Leasing AB, Stockholm (Sweden), 1969.

Long, M.S., Leasing and the Cost of Capital, Journal of Financial and Quantitative Analysis, November 1977, pp. 579-586.

Lüem, W., Le "Leasing", Nouvelle Formule Economique, Informations de Banque Populaire Suisse, No. 51, August 1967.

____, Leverage-Leasing, Industriele Organisation, No.2, 1978, pp. 107-109.

Lüssi, P. Das Leasing-Geschäft, Schulthess, Zürich (Switzerland), 1966.

Lusztig, P., Analysis of the Lease-or-Buy Decision: Comment, Journal of Finance, September 1973, pp. 1017-1018.

McEachron, W.D., Leasing: a Discounted Cash Flow Approach, Controller, May 1961, pp. 213-219.

McGugan, V.J., and R.E. Caves, Integration and Competition in the Equipment Leasing Industry, Journal of Business, July 1974, pp. 382-396.

Mao, J.C.T., Lease or Borrow: a Synthetic View, Cost and Management, February 1964, pp. 59-66.

___, Quantitative Analysis of Financial Decisions, Macmillan, London, 1969.

___, Corporate Financial Decisions, Pavan, Palo Alto, California, 1976.

Marrah, G.L., To Lease or Not to Lease?, Financial Executive, October 1968, pp. 91-104.

Martin, J.D., P.F. Anderson, and A.J. Keown, Lease Capitalization and Stock Price Stability: Implications for Accounting, Journal of Accounting, Auditing and Finance, March 1979, pp. 151-163.

Martin, P., Company Car Policy and Choice, Leasing Digest, August 1982, pp. 31-32.

Merrett, A.J., and A. Sykes, The Finance and Analysis of Capital Projects, Longman, London, 1973.

Middleton, K.A., The Evaluation of Leasing Proposals, Australian Accountant, April 1972, pp. 114-122.

___, Lease Evaluation: Back to Square One, Accounting and Business Research, Spring 1977, p. 127.

Miller, M.H., and C.W. Upton, Leasing, Buying, and the Cost of Capital Services, Journal of Finance, June 1976, pp. 761-785.

Missorten, W., Financiële Huur als Moderne Financieringsvorm, Cahiers Economiques de Bruxelles (Belgium), No. 29, 1966.

Mitchell, G.B., After-Tax Cost of Leasing, Accounting Review, April 1970, pp. 308-314.

Modigliani, F., and M.H. Miller, The Cost of Capital, Corporate Finance, and the Theory of Finance, American Economic Review, June 1958, pp. 261-297.

____, Corporate Income Taxes and the Cost of Capital: a Correction, American Economic Review, June 1963, pp. 433-443.

Moyer, R.C., Lease Evaluation and the Investment Tax Credit: a Framework for Analysis, Financial Management, Summer 1975, pp. 39-43.

Myers, S.C., Interactions of Corporate Financing and Investment Decisions - Implications for Capital Budgeting, Journal of Finance, March 1974, pp. 1-25.

Myers, S.C., D.A. Dill, and A.J. Bautista, Valuation of Financial Lease Contracts, Journal of Finance, June 1976, pp. 799-819.

Nantell, T.J., Equivalence of Lease vs. Buy Analyses, Financial Management, Autumn 1973, pp. 61-65.

O'Brien, T.J., and B.H. Nunnally, A 1982 Survey of Corporate Leasing Analysis, Financial Management, Summer 1983, pp. 30-36.

Ofer, A.R., The Evaluation of the Lease versus Purchase Alternatives, Financial Management, Summer 1976, pp. 67-74.

Ooghe, H., and W. de Groote, Kritische Bespreking van Enkele Voordelen van Financiële Leasing, Bank- en Effectenbedrijf, April 1978a, pp. 145-148.

____, Vergelijking van Financiële Leasing met Schuldfinanciering, Parts I and II, Maandblad Bedrijfsadministratie en Organisatie, No. 979 and 980, 1978b, pp. 382-386 and 430-435.

Peirson, C.G., and R.G. Bird, Business Finance, McGraw-Hill, Sydney (Australia), 1972.

Philippatos, G.C., Financial Management: Theory and Techniques, Holden-Day, San Francisco, 1973.

Pritchard, R.E., and T. Hindelang, The Lease/Buy Decision, Amacom, New York, 1980.

Reilly, R.F., A Cost of Funds Employed Method in Lease vs. Buy Analysis, Financial Executive, October 1980, pp. 14-17.

Reul, R.I., Profitability Index for Investments, Harvard Business Review, July/August 1957, pp. 116-132.

Ro, B.T., The Disclosure of Capitalized Lease Information and Stock Prices, Journal of Accounting Research, Autumn 1978, pp. 315-340.

Roberts, G.S., and A.C. Gudikunst, Equipment Financial Leasing Practices and Costs: Comment, Financial Management, Summer 1978, pp. 79-81.

Roenfeldt, R.L., and J.S. Osteryoung, Analysis of Financial Leases, Financial Management, Spring 1973, pp- 74-87.

Rosenberg, O., Kriterien zur Bestimmung der Vorteilhaftigkeit des Finanzierungsleasings, Schmalenbachs Zeitschrift für betriebswirtschaftliche Forschung, August 1975, pp. 500-516.

Sartoris, W.L., and R.S. Paul, Lease Evaluation - Another Capital Budgeting Decision, Financial Management, Summer 1973, pp. 46-52.

Schall, L.D., The Lease-or-Buy and Asset Acquisition Decisions, Journal of Finance, September 1974, pp. 1203-1214.

Schall, L.D., and C.W. Haley, Introduction to Financial Management, McGraw-Hill, New York, 1977.

___, Introduction to Financial Management, McGraw-Hill, New York, 1980.

Scheffer, C.F., Financiële Notities, Part II, Delwel, The Hague (The Netherlands), 1968.

Schubiger, A., Der Leasing-Vertrag nach schweizerischem Privatrecht, Zehnder, St. Gallen (Switzerland), 1970.

Schwab, B., Conceptual Problems in the Use of Risk-Adjusted Discount Rates with Disaggregated Cash Flows, Journal of Business Finance and Accounting, Winter 1978, pp. 281-293.

Scott, J.H., A Theory of Optimal Capital Structure, Bell Journal of Economics, Spring 1976, pp. 32-54.

Sharpe, W.F., Investments, Prentice-Hall, Englewood Cliffs, New Jersey, 1981.

Sorenson, I.W., and R.E. Johnson, Equipment Financial Leasing Practices and Costs: an Empirical Study, Financial Management, Spring 1977, pp. 33-40.

Spittler, H.J., Leasing, Weka, Kissing (Germany), 1977.

Stiglitz, J.E., A Re-examination of the Modigliani-Miller Theorem, American Economic Review, October 1969, pp. 784-793.

Sykes, A., The Lease-Buy Decision - A Survey of Current Practice in 202 Companies, Management Survey Report No. 29, British Institute of Management, London, 1976.

Terborgh, G., Business Investment Management, a MAPI Study and Manual, Washington D.C., 1967.

Theunissen, L., Aankoop of Leasing: een Vergelijkingsmodel, F.M.P. Newsletter, June 1982, pp. 1-25.

Tobin, J., Liquidity Preference as Behavior toward Risk, Review of Economic Studies, February 1958, pp. 65-86.

Tomkins, C., J. Lowe, and E. Morgan, Leasing: the Gulf Between Theory and Practice, Paper Presented to the Nijenrode Conference on Financial Management of Corporate Resource Allocations, Breukelen (The Netherlands), August 1979.

Upton, C.W., Leasing as a Financial Instrument, in J.L. Bicksler (ed.), Handbook of Financial Economics, North-Holland, Amsterdam (The Netherlands), 1979, pp. 293-306.

Vancil, R.F., Lease or Borrow - New Method of Analysis, Harvard Business Review, September/October 1961, pp. 122-136.

___, Lease or Borrow - Steps in Negotiation, Harvard Business Review, November/December 1961, pp. 138-159.

___, Leasing of Industrial Equipment, McGraw-Hill, New York, 1963.

Vancil, R.F., and R.N. Anthony, The Financial Community Looks at Leasing, Harvard Business Review, November/December 1959, pp. 113-130.

Van Dam, C., Doelstellingen, Waarderen en Investeren in Nederland, Bedrijfskunde, Tijdschrift voor Modern Management, 1978/3, pp. 228-235.

Van der Lande, M.L.B., Fiscaal Bodemrecht Leidt tot Verlies van Werkgelegenheid, Het Financieele Dagblad, 8 March 1983, pp. 31-36.

Van der Schroeff, H.J., Kosten en Kostprijs, Kosmos, Amsterdam (The Netherlands), 1974.

Van Horne, J.C., The Cost of Leasing with Capital Market Imperfections, Engineering Economist, Autumn 1977, pp. 1-12.

___, Financial Management and Policy, Prentice-Hall, London, 1977.

___, Fundamentals of Financial Management, Prentice-Hall, Englewood Cliffs, New Jersey, 1980.

___, Financial Management and Policy, Prentice-Hall, Englewood Cliffs, New Jersey, 1983.

Vial, P., Problèmes Posés par l'Analyse d'une Proposition de Crédit-Bail, Analyse Financière, 3rd Trimester 1974, pp. 10-29.

Voorthuysen, W.D., Leasing, Kluwer, Deventer (The Netherlands), 1970.

Weston, J.F., Managerial Finance, Holt, Rinehart and Winston, New York, 1962.

Weston, J.F., and E.F. Brigham, Managerial Finance, Holt, Rinehart and Winston, New York, 1966.

___, Managerial Finance, Holt, Rinehart and Winston, London, 1969.

___, Managerial Finance, Holt, Rinehart and Winston, London, 1972.

___, Managerial Finance, Holt, Rinehart and Winston, London, 1975.

___, Managerial Finance, Dryden, Hinsdale, Illinois, 1978.

___, Managerial Finance, Dryden, Hinsdale, Illinois, 1981.

Wilson, C.J., The Operating Lease and the Risk of Obsolescence, Management Accounting, December 1973, pp. 41-44.

Wytzes, H.C., Ondernemingsfinanciering, Stenfert Kroese, Leiden (The Netherlands), 1981.

INDEXES

Author Index

Anderson and Martin, 199, 204,
  205-06, 208, 209, 211-12
Ashton, 66, 68

Baker and Hayes, 31, 39, 54
Beckman, 224
Beckman and Joosen, 20, 69-72,
  123, 136n, 148, 179-82,
  183, 198, 217, 220, 240,
  252, 255, 263, 265, 266
Beechy, 12,15,35,54
Bender, 28-31, 35, 43, 166, 234
Bibot, 4
Bierman, 10, 43, 72, 83, 89-94,
  96, 97, 198, 243-45, 253,
  255n.1
Bierman and Smidt, 4, 43, 138,
  145, 157n, 167
Bouma, 145
Bower, 20, 35, 49, 51, 52, 56-
  60, 67, 86, 122, 123, 139,
  238-39, 245, 251, 256
Bower, Herringer, and
  Williamson, 10, 11, 13, 20,
  52-56, 59, 61, 72, 84, 211,
  212-13, 238, 251

Brealey and Myers, 12, 13, 66,
  127, 206
Brealey and Young, 66
Brigham, 12
Burrows, 15

Carsberg and Hope, 12
Clark, 66, 68
Clark, Hindelang, and
  Pritchard, 43
Clark, Jantori, and Gann, 83,
  87, 88
Cohen, 198
Copeland and Weston, 67, 104,
  122, 149, 192
Crawford, Harper, and
  McConnell, 139

Diepenhorst, 13
Dietz, 203-04, 208
Dopuch and Birnberg, 44n
Dopuch, Birnberg, and Demski,
  54, 187

Ecker, 206
Elgers and Clark, 43, 85

Fawthrop, 17

Fawthrop and Terry, 17, 35, 68, 202, 208, 209, 210, 211, 215n

Ferrara, 15, 16, 25, 34, 86, 99, 121, 153, 168-74, 183, 261

Findlay, 57

Franks and Broyles, 66, 144, 218

Franks and Hodges, 66

Gant, 200

Gaumnitz and Ford, 78, 185

Gordon, 10, 11, 20, 60-63, 83, 85, 118, 127, 239, 241, 252

Goudsmit, 5, 219

Goudsmit and Keijser, 5, 25, 148, 163-68, 183, 184, 220, 260, 264, 265, 266

Graf von Westphalen, 221

Haley and Schall, 66, 73, 108-11, 121, 125, 126, 143, 186, 247, 249-50

Hamel, 23, 127n

Hax, 148, 174-79, 183, 184, 191, 262-63, 265

Henderson, 13, 15

Herbst, 66, 69, 78

Hirshleifer, 8, 129

Idol, 66

Isom and Amembal, 12

Jenkins, 148, 168-74, 179, 183, 184, 261-62, 264, 266

Johnson and Lewellen, 10, 11, 13, 16, 25, 35, 60, 73, 83-97, 99, 121, 123, 124, 211, 241-45, 253, 255

Kaminsky, 4

Kim, 129

Koch and Ploog, 102

Koks, 197

Krumbholz and Streitferdt, 7, 10, 36, 73, 100-04, 105-06, 115, 125, 143-44, 221, 246, 254, 255

Lee, Martin, and Senchak, 198n

Lev and Orgler, 83, 94-95, 97

Levy and Sarnat, 10, 12, 13, 66

Lewellen, Long, and McConnell, 9, 78, 143

Livijn, 220

Lüem, 220-21

Lüssi, 3-4

Lusztig, 83, 88-89, 242, 253

McEachron, 12, 20-25, 52, 57, 59, 60, 90-91, 123, 215, 234, 239, 249-50

McGugan and Caves, 4, 205, 210

Mao, 12, 25

Marrah, 201-02, 208, 209

Martin, 206

Merrett and Sykes, 68n

Mitchell, 12, 96, 214

Modigliani and Miller, 8, 62, 64, 82-83, 127, 129

Myers, 13, 42, 49, 76, 127, 182

Myers, Dill, and Bautista, 16,
20, 25, 64-69, 74, 78, 81-
82, 110, 239-40, 249, 252,
255n.1

O'Brian and Nunnally, 212
Ooghe and de Groote, 15

Peirson and Bird, 16, 35, 58n,
148, 160-63, 164, 169, 183,
260, 264, 265
Philippatos, 185
Pritchard and Hindelang, 85,
143

Reul, 20

Sartoris and Paul, 35
Schall, 9, 10, 19, 35, 55, 108-
115, 137, 139, 234
Schall and Haley, 5, 73, 103,
105, 111-15, 125, 247-48,
249-50, 255
Scheffer, 25
Schwab, 10-11, 111
Scott, 129
Sharpe, 8
Spittler, 17, 73, 104-07, 203,
208, 246-47, 254, 255
Stiglitz, 129
Sykes, 203, 208

Terborgh, 144
Theunissen, 73, 115-19, 248,
254, 255

Tobin, 8
Tomkins, Lowe, and Morgan,
204n, 205-06, 208, 210-11

Vancil, 4-5, 10, 14, 20, 25-36,
41, 65, 67, 70, 75, 84,
148, 150-60, 162, 163, 169,
177, 183, 211, 214n, 234-
35, 236, 250, 259-60, 261,
263-64, 266
Vancil and Anthony, 199-201,
208
Van Dam, 12
Van der Lande, 223
Van der Schroeff, 6
Van Horne, 5, 9, 35, 40, 126
Vial, 73, 97-100, 245-46, 254,
255n.1
Voorthuysen, 5

Weston, 37-40, 41, 73-76, 77,
80, 121, 213, 235-36, 251,
252, 255
Weston and Brigham, 1, 5, 8-9,
12, 13, 20, 26-28, 36-52,
65, 66, 68, 72, 73-83, 84,
85, 93, 98, 99, 103-04,
105, 114, 118, 121-24, 126,
143, 144, 179, 211, 234-38,
240-41, 245, 248, 251, 253,
254-55
Wytzes, 144, 191

Subject Index

Abandonment value, 179
Accounting for Leases, 129,
    200n
Anaconda, 66, 249
Assumptions, 8, 13, 18, 108,
    131-36, 148, 168, 193

Balance sheet, 200n, 202, 210,
    223, 224, 225, 226, 227
Bargain purchase option, 224,
    225
Beneficial owner, 224, 227
Bondholders, 1, 144-45
Book value, 68, 155-57, 189-90,
    265, 266-67
Borrowing opportunity rate
    method, 31-36, 70, 84, 150-
    51, 158, 211, 235
Borrowing rate, 10, 13, 26, 36,
    213, 214
Break-even economic life, 155-
    56, 162, 183, 259, 264
Break-even residual value, 155-
    58, 183, 259-60, 264
Business risk, 144

Canada, 199
Cancellation, 4, 7, 147
Capital asset, 1, 5, 6-7, 15-
    16, 219
Capital budgeting decision. See
    Investment decision
Capital lease, 129, 206
Capital rationing, 34-35, 154,
    163, 178, 214

Captive lessors, 4, 198
Cash flow to equity, 78, 99,
    114, 124-26, 137, 185, 192
Certainty equivalent, 51
Characteristics of leasing, 5-
    8, 52, 127-28, 188
Classification of lease evalu-
    ation models, 15, 16, 148
Conditional sales contract, 220
Consumer Credit Act 1974, 218
Consumer Safety Act 1978, 218
Contractus sui generis, 220,
    221
Cost of capital, 9, 13, 62, 64,
    96, 124, 213
Crédit-bail, 100, 219, 222, 225

Debt capacity, 13, 25, 67-68,
    110, 209-10
Debt equivalent, 21, 24, 25
Denmark, 217, 220, 223, 226
Deutsche Leasing A.G., 202-03,
    208
Discounted cash flow rate of
    return, 20-25, 234
Discount rate, 10, 13, 122,
    124-31, 138-43, 256

Economic life, 6, 163, 166, 191
England, 68, 205, 206, 217,
    218, 221, 224
Equipment Leasing Association,
    218
Equity, 1, 78, 106, 123, 134,
    135, 188, 256

Equivalent depreciation, 32, 33, 169
Equivalent depreciation deductions, 32, 33
Equivalent purchase price, 33
Equivalent loan, 12, 64, 74, 123, 213, 230
Expected value, 11, 108, 110, 111, 112, 176, 247
Exposure Draft No. 29, 218, 225

Financial Accounting Standards Board, 129, 200n, 206, 227
Financial advantages, 52-56, 212, 238
Financial lease, 11, 229
  defined, 4-5, 7-8
  -or-purchase, 15-146, 211-15, 233-57
Financial risk, 144
Financing decision, 8-10, 12, 16-17, 121-22, 182, 202
Finland, 217, 220, 223, 226
Firm's goal, 1, 83-84, 125, 197, 229, 230
Fiscale bodembeslag, 223
Flexibility, 147-48, 168, 230
France, 100, 217, 219, 222, 225

Gross present value, 132-36

Hire purchase, 95, 218, 221, 224, 225

Implicit cost of debt, 144
Implicit rate, 129
Income statement, 225, 226

Incremental borrowing rate, 129
Installment purchase, 5, 95, 220, 221, 226
Insurance, 189-90, 192, 195, 197-98, 231, 267-68
Internal rate of return, 11-12, 123, 153, 211
Internal Revenue Service, 130
Investment decision, 8-10, 12, 16-17, 121-22, 182-83, 202
Investment and financing module, 85
Investment opportunity rate, 26, 34-35, 154, 163, 166-67, 202

J-policy, 197

Landlord and Tenant Act 1954, 219
Laplace Insufficient-Reason Criterion, 185
Lease obligation procedure, 21, 90
Lease-or-borrow, 16-17, 20-72, 83, 95, 100, 123-24, 229-30
Lease-or-buy, 16-17, 37, 60, 73-119, 123-24, 229-30
Lease Plan Holding N.V., 5
Lease project approach, 85
Leasing, definition of, 7
Lending rate, 35
Lessee, 7, 128, 129, 144, 147, 229
Lessor, 7, 128, 129, 144, 147, 229
Leverage lease, 5

Lloyd's, 197, 206
Loss protection, 130-31, 189,
    267

Maintenance lease, 5
Maintenance services, 149, 165
Market imperfections, 9, 126,
    143
Mathematical notation, 2, 17-
    18, 231
Methods of analysis, 17
Mortgages, 95

Net Advantage to Lease, 49-50,
    237
Netherlands, The, 5, 104, 128,
    136, 197-98, 204n, 217,
    219, 225, 257
Net present value, 6, 9-10, 11-
    12, 123, 124, 193-96
Norway, 217, 220, 223, 226
Numerical example, data of, 18-
    19, 150

Obsolescence, 7-8, 147, 149,
    183, 187, 191, 197, 198,
    215, 219, 223
Off-balance sheet financing,
    209, 210, 217
Operating advantages, 52-56,
    238
Operating lease, 5, 11, 67,
    123, 229
  defined, 4-5, 7-8
  -or-purchase, 147-98, 230-31,
    259-69

Optimal capital structure, 129,
    145
Option, 218, 219, 224, 226

Percentage leases, 127n
Premium, 45, 153, 170-72
Primary risks, 197
Probability, 111, 168, 176-77,
    180-81, 184-85
Probability distribution, 131,
    167, 173, 184, 186, 261-63,
    266
Profitability Index, 20, 23
Project hurdle rate, 13, 60,
    127, 137, 182, 185, 194
Promised payments, 10-11, 19,
    112
Pure expected return model, 19

Qualitative considerations,
    145-46, 168, 196, 210, 215,
    230
Quasi-expected return model, 19

Refunding, 44-45, 47
Rent, 3, 6, 218, 219, 220, 221,
    223
Rental arrangement. See Rent
Replacement asset, 149
Required rate of return, 103,
    125, 137, 143-45, 175, 192
Requirements, 8-14, 121-25,
    147, 182-84, 197, 229-31
Residual value. See Salvage
    value

Risk-adjusted discount rate, 19, 51, 108, 126, 139, 230, 231
Risk advantages, 52, 56
Risk-free rate. See Riskless rate
Riskless debt, 11
Riskless rate, 44-45, 99, 118-19, 126, 130, 186
Risk premium, 63, 118, 126, 213
Risky debt, 11

Sale and leaseback, 5, 45
Salvage value, 9, 46, 143, 159, 186-87, 189, 265-67
Secondary risks, 197
Secured loan, 220
Sensitivity analysis, 57-59, 122, 139-43, 196, 230, 239
Separation theorem, 8
Service lease, 5, 45, 149
Standardized method of notation, 249-55, 257, 263-66, 268-69
Stockholders, 1, 78, 84, 100, 104, 114, 124-25
Sweden, 217, 220, 223, 226
Switzerland, 204, 217, 223-24, 226

Tax deductions. See Tax savings
Tax depreciation life, 18, 41, 46, 148, 163-64, 185
Tax savings, 10, 28, 57-59, 130-31, 138-43, 186
Technical service life, 6, 191
Terminal values, 12
Tolley Publishing Company, 206, 208
Two-step analysis, 153, 158

U.K. Inland Revenue, 221
Uncertainty, 139, 148
United States, 68n, 199
Useful life, 6-8, 128, 130, 168-74, 185, 224, 225

Value-addivity principle, 126, 137, 192, 193, 230, 231
Venus Air Lines, 36
Vermogensaanwasdeling, 104

Western Europe, 217-27, 231
West Germany, 17, 199, 203-04, 217, 221, 224, 227
Wet Investeringsrekening, 222